Essayist, poet, dramatist and traveller, Enzensberger is – in the words of the *Times Literary Supplement* – 'a phenomenon'. He is one of Germany's, and Europe's, leading writers and one of her great public intellectuals. His long narrative poem *The Sinking of the Titanic* was published to great acclaim in 1987.

Hans Magnus Enzensberger

EUROPE, EUROPE
Forays into a Continent

Translated from the German by
Martin Chalmers

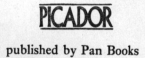

published by Pan Books

First published in slightly different form 1987 by
Suhrkamp Verlag, Frankfurt am Main, as *Ach Europa!*
First published in Great Britain 1989 by Hutchinson Radius
This Picador edition published 1990 by Pan Books Ltd,
Cavaye Place, London SW10 9PG
9 8 7 6 5 4 3 2 1
© Suhrkamp Verlag 1987
© translation Random House, Inc., 1989
ISBN 0 330 31234 0
Printed in England by Clays Ltd, St Ives plc

Grateful acknowledgement is made to the following for permission to
reprint previously published material:
Princeton University Press: excerpts from "Bohemia Lies by the
Sea", from *In the Storm of Roses: Selected Poems by Ingeborg
Bachmann*, edited and translated by Mark Anderson, © Princeton
University Press 1986.
Random House, Inc: adaptation of selection on p. 210 from *A
Warsaw Diary, 1978–1981*, by Kazimierz Brandys, translated by
Richard Lourie. Translation © Random House, 1983

Translator's note:
I should like to thank my friend Bob Lumley for so much perceptive
advice during the preparation of this translation, and my editor,
Helena Franklin, of Pantheon Books, for being so patient.

C O N T E N T S

SWEDISH AUTUMN
[1982]
....

THE ELECTION PARTY

"It doesn't matter who we vote for or what the result is, because we're all Social Democrats," said the gentleman in the well-worn tweed jacket, raising a tumbler of red wine.

His remark did not surprise me. The election party to which I had been invited was taking place in the Old Town of Stockholm in the apartment of a prominent intellectual in the working-class movement, and I had the impression that it was to be a gathering of the party faithful to celebrate the forthcoming victory of Olof Palme. It was 1982 and Palme was at the height of his career, which was to end so tragically four years later. The apartment was furnished modestly and without much care. It was almost a little shabby: oddly assorted chairs, old posters on the walls, books in rough-hewn bookcases. Young married teachers in Frankfurt or Berlin live just this way, as do writers of radio plays or art historians who have managed to get a postgraduate grant. The apartment did not have an air of money, prestige, ambition. Reassured, I leaned back in anticipation of the first computer projections and ate a piece of smoked meat from the paper plate. After all, the intellectual in West Germany is used to such comfortable corners and niches far from the seats of power.

Then, however, at the improvised bar in the passageway, a helpful soul began to enlighten me. The gentleman in the tweed jacket was, it turned out, not the secretary of the local teachers' union but a much-feared journalist who wrote notorious lead articles for the country's largest Conservative newspaper; the almost too elegant man just fetching a piece of cheese from the kitchen was a star architect in Stockholm; the morose woman in running shoes had for years been in

3

charge of the Ministry of Social Affairs; the art teacher with graying temples was not an art teacher at all but a former ambassador; even the lady with the camera who took snapshots all evening without anyone paying the least attention to her was by no means an ordinary reporter, or the host's aunt, but one of the richest heiresses in Sweden.

Unsuspectingly I had stumbled into a gathering that any research sociologist would call, without hesitation, the country's power elite, even if those present would have completely rejected such a description. "Power elite" is a horrible expression, and nowhere could it sound less appropriate than here in Stockholm—not even in Tirana or Phnom Penh.

Somewhere in a corner a small television is on. The guests talk animatedly, drowning out the commentator's voice, and only occasionally glance at the early returns. Not a trace of tension or excitement, no "election fever." I had already been struck, in the days before the poll, by the extraordinary calm with which the Swedes approached their election campaign and by the stoical politeness of the speakers. In most democratic countries the campaign season is the time when the gray routine of party politics is transformed into public theater. An election is an exhibition bout, a carnival, a purification rite—a kind of football championship of rhetoric in which pent-up aggressions and suppressed emotions surface. It's an outlet for the frustrations, defeats, and disappointments of everyday politics. And especially when nations feel that their future might be at stake, the election is like a destructive potlatch, a national brawl in which what normally is forbidden is briefly permissible: open rivalry, ruthless polarization, the eruption of hatred, dissatisfaction, and ill will.

No one can say that the Swedes are simply short of reasons for getting excited. I'm told that the national budget shows a deficit of 78 billion kroner for 1981—more than 11 billion dollars.* Every Swede who reads a newspaper knows that his personal share of the national debt is 38,000 kroner (approximately $5,400), which amounts to more than 300 billion ($43 billion) for the state as a whole. And while official statistics cite 170,000 unemployed, everyone realizes that it's a cosmetic figure, that the real number is closer to 500,000. As if all this were not enough, the trade unions have placed a monster of a plan on the political agenda, just in time for the election. The famous Employees' Fund, which has been called a utopian white elephant by some and an economic King Kong by others, makes an almost ideal bone of contention. In any other Western nation it would have triggered an ideological civil war. If I have understood this proposal correctly (and if not, I won't be the first person to have lost his way among its pitfalls and elastic clauses), it amounts to a demand as simple as it is audacious: the capitalists are to pay for the rope by which the trade unions want to hang them.

Of course, in an orderly country like Sweden no one puts it so bluntly. Perhaps it's not even meant to be taken quite seriously; perhaps the trade unions were only sending up a trial balloon. Perhaps some left-winger only wanted to breathe a bit of life into the proceedings, and after a few hostile election posters, a few cautious interviews, and examination by a couple of parliamentary committees the plan will end up being shelved. A number of those present at the party, including a man who plays tennis with Olof Palme and another who goes on summer trips with him, assure me that the future prime minister is not very happy with the idea and took it up only to pacify some of the trade union leaders.

Maybe. But the more I think about it, the more threadbare such superficial explanations appear. The deep note of

* *All currency equivalencies given in this book reflect rates of exchange at the time of writing.*

harmony that accompanies every political statement in this country must have a far more profound source. When faced by a problem, an intellectual usually reaches for a concept. This time it's Gramsci who comes to my rescue. The concept of hegemony plays a central role in his theoretical writings. It seems to me that the Swedish Democratic Party is no ordinary political party. It plays a hegemonic role, which means it determines the rules that everyone else must follow for political survival.

On the eve of the election the leaders of all the parties represented in the Riksdag took part in a televised discussion. As was to be expected, it was conducted in such a fair, decent, and restrained manner that many viewers dozed off in front of their televisions. From the first it was obvious who the dominant figure was. Not the prime minister but the chairman of a party that, formally speaking, was part of the opposition. Olof Palme acted as if he were the host or the reigning champion, and his domination was not due to charisma or rhetorical skills. (He lacks the *gravitas* of the born father of the people; he is too intellectual, too versatile, too urban to arouse adoration or even respect.) If he was, nevertheless, in command of the situation, it was thanks to his office. He had the last word because he represents an organization that dominates Swedish society ideologically, morally, and politically, whether it is in office or not. Its power is so great that it determines every move its opponents make. Anyone who opposes the Social Democrats tends to apologize for his stance, often without noticing it. This habit extends even to the other parties' choice of names. The Conservatives call themselves the Moderate Unity Party, as if they were ashamed of being Conservatives. The Liberals clearly find their own Liberalism suspect, so they've settled on a folksier name, while the old Farmers' Party hides behind a title so neutral that it hardly means anything at all.

* * *

It is an old, tired Marxist misunderstanding to believe that political power resides in bank vaults. What goes on in people's heads, which unwritten laws they obey, and which language they speak count just as much. The Swedish bourgeoisie has no language of its own anymore, no identity, and no political culture. Even the word *borgerskapet* has a disreputable or at least a defensive sound to it. So it's no surprise that, apart from a few minor changes, the so-called "middle-class governments" in power after 1976 merely continued Social Democratic policies. They increased the tax burden and raised both public expenditure and the state's share of the gross national product.

It appears that the rich do not have much fun in such a society. This isn't just a matter of paying taxes! As respectable citizens they would be glad to pay them punctually, even if unwillingly. What hurts them far more is that no one shows any understanding for their difficult position. They open their front doors apologetically. It was, as it were, only by chance, almost by mistake that they acquired their money, their villas. And it's not as if they flaunted their wealth. Quite the contrary: wealth is a burden, it makes them conspicuous, it gives rise to misunderstandings. They might be thought vulgarians or even speculators, and they would find that extremely offensive. In short, they feel they are superfluous, ignored, and excluded. Whenever they do manage to rouse themselves to a mild protest, the result is a bit forlorn and shamefaced. I always have to smile when I think of the dark-blue Jaguar in front of the Grand Hotel Saltsjöbaden on election Sunday. Its rear window bore a sticker reading *Folket mot löntagerfonderna* (The people oppose the Employees' Fund).

Meanwhile the ranks of the guests had thinned. No one paid any attention to the columns of figures on the screen. The most important people, distinguishable to the outsider only by their extreme inconspicuousness, had disappeared as soon as victory seemed imminent. Presumably, they had driven to party headquarters, where the first decisions about government appointments were being made. The remainder had got as far as dessert (wild-strawberry ice cream in paper cups) by the time the evening's winner appeared on the screen. What he said no longer surprised me. He generously offered his opponents "his outstretched hand," paternally exhorted them to bring confrontation to an end, and promised to respect the views of the losers. Like a good shepherd, he promised forgiveness and reconciliation to all lost sheep. The country could return to business in the mild glow of Social Democratic hegemony.

However, I picked up a glass of port, and while the last guests were buttoning up their coats, I fell deep into thought. I probably stayed too long. The longer I thought about the evening, the more remarkable and exotic this Northern country seemed to me. Everything I'd heard during the election campaign suggested that I had arrived in the kingdom of reason and good sense, of solidarity and consideration. I had been able to observe a noble contest in which all the contestants were racking their brains about just one thing: how to help the unemployed and the disabled, the pensioners and the needy. No one appeared to be thinking of his own interests. No one appealed to the lower, selfish instincts that obsessed other societies. When I thought of my own country, the Federal Republic of Germany, I experienced an ugly feeling of envy. My compatriots seemed like a horde of egotists and delinquents surrendering themselves to extravagance, ostentation, and aggression.

It really looked as if the Social Democrats, the hereditary tenants of this political culture, had succeeded in taming the human animal where other quite different regimes, from theocracy to Bolshevism, had failed. Stumbling back to my hotel through the deserted streets of the capital, I asked

myself how they had managed to achieve this miracle. I saw
the neon logos of the multinational corporations, the deluge
of goods in the shop windows, the police, and the drunks.
So much harmony, so much solidarity, so much altruism in
the midst of capitalism? I came to the giant brick, granite,
and sandstone castles of the Östermalm with their green
copper towers, stony monuments to the Swedish bourgeoisie,
and was—dare I admit it?—suddenly gripped by a cold
shudder of doubt. I asked myself, What was the price of this
peace, what were the political costs of this re-education? I
began to suspect the suppressed and its return everywhere
around me, and to discern the suffocating presence of a
remorseless, soft, omnipresent pedagogy.

At Nybroplan I was close to a mild depression. Then I
remembered a man I had met a few days before in an ugly,
modern office building nearby; an upstart, a *nouveau riche*, a
self-made man. Well-meaning friends had warned me about
this "ugly Swede." "What do you hope to learn from meeting
him?" they had asked me. "He's a speculator, a shark, a
moneylender." Their warnings had no effect; on the contrary,
I was eager to meet this black sheep who had risen from coal
merchant to company boss. He received me in a comfortable,
rather ordinary office whose walls were hung with brand-new
paintings. The laugh lines around his eyes multiplied as he
told me about his fabulous successes. He showed not a trace
of hypocrisy. He talked about his wealth with awe, about his
enemies with satisfied hatred, and referred to the newspaper
campaigns against him without self-pity. He gave me his
company newspaper when I left. It was illustrated with
fourteen photographs. He himself could be seen in eight of
them: statesmen congratulated him, diplomats offered him
greetings, society ladies smiled at him. There was something
disarming about his naïve vanity. He was tough, clever, and
a little vulgar, but there could be no doubt about his energy
and his determination.

It is difficult for a Central European to rid himself of the residue of cynicism he needs to survive morally and intellectually in his homeland. Perhaps that's why I liked this ugly Swede. His views don't interest me and his successes leave me cold. But I think his existence lays bare a suppressed truth. I think his fellow Swedes resent not only his millions but also the shameless candor with which he displays his success. There are people on whom even the most benevolent welfare and educational system breaks its teeth. I don't know why, but this truth comforts me.

THE ARMOR OF INSTITUTIONS

One fine autumn evening in September 1982 a couple of dozen schoolgirls and schoolboys in bright-colored clothes met on the Fridhelmsplan. Not a motorcycle gang, quite ordinary young people. There were only a few representatives from the sparse punk and anarcho milieu. More and more young people appeared out of the depths of the pedestrian underpass. No one knew where they had come from or what they wanted. They didn't want to demonstrate for or against anything. They were simply there, standing around in loose groups and talking to one another. When the crowd had swollen to almost a thousand, it moved off in the direction of Rålambshovspark without forming itself into any kind of order, without slogans, and without any preconceived plan.

After half an hour the police arrived, over fifty men with vans, truncheons, and ferocious dogs. Within seconds the peaceful scene was transformed into a threatening confrontation. The officers in charge were determined to disperse the young people. The police hit a few with their truncheons, the dogs became restless, there were bruises and torn clothes. Then the first stones were thrown. Three hours later the park lay quiet and empty in the darkness again.

Not until the next day did the people of Stockholm learn

from the morning papers that a very interesting social innovation had led to this violent action against the adolescents. A couple of smart kids had discovered an interesting technical deficiency in the public-telephone network whereby anyone who dialed certain unallocated numbers could talk to anyone else who did the same thing. The numbers spread through the Stockholm schools like wildfire, and an enormous, spontaneous conference circuit came into being, a new mass medium: the "hot line." It's hardly possible to use modern communications technology more intelligently. I don't know if the city of Stockholm awards a cultural prize. If it does, then the unknown discoverers of the "hot line" have done more to deserve it than all the aspiring performance artists in the kingdom. Even the highly paid experts who have been boring the public for decades with their anxious observations on the aimlessness, lack of motivation, and anomie of today's youth should be able to understand that.

But the authorities preferred a different kind of response. After all, what are police dogs for? In any case, the police department was mildly reproached in a few carefully balanced newspaper articles. However, the critics didn't even mention that the police action was in clear violation of the constitution, which guarantees freedom of assembly to all Swedish citizens, and as far as I know none of those responsible have been called to account.

Now, as I know from my own experience, the arbitrary power of the police is far from being an exclusively Swedish phenomenon, and although I find the incident repugnant I wouldn't go on about the authorities' obsession with order if it were only a matter of some torn jeans. The terror practiced by the French or West German police (to say nothing of the East German) takes much more dangerous forms, ones with which their Swedish colleagues can hardly compete. But it seems worth noting that their excesses have quite a different meaning. There were no illegally squatted houses in Rålambshovspark, no masked faces or Molotov cocktails—only a few hundred young people who wanted to talk to one another.

Their crime was simply that they had not called upon any of the responsible *institutions* available for this purpose. If they had applied to the appropriate office with a request to *organize* a meeting place for aimless, weakly motivated, anomic young people, they would have been met with subsidies instead of police truncheons. Crowds of social workers, youth workers, and community art workers would have descended on them to help them achieve socially desirable forms of communication.

Proof of this theory came within a week. Hardly had the bruises healed and the jeans been patched than the responsible agency came forward offering to institutionalize the "hot line." "We understand," a communiqué stated, "that many young people feel a genuine need for the 'hot line.' We intend, therefore, to set aside a telephone number just for group conversations, and we suggest that five persons at a time can use it for up to five minutes at a time." The logic of state intervention is quite clear: first the stick, then the carrot. The social imagination and independent initiative of the young people are crushed in a kind of pincers movement—repression on the one hand and the state's embrace on the other. A few hundred young Stockholmers' taking the liberty to move around and talk to one another appears to both police and social workers as an unauthorized and irresponsible activity that is not to be tolerated.

In the long run the young people themselves—or some, at least—have come to the same conclusion. They form a committee to negotiate with the appropriate agencies, the social-welfare office, and the telephone company. And from then on the vicious dogs can be left in their kennels. There's nothing but helpfulness and understanding for the lost sheep that have found their way back to the fold.

* * *

Max Weber called this fold "the armor of institutions." Of course, there's nothing new in the argument that, as inhabitants of modern, industrial states, we long ago became reconciled to spending our lives inside a labyrinth of visible and invisible walls, and to the inexorable growth of bureaucracy as our societies become larger and more complex. Criticisms of this situation have themselves become banal. Our resistance to it is usually as silent as it is futile, and the reason is very simple. It is quite half-hearted. The very thing that worries and limits us at the same time promises protection, release from responsibility, fewer complications in our personal lives. We demand that Leviathan give back to us the ability to determine our own lives when in fact we usually have only delegated it. The risks of freedom seem much too high, and indeed the individual is hardly capable of bearing them anymore.

I don't think there's anything specifically Swedish about this dilemma. And yet the general analysis fails to do justice to the specific character of the strategies the Scandinavian welfare state uses to resolve the fundamental conflict between people and the institutions in which they live. The two sides confront each other in a condition of historical innocence that would be unthinkable elsewhere. Whether it's a matter of dealing with the "hot line," alcoholism, the education of their children, town planning, health, or income tax, the citizens of Sweden regard their institutions with a trust and lack of suspicion that takes good intentions entirely for granted. Such an attitude would be incomprehensible to a Spaniard, an Irishman, an Italian, or a Frenchman, to whom skepticism, lack of enthusiasm, and mistrust have long been second nature. Even the Germans, traditionally prone to defer to authority, can no longer compete with the Swedes, who hold a record for docility.

There are probably many reasons for this trustfulness. Perhaps the most important, though, is a lack of experience, for which the Swedes can only be envied. Generations ago those in power abandoned a pastime that is still quite common in other parts of the world: the armed hunting-down of human beings. That's why the Swedes believe the authorities have only the people's best interests at heart.

And the Swedes are right in making this assumption. The institutions whose concrete boxes occupy the center of every town embody a power that is alien yet always benevolent. It's precisely their benevolence that places them beyond criticism. Consequently, these institutions have increasingly acquired a moral immunity unknown to other societies. To limit, supervise, and resist the forces of good can only help the forces of evil. And so it's not surprising that this power expands irresistibly into the farthest corners of everyday life and regulates the affairs of individuals to a degree unparalleled in other free societies. This means that the institutional apparatuses have been able to appropriate the citizens' moral values along with the lion's share of their incomes. It is the apparatuses that take care of community and equality, shelter and aid, justice and decency—all things much too important to be left to ordinary people.

Impersonal reason seems to dominate every statement about life. It's present in the smallest trade union local and the remotest farm house. Its embodiment is the *ämbetsverk*, an administrative board or office. No one in Sweden could tell me how many of these administrative monsters there really are. One M.P. estimated their number at seventy-five, a professor of constitutional law reckoned almost two hundred. However, everyone I asked agreed on one thing: all these bodies—*nämnder, expeditioner, ämbeter, enheter, styrelser, verk*—enjoy an autonomy hardly conceivable anywhere else. The supervision that Parliament exercises over them is extremely weak, and any minister who dares to intervene in their management is soon put in his place. I suspect they

14

derive their sense of identity from the age of enlightened absolutism. They are like huge, ingenious, somewhat old-fashioned pieces of theater machinery that, despite cumbersome creaking and groaning, keep the wheels of state in motion while the politicians conduct their sham fights on stage.

It is as if the civil servants in fact stood above the parties whose instructions they are supposed to carry out. The same could be said of the trade union leaderships. They believe they are able to speak and act not only in the name of their own organizations but of society as a whole. Certain characteristic phrases recur in their statements: "Society must intervene here." "Society cannot allow this." "Society must concern itself with this." Reading the sentences more carefully, one soon realizes that the word *samhället* (society) is synonymous with "the institution I represent."

The good shepherd—to return to him—is always convinced that he is right, since he only wants what is best for his flock. It is virtually his duty to "know it all." If he meets with criticism he may make a tactical withdrawal here and there, but he sticks unswervingly to his plan, determined to force it through at the next possible opportunity. Not that he's infallible; only the ideal totality he embodies, inadequately and provisionally, is infallible. Since he is also a teacher down to his fingertips, he knows that his goal—the improvement of humanity—can be advanced only one step at a time, and that he must be patient with his pupils when they prove unreasonable.

It is difficult to pass judgment on the good shepherd. That is because of the ambiguity of his actions. He provides a service: an unparalleled degree of care and welfare. But at the same time he practices a kind of "soft terror" that frightens me. It's easy to feel indignant about the good shepherd when he kidnaps children, imprisons journalists, and sets fierce dogs on young people—all with the best intentions, of course. But he's to be applauded for providing free wheelchairs and establishing equal rights for women in the workplace. Maybe it's not even possible to be objective about him. Each particular case will determine whether one regards the advance of this social figure with satisfaction or dismay. For, of course, the good shepherd is not an individual but a collective entity that reproduces itself exponentially. It is unlikely that any other segment of society has grown so rapidly. And the good shepherd's benevolence stops where his own corporate existence is called into question. Here he is not to be trifled with.

A little while ago the central organization of state nursery school teachers strongly criticized a group of Swedish parents who had announced that they intended to care for their own children in the future. Such blatant interference in their duties, said the good shepherds, threatened not only their jobs but also the humane goals of a society based on a community of interest.

One can hardly counter such a forceful argument with mere citations. Nevertheless, I reach for my Swedish dictionary and find the following entry: *myndighet* [noun], derived from *myndig* [adjective]. The word literally means "who has power," and is derived from Germanic *mundô*, "hand." It refers in particular to the power exercised over dependent members within the family: Anglo-Saxon *mund*, "hand, protection, guardianship, guardian; also bride-price and the rights of guardianship over the bride acquired through this purchase." One derivation is *myndling*, "someone in the power of another; see also *formynder* (guardian)."

I seem to remember that long, long ago the left hoped to liberate human beings from their dependency. I've never quite understood why in so many countries—including Sweden, unfortunately—worship of the state became the credo of the left, while the desire for self-determination came to be regarded as the quintessence of middle-class obduracy.

THE CONSTITUTION NO ONE KNOWS
....

On a wonderfully clear morning—from Riddarsholmen all the spires of the capital can be seen gleaming gold—Executive Councillor Gustaf Petrén, one of Sweden's most senior judges, is sitting in his office on Birger Jarl Torg. Really, he's got better things to do than entertain the questions of an itinerant ignoramus. Apologetically he indicates the piles of documents covering the floor of the room. But as soon as he begins to talk about the foundations of the Swedish political system, this large man with the disheveled hair and bushy eyebrows forgets to look at the clock. He has no time for the measured language of civil-service routine, and he displays something very rare: the single-minded commitment of a born lawyer.

"In Sweden," he says, "the law is not much more than a branch of the administration. The judges usually come from the civil service, and they think of themselves as part of the apparatus. They don't see it as their job to protect the citizen from the state; they're more concerned about protecting the state from the citizen. Perhaps you remember the so-called Law of Exception, which tried to prevent members of the public from taking senior civil servants to court?" I have heard of it, but I also know that the law, passed by a sleepy Parliament, has been repealed. "Yes, the Riksdag seems to have too much to do," remarks Petrén drily. "I know at most half a dozen M.P.'s who are in a position to really understand the bills on which they have to vote."

The sarcasm this judge displays does not tempt him to draw any simple conclusions. His intelligence is too dialectic, too alert for that. Spurred on by a highly productive restlessness, he jumps from one subject to the next, first emphasizing a good point or strength of the system (he praises the openness of the Swedish authorities and explains the benefits of the appeals procedure) then sharply criticizing what he

17

sees as defects. He makes brief digressions into history and draws on examples and comparisons from other countries. Sometimes I'm not quite sure whether he intends an argument to be taken seriously or ironically. "There was one good thing, at least, about the Law of Exception," he remarks in passing. "Approximately five thousand gentlemen could sleep peacefully in their beds knowing that no crowd of litigious troublemakers was going to make their lives hell."

I've always suspected that it would not be difficult for a good lawyer to become a good satirist. "Our system," continues Councillor Petrén, "has very ancient foundations, which date back to the time of Oxenstierna.* The concept of separation of powers is foreign to us. The Swedish philosophy of state is concerned not with checks and balances but with the continuity of a neutral administration. As a result we have a state that places more emphasis on laws than on rights. Anyone who is too insistent about his rights is considered a legalist."

But the institution of the ombudsman is a Swedish invention, I object.

"Just don't talk to me about it," replies the judge angrily. "I was Justice Ombudsman for many years and perhaps could still have been today. But I lost interest in the job after it was stripped of all real power in 1976. Since then the authorities have been able to disregard the ombudsman's verdicts without losing any sleep. The office is in danger of becoming mere window dressing. I didn't want to be party to it."

A secretary has brought the judge his lunch. The frugal meal lying on the desk consists of a foil-wrapped tomato sandwich. Apparently, the judge doesn't even allow himself a cup of tea. Perhaps, I think to myself, it's time for me to

* Axel, Count Oxenstierna (1583–1654), who as chancellor and regent for Queen Christina exercised almost unlimited power in Sweden.

take my leave. But Councillor Petrén shakes his head. This is his subject.

"In case of doubt, it's always the Executive that has the last word in Sweden. The Riksdag's role is relatively modest. The experts in the *ämbetsverk* or in the commissions draw up the bills. Even the ministers' influence is comparatively small. It's only in cabinet that they carry much weight, and even there the opinion of the state secretary, who has a very strong position, is decisive. Then the bill goes to the appropriate committee. The Riksdag's blessing is almost automatic after that. It hardly ever initiates its own bills."

I inquire whether this distribution of power corresponds to the provisions of the constitution.

"No one in Sweden is interested in the constitution. No one knows it. There are historical reasons for that too. The constitution that was valid until the 1970s had been imposed from above in order to legitimate a *coup d'état*—an event in which the Swedish people played no part. The constitution was not even incorporated into the Swedish legal code. Strictly speaking, the parliamentary system was not introduced in Sweden until 1969.

"The king had a very central position under the old constitution. The politicians didn't like that, so they decided to give all power to the people—only to reclaim it in the very same breath. Apart from that, they completely forgot to include a bill of citizens' rights in the draft of the new constitution, and the omission was rectified only after some people had drawn attention to it. Perhaps it's also significant that the new constitution, just like the old one, was adopted without the sovereign people having had any opportunity to vote on it."

I expressed my thanks and took my leave of this frank man, depressed by the thought that he'd now have to turn his keen mind to a pile of dusty documents. And while he ate his sandwich bent over his files, the excellent restaurants of the Old Town were filling up with smart businesspeople who at about half past three, after a very satisfying meal, would snap shut their attaché cases and pull out their credit cards.

Meanwhile I visited two or three nearby bookshops to buy a copy of the Swedish constitution. This request produced only helpless apologies. Eventually I thought of the last resort of the ignorant foreigner, the Svenska Institutet (Swedish Institute). After a lengthy search in the storeroom, an elegant lady handed me a free copy of the desired text, in Swedish and English, and I made my way back to the hotel to study the document.

I actually rather enjoy reading constitutions. True, I'm only an amateur in the field, but I believe that they are one of the most admirable inventions of the bourgeois epoch. My Marxist friends' view that they are merely a ruling-class deception, a pure meaningless formality, has always seemed idiotic to me. The left's abandonment of so-called bourgeois rights and freedoms has always had dire consequences, sometimes of the bloodiest kind. So it was with pleasure that I read the first two chapters of the *Regeringsformen* (Instrument of Government), as the Swedish constitution is officially titled, which deal with the basic rights of the Swedish people. Here there is even a declaration of intent missing in the constitutions of other countries: "In particular it shall be incumbent upon the community to secure the right to work, to housing, and to education, and to promote social care and security as well as a favorable living environment." This provision, along with the absence of a clear guarantee of property, presumably expresses what one may call the Social Democratic hegemony.

But unfortunately, I also had to conclude that Gustaf Petrén's criticisms were correct. It seems especially incriminating that there is no provision for a constitutional court.

What happens if the Riksdag or the government or some other authority passes a law, decree, or regulation that is unconstitutional? Nothing happens. For according to Chapter 11, Article 14: "If a court or any other public organ considers that a provision is in conflict with a provision of a fundamental law or with a provision of any other superior statute, or that the procedure prescribed has been set aside in any important respect when the provision was inaugurated, then such provision may not be applied. However, if the provision has been decided by the Riksdag or by the Government, the provision may be set aside only if the inaccuracy is obvious and apparent." This provision is so odd that no one, so far, has thought of implementing it.

Other parts of the constitution also show evidence of confusion and badly thought-out compromises, for example the section on the monarchy. The poor king, who is treated like some stage extra, has even lost his title in the chapter heading. He is not granted any rights; in their place is only a pedantic list of limitations, as if the authors of the constitution wanted simultaneously to keep and get rid of the "head of state." The same appears to be true of the state church, which the fathers of the constitution want neither to endorse nor to abolish and which is therefore relegated to an obscure footnote under the heading "Transitional Provisions." In fact, the whole text gives the impression of having been a burdensome duty. Even a stumbling foreigner will notice the stiffness of this prose, especially when compared to the old Swedish royal oaths and pledges. Can one blame a nation for not taking to its heart formulations like the following?

"A statement by the Law Council should be obtained before the Riksdag takes a decision on a fundamental law concerning the freedom of the press, on any Act of law limiting the rights to have access to public documents, on such Act of law as referred to in the first paragraph of Article 12, in Articles

17 to 19, or in the second paragraph of Article 20 of Chapter 2, or on any Act of law amending or repealing such Act, on any Act of law as referred to in Articles 2 or 3, or any such Act of law as referred to in Chapter 11, if such Act is important to private subjects or from the point of view of public interest. However, the foregoing provision shall not apply, if obtaining a statement of the Law Council should, on account of the character of the relevant matter, be without importance or should delay the dealing with the legislative matters in a manner which would entail considerable disadvantages."

These sentences are painfully reminiscent of the endless and incomprehensible phrases that appear on giant blue signs in every Swedish town, with the purpose of impeding Swedish drivers in their use of the streets and squares. However, it takes so long to read through these no-parking signs that a driver would first need to find a parking space to have the time to peruse and understand them—a logical dilemma that can be solved only by remitting 200 kroner (about $32) to the authors of these works of prose.

Now perhaps the Swedes are right to overlook such absurdities with a resigned smile. Perhaps my taste for studying constitutions is only a typically German obsession, a product of the unhappy history of a nation that has had all too much reason to fear its rulers like the plague. German democracy—such as it is—would be unthinkable without the constitutional struggles of the nineteenth century. The tenacious and heated debate over the interpretation of the Bonn Basic Law, which has been going on since the foundation of the Federal Republic, can only be understood when one remembers that what is at issue is the completion of the failed revolution of 1848.

It's quite possible that such disputes are unnecessary in Scandinavia and that people don't need a piece of paper to defend their freedom. Some Latin American dictatorships have constitutions that are a pleasure to read. It is well known that in 1936 Stalin had a constitution drawn up that guaranteed Soviet citizens every possible human right, just at the time he was preparing to inflict an unparalleled mass terror on the Soviet Union. Chasms can open up between constitutional law and constitutional reality. That is true not only in a negative but also in a positive sense. Why allow oneself to be intimidated by the oppressive features of the *pays légal* as long as the *pays réel* lives on happy, free, and unconcerned?

I put the books aside and looked out of the window across the glittering surface of Lake Mälaren to the proud city lying in the slanting light of the October sun. The newspaper clippings of my little archive, articles that threw a harsh light on the paradoxes of Swedish freedom, rustled on the table. Perplexed, I remembered the excited rhetoric of the critics. Their attacks bore witness to the arrogance and stupidity of officialdom and of the narrow-mindedness of power. The articles were read, discussed for a few days, and then forgotten.

Their tone was often shrill, sometimes even seemed hysterical, but that only showed that they were in the minority. The more concrete their examples, the more firmly convinced I was that they were right. Only when they tried to sum up their worries did they seem strangely unconvincing. They had borrowed their theoretical terms from other, distant societies; they spoke in terms of collectivism, corporatism, totalitarianism. I understood only too well what they were trying to say, but some of the regimes in which these abstractions had become reality I knew at first hand, not just from books.

I look out the window and think of the depopulated settlements of the Värmland region, of the fourteen-year-olds on Sergelstorg Square cutting off the telephones in the phone booths, of the crazy old ladies wandering through the rocky parks in the Södermalm district. I try to imagine the real lives of the real Swedes, and as the view over Lake Mälaren gets darker, I'm less and less convinced by those who are reminded of Mussolini's Italy or Honecker's Germany when they think about the problems of this odd country. I switch on the light and look through the intelligent, serious, urgent articles again, and suddenly I think I understand what makes their analyses so barren, so lacking in light and shade. They have forgotten something: the past. It makes their explanations flat and short of breath. I must say, I don't like to hand out advice without being asked; I'm just talking to myself, saying what's on my mind. But I think that anyone who tries to ignore Sweden's history will hardly be able to solve its present-day riddles.

THE WALL AGAINST THE WOLVES

Less than two hours by car from Stockholm, in northern Uppland, the Swedish landscape already looks desolate and unpopulated. But this impression is deceptive. Anyone who began to dig here would stumble on prehistoric remains or find the foundations of an abandoned church or the ruins of an ironworks. And the traveler who is patient and armed with a good map will discover even more in the middle of this featureless, flat forest region: a small miracle of early industrial civilization. Leufsta Bruk, today a quiet, idyllic settlement, far from the main roads, presents the visitor with an almost intact picture of an eighteenth-century utopian community. In the center, surrounded by a large park, is the manufacturer's mansion, reflected in a large reservoir that is part of an artificial hydraulic system putting the forces of nature at the services of human reason. The houses of the manager, the smiths, and the laborers are symmetrically arranged on the other side of the lake. Beside them are the school, the apothecary, the doctor's house, the wooden tower whose bell called the whole community to work, and a small church, at once plain and magnificent, which contains one of the most beautiful baroque organs in Northern Europe.

The ironworks itself, the actual raison d'être of this fantastic place, no longer exists; its last remains were demolished in the thirties. Only the old engravings that slumber in the inaccessible library of the stately home could vividly convey to the visitor the astonishing technological energy of its builders. Today it still sounds like a miracle that three hundred years ago this traditionally poor, underpopulated country could become the world's leading exporter of iron and steel. This achievement would have been impossible without the social imagination embodied in the structure of these model communities. The Bruk company provided work, housing, spiritual and medical care, and retirement pensions for all its workers and their families. The voice of culture, and that means the voice of Johan Niclas Cahman's organ— pipes, stops, reed flutes, vox humana—was there for everyone too. One would have to be deaf and blind not to recognize the basis of the modern Swedish welfare state in this patriar- chal utopia.

Leufsta Bruk is an enclave in the wilderness, a quadrilateral figure of order, security, and discipline. A high, yellow wall separates it from the unpredictable animal forces that lurk in the outside world. This wall had not only a symbolic meaning but also a practical purpose: it protected the com- munity from the wolves.

L., a seventeen-year-old from Västerås, is passionately interested in the history of her country. She wants to be a historian. Two years before her graduation from school, one of her teachers explains to her that she is on the wrong track altogether. "What's the point of all this worn-out rubbish? Do you think it means anything? You'd be much better off worrying about the future. History isn't a proper subject at all. Look at our curriculum. Social studies and more social studies, that's what we have to concentrate on!"

The Stockholm Museums Guide by Bo Wingren lists forty-nine institutions, from Liljevalch's Art Gallery to the Tobacco Museum, from the Millesgården to the medical history collection. One can find old brewery equipment, old handicrafts, old cannon, old post horns, Chinese bronzes, Strindberg's desk, the genuine clothesbrushes and fake Breughels of Countess Hallwyl, motorcycles from the twenties, and exotic butterflies. But there is no museum for the political history of Sweden. Anyone who makes a pilgrimage to the Historical Museum hoping to learn something about the fabulous expansion of Swedish power in the seventeenth century faces a severe disappointment. The collections have an ethnographic and cultural orientation rather than a political one and extend only up to the beginning of the Vasa period in the sixteenth century. Beyond that, there's a vacuum that seems to interest no one.

Ideological repression? Political self-censorship? Fear of a past that might not fit into the self-portrait one would like to draw? At any rate, officially approved historical memory hardly seems to stretch any further back than the 1870's. Great value is placed on the social history of the popular movements, the trade unions, and Social Democracy. It is presented in feature films and textbooks, in academic monographs and exhibitions, in novels and television series. A degree of triumphalism is often evident in these portrayals; the understandable but self-righteous motto appears to be "From the darkness into the light."

It is precisely the very greatest achievements of their nation that Swedish intellectuals seem to find strange, even burdensome. There are historians who believe that Sweden is the oldest modern nation-state. The "motley feudal ties" to which Marx alludes in the Communist Manifesto were torn asunder here earlier than anywhere else, to be replaced by a strictly organized centralized state. Oxenstierna, an administrative genius, invented the prefectorial system two hundred years before Napoleon. He sent governors armed with executive powers into all the regions of the kingdom. They even had military means at their disposal to enforce the king's policies against the interests of the provinces. He created the first national atlas and the first central bank in the world. And so on. Does all this have no implications for the present condition of the country and for the problems of its institutions? Why is no one interested in the so-called "Era of Freedom"—a period in the eighteenth century when party strife was supposedly intolerable, but which gave a much-needed breath of intellectual fresh air and political "chaos" to future Sweden. It may be an admirable reflection of the international solidarity practiced by the Social Democrats that Swedish schoolchildren know more about repression and exploitation in the Third World than they do about Sweden's own period as a great power. But is it possible to understand why Sweden is the way it is by studying the apartheid system in South Africa and liberation movements in Central America? I'm only posing a question.

"The liquidation of their own history," I was told by a Norwegian historian, "is perhaps Swedish Social Democracy's greatest mistake. How can such an old nation know what it's doing if it doesn't know what it has inherited? This systematic forgetfulness will have to be paid for, at the latest in the times of crisis that lie before us."

Hans Hagnell, *landshövding* (provincial governor) of Gävleborgs Län, resides in the northernmost palace in the world. In the spacious rooms eighteenth-century Gustavian fauteuils stand next to spartan fifties furniture. The feudal character of the surroundings irritates the old metalworker. He resists it by refusing to throw away his old shoes and his patched trousers. Instead, he had the porcelain collection that his predecessor left him transferred to a museum as soon as he learned that it was worth several million kroner. Before I leave, this immensely upright, lean, white-haired man shows me an eighteenth-century paravent. On one panel of the richly painted folding screen, four apes can be seen dancing to the tune of a flute-player in the foreground. Who are the apes? Who is the flute-player? Why does the *landshövding* show me this picture, and what does his bitter smile mean?

Three days after the election, B., a member of Parliament, hands me a slip of paper across his desk. "This is the only written proof that I am one of the elected representatives of the Swedish people," he says, shrugging his shoulders. I look more closely at the document. It's a computer printout issued by the tax office and signed by some office worker. "As you can see, an M.P. is nothing very special in this country," says B.

Despite being a hard-headed, cynical Central European, I'm shocked. The technocratic shabbiness, the repulsive rationality of the procedure seems incomprehensible to me. "Once upon a time," adds the M.P. with a deprecatory gesture, "such documents were made out in the name of the king."

It's certainly difficult for a foreigner to understand why Sweden's internal revenue service should be responsible for its elections, when it is an institution that in most other countries would long ago have gone up in flames had it made such shameless, confiscatory demands on the citizens. Yet the aversion that B.'s computerized letter arouses in me has nothing to do with Swedish tax rates. What strikes me as scandalous about this communication is the brutal disregard for symbolic forms it shows. The bureaucracy is telling

Parliament in black and white to harbor no illusions about its dignity. In the bureaucracy's eyes only one law counts, the famous "Jante Law" formulated by the Norwegian writer Aksel Sandemose: "Don't imagine that you *are* someone, don't imagine that anyone is interested in *you*, don't imagine that you can tell *us* anything."

The elimination of formalities is another indication that the historical consciousness of this society is threatened by decay. The hegemonic culture of Social Democrats has forgotten the symbolic dimension without which politics cannot exist. They may have to pay dearly for this mistake.

As for B., he belongs to the Conservative Party. Yet his militant efficiency and smart insensitivity seem very much a part of the problem.

Lesjöfors in Värmland is a typical old Bruk company town. The ironworks, which still employs two thousand people, is partly out of date despite enormous efforts to modernize it, and it has fallen on hard times with the industry's structural crisis. For a century its location was ideal. The ore came from mines in the hinterland, the forests supplied charcoal, and water provided cheap energy, while the railway and the great lakes gave access to markets. In the time of the "old baron" who liked to ride through the rolling mill on horseback, business was still good and the company could take care of everything the community needed: housing and shops, sewage disposal and electricity, parson, druggist, running water, streetlights. The company was employer, health insurance fund, and retirement home rolled into one, and no one was forgotten, not the choir or the athletic club or the brass band.

Today the historic plant faces bankruptcy. When the family who owned it was on the brink of giving up, the workers decided to take it over themselves. After strenuous negotiations they were still 30 to 40 million kroner (5 to 6 million dollars) short of capital.

At the end of September (1982), even before the new government had been formed, a delegation traveled to Brommersvik in Sörmland. The leadership of the Social Democratic Party was holding a closed meeting in a trade union center there. Olof Palme had had a small apartment in its gatehouse for many years.

The delegation is said to have been admitted only after considerable discussion. The cabinet had not yet been named. No one felt like setting a precedent for the government's program with an ad hoc decision. After lengthy deliberation the requests of the workers from Lesjöfors were rejected. They left in a depressed mood. The designated finance minister drove back to Stockholm.

But the workers from Värmland did not give up. Two veteran metalworkers invited Palme to take a walk with them along the banks of the Yngar River. When they returned in the blue-gray twilight, the future prime minister had come to a decision alone. The workers of Lesjöfors were to get their 30 million.

Perhaps this story is a legend, and perhaps not. But its significance is obvious. The Swedish Bruk has got problems. The managing director is doing his best to save what can be saved. Meanwhile outside the walls of the community the wolves of competition, debt, and unemployment—the wolves of crisis—are howling.

THE CRISIS

One needs only to hear an opinion often enough for it to become suspect. The Swedes worship consensus, they are compliant, even conformist, and they display a touching trust in their governments. Some even say they're a little complacent and value security above anything else. Such judgments are rarely without a grain of truth, but basically they have all the reliability of rumor. Perhaps they're true, and perhaps not. Perhaps the one who keeps on repeating them fails to notice the symptoms of change, the subtle omens. Perhaps he misses what's really important.

Most of the Swedes I met this autumn were deviationists. Sooner or later, cautiously or vociferously, full of regret or anger, they expressed their doubts about the great model, about that best of all possible societies, which only twenty years ago still seemed within reach.

Of course, the faithful supporters of this project have not died out overnight. There are many, particularly in the headquarters of the trade unions and in the upper ranks of the Social Democratic Party, who maintain a furious optimism. "We can be proud of what we have achieved," they say, "and we will achieve even more." They are firmly convinced that things will go on as they are. They intend to respond to the increasing malaise affecting Swedish society by increasing the dosage of the medicine. With regard to the economy, that means more deficit spending, more public expenditure, sharper controls, growth at any price. Anna Hedborg, for example, a leading trade union economist, explains the growth of unemployment in the simplest way possible. It is "the result of regional imbalances, outdated gender roles, inadequate education, neglected kindergartens, and a lack of responsibility in taxation matters." The solution is simple: even more welfare, even more central planning, even more state. And she answers with a straightforward "no" when asked whether she sees any limits to industrial wealth or to state welfare. She is not alone in this point of view. An adviser to the prime minister has assured me that in the future Sweden would continue to be a model for the whole of Europe. Discipline, decency, and cohesion would allow considerable and uninterrupted growth rates to be achieved. The technocrats of left and right are united in this certainty at least, even if their methods differ.

But it's possible that they, and their confidence, are quite isolated. It sometimes happens that nations are a step ahead of their ideologists, that their ideas go further than the doctrines the politicians want to fob off on them. It may be that the Swedish crisis is more than a temporary liquidity problem, more than a passing case of economic hiccups, cured by the usual tricks. It could be that the all-encompassing service society was a fair-weather construction whose hidden political and moral costs have become apparent only as times grow harder.

One index of that is the so-called "contempt for politicians," a phenomenon that causes some well-intentioned observers to furrow their brows anxiously. "There must be a situation of trust!" exclaimed a liberal professor of politics. But why?

It's not only young people who are having second thoughts. A vague uneasiness is also spreading among the victors of yesterday and the day before. The veterans of the working-class movement, whom the Swedes affectionately call "gray socialists," are not people who have learned to conceal their thoughts. It's easy to see why the whole country trusts them. They find it difficult to express their doubts. They do so carefully, keeping within the bounds of loyalty.

Per Nyström in Göteborg, one of the architects of the welfare state, quotes Tage Erlander: "When people start talking about *them* instead of *us*, then the working-class movement is in danger." He criticizes the concentration of power in the trade union leadership, the arrogance of government departments, and the swindle of so-called decentralization, which consists of transferring a couple of the powerful administrative headquarters to the provinces, as if it were enough just to change an address.

Hans Hagnell raises a moistened index finger in the air and says, "That's how the politicians in Stockholm make politics." The civil-service unions have become nothing but self-service stores, and the official unemployment figures are good for nothing but self-deception. He tries to make sure that his own office goes against the administrative grain. He uses it to assert the region's interests against the unwieldiness, ignorance, and narrowly managerial attitudes of central government.

Bengt Göransson, the new minister of culture, whose political home is the clubs and associations, complains about the loss of variety and initiative that has resulted from the state taking over responsibility for social needs in Sweden. "People have gotten used to regarding the community as an insurance company. The citizen pays his premium, and the higher it is the more service he expects, the more passive he becomes, and the more certain he is to end up isolated."

The criticism expressed by those not so close to the hegemonic culture of Social Democracy is much more radical. I have been present at merciless discussions among Stockholm intellectuals who, not without some irony, describe themselves as "free thinkers," and who are not only ready to challenge the very foundations of the Swedish consensus but even feel it is their duty to do so. Others, perhaps the majority, simply turn their backs, like John, a young man who voted for the Conservatives not because he sympathized with them but because the trade union had screwed up his vocational training with its pig-headed regulations. Or like the former minister of industry who has lost the will to resist being ground down by party politics, and intends to write poems instead. Or like the kids to whom the "hot line" matters more than any official program for young people. And like the old lady who commits her first "economic crime" by hiring an "unauthorized" tradesman to paint her apartment because he is so nice, and because, if it were left to the whims of the tax office, she would end up spending the last years of her life in a dark, dirty room.

Harald Wigforss, one of the grand old men of Swedish journalism, whose home away from home is the Royal Bachelors Club in Göteborg, puts it coolly and cheerfully: "Everywhere in Sweden you now find a sense of unease, mistrust of officialdom, grass-roots movements, citizens' groups, the shadow economy, resistance in the trade unions, deviationists in the parties—in short, you catch a whiff of anarchy everywhere."

It's difficult to be precise about what's happening. Some say that it's simply a kind of normalization. In becoming more like the other Western industrialized countries, Sweden is losing the special role it has played since the Second World War. But perhaps it's also a slow, molecular learning process that may lead to new and unexpected results. At any rate, those who simply denounce such subterranean movements as immoral, and damn everything that doesn't suit them as renegade, egotistical, and lacking in honesty and a sense of community, are making things too easy for themselves.

The moral rigor that comes to the fore in such denunciations is itself more a part of the dilemma facing Swedish society than a solution to it. Anyone who understands politics only as a struggle between good and evil simply cannot cope with a crisis of the system like the present one. The eternal guardians want to make the people see reason and free them from their sinfulness. But their efforts are futile. Each new regulation tears open new holes; each additional measure of control increases the risk of malfunction, and the denser the mantle of institutions the greater the vulnerability to internal and external disturbance.

This increasing ungovernability bewilders and irritates administrations, and not only in Sweden. But here, where Manichaeism has struck particularly deep roots, the temptation to depend on good intentions is very strong. Only, good intentions are no longer enough when there's a problem that no longer fits the black-and-white grid.

The good shepherd believes that the world is governed by intentions, good or evil. He believes that social processes can be calculated and therefore controlled. But perhaps that's a delusion? Perhaps the good shepherd is an absurdity? Perhaps—to put it theoretically—human evolution is a stochastic process, a matter of guesswork rather than computation?

It's a very old idea. It was familiar to the Greeks. It surfaces again and again, in the idea of tragic irony as much as in the conception of the "invisible hand." Marx too was convinced that historical developments take place behind people's backs and without respect for their intentions.

Therefore, if the citizens of a country withdraw from their institutions, if an increasing proportion of the economy "submerges," if quite new social visions, from self-help to self-sufficiency, develop, then there is little sense in lamenting declining moral standards, instability, and polarization. In fact, these are all signs of life. Even if they cannot name their own goal, people's self-directed activity expresses a practical critique of existing conditions.

If there is any truth to that, then the crisis of the Swedish system is not merely an economic mishap that can be rectified by a few technical tricks. Of course, the outcome is extremely uncertain. But the prospects opened up by the crisis are not necessarily only depressing ones. The crisis also presents an opportunity. Perhaps one day it will lay bare the oldest stratum of Swedish history, its often hidden democratic bedrock.

ITALIAN EXTRAVAGANCES
[1983]

THE MAGICIANS

In the Hades of Milan, beneath the cathedral, in the endless, dark-brown corridors of the subway station, in this limbo of mass transportation, I learned of the existence of a German educational establishment previously unknown to me: The High International Academy of Artists of the Occult Sciences of Berlin.

Right next to a dazzlingly bright window display of pajamas and underpants in every possible color, I had noticed one dusty glass showcase. The following objects were laid out in the dim pink light of a flickering neon tube: a red devil's cap pulled over a white polystyrene skull . . . an aluminum teapot with a black plastic handle, which could, if desired, give birth to a crowd of little foam-rubber animals (90,000 lire—or 54 dollars) . . . a sad bunch of flowers made of lollipop-colored feathers . . . a mysterious little box with whose help any number of doves could be conjured up (100,000 lire—60 dollars) . . . a death's-head and a small pile of bright-colored play bank notes with a face value of 100,000 lire. Issued by the "Banca d'Amore," they were adorned with the portrait of a bearded gentleman who vividly reminded me of the sociology students of the early seventies. A hand-painted poster hanging over this wide selection of articles read as follows:

Warning: Italian certificates and diplomas are not recognized by the state. Anyone who wishes to obtain an internationally recognized diploma must call 059–685323. SILVA THE MAGICIAN is authorized by the High International Academy of Artists of the Occult

Sciences of Berlin to confer diplomas on professional and amateur practitioners of the occult arts.

I hesitated. Tempting though the prospect of a conversation with Silva the Magician might be, the area code puzzled me: 059 . . . that must be somewhere in the mountains, past Reggio Emilia, probably near Canossa. But I didn't want to go so far. It wasn't necessary anyway, as I learned from the telephone books. Every large town in Italy has dozens of magicians listed in the yellow pages.

Unfortunately, I have space here to mention only a few of them: the Magician of Florence, Joseph Cervino (National Chairman of the Magicians of Italy, A.N.D.D.I. Association) . . . the Sorceress of the Seven Rings . . . Dr. Marco Belelli (President of CISA, the International Center for Astrological Studies, Grand Master of the Theurgical Order of Elios) . . . the Magician Pharaoh Tutankhamen . . . and Professor Joseph, the Magician, who was blessed by His Holiness Pope John XXIII for his humanity and great kindness (Honorary Member of the National Association of Magicians and Spiritual Healers of Italy and holder of the Honorary Diploma of the Venerable Institute of Metaphysical Sciences in Paris).

For further information I must refer the reader to the appropriate trade press, especially to *Astra* (the astrological monthly published by *Corriere della Sera*), whose classified pages are a mine of information on the occult. The number of practicing *maghi* in Italy is estimated at a hundred thousand. The range of specialization is wide. Exorcists and pendulum-healers, astrologists and palmists, clairvoyants and pranotherapists, hypnotists and parapsychologists, readers of coffee grounds and experts in extrasensory perception, demonologists and radium healers, card-readers, and those gifted with second sight earn many hundreds of billions of lire every year and in return "solve any problem, whatever the distance."

A few years ago workers in the supernatural professions

began to unionize to overcome the one problem that still defeated them: the integration of magicians into the welfare state.

The magicians' trade union, Uaodi (Union astrologico-occultistica d'Italia), has already set up an official register and placed before Parliament a draft law that even provides for a state-approved examination for magicians. "We demand," states Mario Davano, the union's secretary-general, "that the following titles finally be given state recognition: Chartered Astrologist, Chartered Occultist, Consultant in Bioplasmology and in the Occult . . . Anyone abusing these titles must be subject to disciplinary proceedings. Yes, and in particularly serious cases may even be struck from the professional register . . . Our members are required to keep proper accounts and to deduct value-added tax at the legal rate . . . In return we demand equal status with other professions, especially with regard to pensions and health care."

"I don't know what you're trying to get at with your magicians . . . Or rather, I know only too well . . . I can already see him before me, the superstitious Southerner who pulls out a piece of coral the moment he encounters someone with the evil eye . . . the pilgrim who believes in miracles, in quest of the blood of some saint . . . the Mafia boss who bursts into tears because he's lost his amulet. But these are the clichés of folklore! Italy isn't the Third World! We're not some tribe of wild Indians! Try to remember that . . . A pocket edition of the savage mind—Lévi-Strauss in the pizza bar—that would just suit you down to the ground! In fact, superstition is about as Italian as IBM or Coca-Cola. Or do you really think Germans don't read horoscopes?"

There was little I could say to counter the reproaches of my friend from Turin. It was in vain that I quoted Camilla Cederna's book *Cosa Nostra* to her. In the first chapter, entitled "Satan in Turin," Cederna makes the astonishing claim that the city's magicians earn more than the Fiat factories.

"So what? What do you think that proves? That Piedmont's part of New Guinea?"

"I don't want to prove anything . . . I board my plane in Frankfurt, and an hour later I disembark in a quite fantastic region, in a country swarming with mythomaniacs. I page through the very first Italian newspaper I come across and immediately find myself at a giant fairground . . . I pay 500 lire at the turnstile and I'm riding a ghost train! Conspiracies, wire-pullers, secret lodges, melodramatic gang wars, incomprehensible palace intrigues . . . Facts simply evaporate. Reality becomes a comic strip. I only need to turn on the TV and what do I see? The deserted hallway of an apartment building in Geneva. The camera zooms in on an elevator door. The door opens. The elevator is empty. Upstairs, sinister shadows along the corridors, just like in *The Cabinet of Dr. Caligari* . . . A perplexed cleaning woman is interviewed . . . That's how the evening news begins, with a scene from a thriller that makes no sense at all. It's episode 100 of a pulp novel whose invisible hero is a mattress manufacturer from Arezzo. A shadowy demon, a paranormal personality—and the most powerful man in Italy. Grand Master of the mysterious lodge to whose tune ministers, generals, party chairmen, and secret services dance. A mattress manufacturer! Surely one is at least permitted to ask what's going on here. Melodrama or paranoia? TV series or black magic?"

"So you think we're out of our minds?"

"Let's say rather that madness is your daily bread."

"In other words, we're subnormal."

"Not at all, quite the opposite."

"What does 'quite the opposite' mean?"

"I don't know exactly. Perhaps the same as paranormal. That's why I'm interested in your *maghi*."

"And you think you can find them in the phone book? I feel sorry for you! A really good magician isn't listed in the yellow pages."

"Where do you find one, then?"

"I'll give you a couple of addresses. But on no account mention my name."

"Why not?"

"Because it's bad luck."

"The Italian peninsula as a whole may be under the dynamic sign of Aries, but the republic's horoscope is dominated by Gemini. Apart from that, every horoscope consists of four elements: earth, water, fire, and air. But the republic was declared on June 18, 1946, and there were no planets in Earth signs on that date. That's why this state lacks authority. It's unable to act effectively. Alternatives exist only for the individual. That makes survival possible."

These are the opinions of Francesco Waldner, a renowned astrologer from the South Tyrol who has been practicing in Rome for more than thirty years. Anyone who wishes to consult him is led into a small, elegantly furnished waiting room, high above the Tiber, where, just as in a fashionable doctor's office, one can while away the minutes reading glossy magazines. After a suitable interval the client is admitted to the imposing consulting room.

Behind a desk covered with gilded magnifying glasses and astronomical tables the small, robust *mago* almost seems to sink into his huge armchair. For a moment I'm irritated by his disconcerting resemblance to Franz Josef Strauss. The self-possessed man with brown-dyed hair and small, veiled eyes sits sideways in the armchair with his knees drawn up. Gesticulating vigorously, virtually unable to keep still, he lectures me on "the oldest science in the world that has been tested by experience." Again and again he drops names like Kreisky, Pompidou, Spadolini. But his judgments aren't fashionable ones—they're quite sound. And, far from cloaking himself in the mysteries of the supernatural, he delivers measured, sensible advice.

I'm disappointed. Pleasantly disappointed . . . My search

for the fantastic has had a paradoxical outcome. It seems as if in this country astrologers are the last resort of common sense, as if pragmatic thinking, reduced to an old-fashioned and slightly philistine core of aphorisms, has locked itself into the headquarters of "superstition"—while outside in the world of banks and political parties, of health plans and TV networks, reality is becoming ever more illusory, illusion ever more real. It's not the sorcerer in his salon who's demonic but the city outside his door, with its financial scandals, its addiction to luxury, its gang wars, corruption, and prisons.

But perhaps I've got Italy wrong. Perhaps I allow the mere surface of everyday life to deceive me—am I a victim of my own prejudices?

Of course, says Dr. Giampaolo Fabris, professor of sociology at the University of Trento, a lively gentleman who sounds very authoritative . . . The Italy you are looking for is an illusion . . . It doesn't exist! The reality, he says, is much more complex than you suspect. There are, he says, seven different Italies, no more, no less . . . And I can prove it to you!

The social scientist has a wiry physique. His high-domed skull is suntanned and bare. He has a carefully trimmed black goatee, and when he removes his round, nickel-plated glasses, his eyes are strangely penetrating. The walls of his Milan office are decorated with the results of "the largest ethno-anthropological investigation of Italian society" that has ever been carried out. This research project is named "Monitor 3Sc," or "the systematization of sociocultural currents and transformation scenarios," and it is run by the Monitor Demoskopea company headed by Dr. Fabris.

No one can say that he and his team have made things easy for themselves. First of all, they identified approximately thirty "currents" or "values" that could be used in their delineation of society. Among them were concepts like "poly-sensuality," "sexual permissiveness," "sensitivity to nature," and "secularization." Then they thought up a few hundred questions and formulated them in such a skillful way that the interviewees would, as far as possible, be unable to recognize the overall purpose of the survey. And no fewer than 2,520 Italians allowed themselves to be subjected to this hour-long test. (Sample: "It is always somewhat embarrassing to get to know an unmarried couple who are living together. Yes or no?")

The replies were fed into a computer, which balanced factors, calculated correlations, and located zones of minimal variability according to an elaborate mathematical-statistical model. "From the moment we commit our data—i.e., the coded answers on each topic covered—to the computer, we no longer have any influence on the outcome," says Dr. Fabris, with a touch of satisfaction.

Yet one can hardly describe him as a narrow-minded empiricist. For as he explains his methodology to me, he quotes Horkheimer, Max Weber, Agnes Heller, and Gramsci with ease. He also lets me know that he sympathizes with the Italian Communist Party, even if his clients . . . regrettably . . . tend to be found among the big capitalist companies . . . But what has he got to show them?

First of all, there is not, as we thought, one Italy—there are seven of them. The computer has discovered that in the future the following will have to be distinguished from one another: a conservative Italy; an archaic, a puritan, a consumption-oriented, a progressive, and a blue-collar Italy; and an Italy of the future (*emergenti*). The populations of these imaginary countries range from 3.2 to 7.6 million. If required, Dr. Fabris is able to say at once which newspapers these nations read, what they buy, who they vote for, what their favorite food is, and how often they go to the hairdresser.

But what relation do the seven tribes bear to one another, and what is their future likely to hold? The Demoskopea computer can answer these questions too. It prints out on request the coordinates of a map on which each clan can find its own sociocultural home. The vertical axis of the system stretches from the South Pole of the "social" to the North Pole of the "private," while the horizontal "axis of modernization" extends from the "umbilical cord" of the old, in the East, to the "new frontier" in the West. And in which direction is society as a whole moving? It's hard to believe, but figures don't lie: society is leaving tradition behind and, avoiding the "triangle of alienation" by a hairsbreadth, making for the "northwest passage"! That is the "megatrend" . . . "For anyone who can read the signs," says Dr. Fabris, "it's already clear what Italy is going to be like at the end of the millennium."

The country's leading newspapers commented respectfully on the results of the Monitor 3Sc project. In some quarters there was even a sign of satisfaction. Apparently no one asked himself why there should be just seven Italies. Why not five or eight or twenty-two? Is it because seven is a magic number? And why do the *emergenti*, these mutants of modernization, appear on the horizon of the future? Perhaps because Dr. Fabris gave them this fine name himself. Is it because, although tautologies don't prove anything, they do have the advantage of being impossible to disprove? And why, indeed, is the "private" to be found in the North, while the "social" is at the South Pole? Why not the other way around? And what do "private" and "social" mean anyway? Why this antithesis and not another? Why doesn't Dr. Fabris divide up his map of values differently, setting up an opposition between "corrupt" and "honest," for example, or "hardworking" and "lazy," or "rich" and "poor"? Ah, says Dr. Fabris, I think I know what you're getting at. But the concept of class is totally obsolete! A useless instrument!

I see . . . Well, who wants to be stuck with the good old facts? Certainly not Monitor Demoskopea Ltd. It wants to know about "currents," "values," and "lifestyles," and its data are attitudes, opinions, views . . . or rather attitudes about attitudes, opinions about opinions, views about views.

But what has come out of it all in the end, and what will the Mark 2000 Italian of the future be like? "Seeks a balance between home life and the outside world . . . Likes to spend as much time as possible in the open air . . . Prefers 'creative' hobbies . . . Takes one long or two short vacation trips . . . Has a pronounced need for spiritual values."

Doesn't that sound a little familiar? Max Weber? Not at all. It's an all-purpose description, not an ideal type. Demoskopea's electronic computer has drawn up a horoscope, just like the ones in *Astra*! And Dr. Fabris, the man with the black beard and the penetrating eyes, is the real astrologer, reading the imaginary future of Italy out of the coffee grounds of his theories and the entrails of his computer. The sociologist as fortune-teller! The magician as a figure of the Enlightenment! And who are his clients? The automobile industry, the soap business, and the secretary-general of the Christian Democrats!

My Roman acquaintances laughed at me when I told them about my researches. It's really nothing new. Everyone knows that! They could have told me all about it! Clearly, like most foreigners, I hadn't noticed that Italian culture has been dominated by a horde of secular witch doctors and shamans for years. By specialists in debate, commentary, interpretation, and "discourse" who have established themselves everywhere, in television, in the think tanks, in the press, in the political parties, in literature, and in Parliament, and whose never-ending torrent of words no one can escape. Political scientists, novelists, psychoanalysts, professors, editorial writers, sociologists . . . an undifferentiated dough out of which a worldly caste of priests had taken shape and in whose hands the whole cultural output of the country had been reduced to one thing: journalism. "In this tribe of ventriloquists and everyday prophets your Dr. Fabris is only a little fish, a beginner. The stars of the industry don't need a computer— they can be found in every newspaper and on every channel. We even have a name for them. We call them *gli intelligenti*."

They pronounced this term as if it were an insult or a curse. "Do you really think it's so bad for an intellectual to be intelligent?" I asked. I had the unpleasant feeling that they were amused by my naïveté. We were sitting in one of those exquisite restaurants that no American tourist is ever able to find: a melancholy young man who published beautifully printed but somewhat esoteric books; an uncompromisingly militant translator from Naples; and a mischievous dandy who had studied constitutional and administrative law for many years. The terrace doors were wide open . . . Duse may once have dined with D'Annunzio on these little art nouveau easy chairs, and the green salad was mixed with white truffles . . . But from time to time a shrill howl came up from the street. Then one of the party rose to check his car. The sound of the alarm obviously seemed to belong in the score of a Roman night.

"Say what you like," I continued. "I, at any rate, admire your intelligent sorcerers. When I listen to them, I feel like a provincial."

"You're making fun of us!"

"On the contrary. Here even the cretins are able to see through everything and take nothing at face value. There's not an intrigue or a plot that they couldn't uncover in next to no time, or a motive that could stay hidden from them. But if I think about our own press, the German, Swiss, and Swedish newspapers! Their ingenuousness, their gray conformity, the way they stick to mere facts . . . the lack of audacity, tempo, brio!"

"But your journalists actually go and do research on the spot, they're concrete. Our *maghi*, on the other hand, never leave their desks and hotel rooms—and that's precisely why they're so omnipresent and omniscient! You can't tell them anything they don't already know, you can never disturb their equanimity. The collapse of our institutions, terrorism, the crisis, the Italian catastrophe, it's all just more grist for their mill. They're always up to date, and their privileges are unequaled anywhere else in Europe."

"That's just not so! It's only true of half a dozen stars! I know plenty who earn so little they can't even afford to buy themselves a new shirt."

"So they try to push themselves forward even more frantically. They register every little fart *Le Monde* makes. To say nothing of the dozens of Italian papers they seem to read every day . . . 'So-and-so has stated in *Manifesto*' . . . 'She has just argued in *La Stampa*' . . . 'X responded in *La Repubblica*' . . . 'Have you seen Y's letter in *Unità*? Ridiculous. Utter nonsense' . . . 'That may have been the case three months ago, but now I couldn't care less' . . . And so they keep working away, getting this skein of opinions tied up in more and more knots, and their productivity borders on madness."

"They don't miss anything? All the better!" I exclaim. "This voracity has a positive side, and I think it's a considerable virtue to take an interest in what's happening abroad. Italy is not only the largest importer of malt whisky and champagne, it's also the European country most enthusiastic about translations."

"It's all just showing off! Overcompensation! An inferiority complex! We're allowing ourselves to be colonized, we simply echo the French and the Americans. Our journalism soaks up everything it hears about, like a dry sponge. And the invisible hand of the market wrings out the sponge at shorter and shorter intervals. The result is a boundless forgetfulness. Apart from that, our *intelligenti* are completely incapable of constructing a normal Italian sentence."

At this point I was forced onto the defensive. I had to

admit that I was often unable to decode the Italians' "discourse." Certain peculiarities of their vocabulary that I found disturbing could simply be put down to the carelessness of people who are in a hurry. It was possible to guess what a "maxisitting," a "megatrial," and a "micromimesis" might be. But no one could explain to me what "virtuosic projectuality" means, or "interaction compensation," to say nothing of "metavulgarity" or the "polytheism of consumption" . . . and all of these not in some esoteric journal but in the popular press with its printings of hundreds of thousands of copies. What does the public think of this, those who are not counted among the *intelligenti*?

"They're fed up with it," said my host. "That's why sales are declining. Give me the old crime pages, the black chronicles of traditional criminal reporting . . . newspapers as fantastic opera libretti . . . the transfiguration of reality into a gangster's smoking gun, into pulp fiction, the way it used to be. Anything is better than this pretentious, inconsequential nonsense!"

By dessert they had almost convinced me. Almost, but not quite. "And you?" I inquired maliciously.

"Oh, we're part of it too, of course . . . Maybe we lacerate ourselves a little less than others do. But we don't accomplish anything. Everyone wants to talk and no one listens."

All in all, it was a depressing evening, despite the excellent truffles in the salad and the luxuriant vegetation on the terrace.

THE HATRED OF EQUALITY

Customs Declaration. I was relieved when the bill of lading came. The house I had found in the Alban Hills was no noble villa, but my family was small and it would do very well for a year. The lease had been signed; I had been initiated into the secrets of the *carta bollata* (the taxable paper on which

Italian legal documents are drawn up); the notary had explained to me the contract's more obscure clauses. Now only one small detail was left: my baggage for the move to Italy had to be brought through customs.

One morning, I went to the appropriate government office. It was located in an old, seedy, barrackslike building on the outskirts of Rome. I even let the taxi driver wait, because I thought it was all a mere formality—no merchandise, no valuables, just a few boxes with household goods, clothes, books.

I spent three days of my life in this barracks, in a labyrinth of storerooms, offices, corridors, antechambers, and counters, unbelieving at first, then outraged, and finally embittered and demoralized. All around me everything was running like clockwork. Brisk, businesslike, but mysterious people wearing thick gold watches on their wrists hurried past me, laughing and exchanging greetings and jokes with the officials. Countless cups of coffee were being drunk. I was the only person who had to wander from one counter to the next with my forms (five copies of each), with duty stamps, clearance vouchers, receipts, and certificates. I had to plead my case a dozen times, was forced to wait, was put off with fine words, was sent from pillar to post, and was ignored.

On the evening of the third day I received my possessions with a stony expression. There were no fewer than thirty-eight rubber stamps on my bill of lading and my customs declaration. I had fought doggedly and resentfully for each one. That was more than twenty years ago, but even today I'm gripped by an unreasonable repugnance when I catch sight of an Italian customs official.

Of course, I learned long ago that this absurd adventure was my own fault. If I tell my Roman friends about it, they listen with amusement, but there is also a note of admiration and alarm in their laughter. What? You went there yourself? Alone? They treat me as if I were a lunatic who had crossed the Alps on foot. Today I too know how to interpret the sullen, bored, offended, and irritated faces of the minor officials who made me so indignant. Without suspecting it, I had broken the basic rules of the game. I had behaved like an American from the Midwest preparing to set up a vegetable stall in the middle of Nepal, or like an Irish hippie who had hit on the idea of competing with the porters at the Stazione Termini railway station in Rome.

I had no idea that a customs official who tried to live off his salary would be virtually condemned to death by starvation, and that by trying to deal with things on my own I was behaving like a dangerous madman. An Italian would never conceive of such an eccentric notion as going through customs by himself. Today I also know who the brisk creatures were who whisked past me in the halls of the customshouse. They were the *galoppini*, the professional intermediaries and agents. Pay them and all thirty-eight rubber stamps can be effortlessly mustered in half an hour. Everything works out, everyone makes some money, everyone benefits.

The Broad Road and the Narrow.   A foreigner will never understand all the nuances, undertones, and subtleties, but the principle is clear enough: the direct route is not the direct route. There is no point, under any circumstances, in appealing to a right that is common to everyone. It's much more important to acquire a favor, an obligation, or a privilege—and that demands a detour, a recommendation, a middleman.

A world of fabulous richness opens up, displaying an inexhaustible variety of forms. We meet the fireman who always has a ticket for the sold-out performances at La Scala; the neighbor who is a friend of the janitor's daughter, and who can find out in advance the test questions for the high-school graduation certificate; the Mafia boss who has a teleprinter brought into his cell; the male nurse who obtains for a patient a *turno*—a numbered slip that allows him to attend a clinic, and for which others have to start lining up at six a.m.; the industrialist's wife who hasn't a clue how to mail a registered letter or renew a driver's license, because a crowd of *galoppini*—her husband's secretaries—relieve her of every conceivable errand; and the ironing lady who brings a chicken for this same woman, her employer, because the latter's nephew is a dermatologist. She looks to the nephew to cure her breast cancer (which is not his specialty), because she is frightened that the obscure, nameless machinery of medicine will kill her . . .

Yet everything has its price. It will take the outsider years to learn all the rules of the game. True, it's easy enough to understand the 50,000-lira note (30 dollars) placed between the pages of the passport, but what about the visiting card with a couple of friendly, vague, handwritten lines addressed to the bursar? The visitor from the North who immediately cries "Bribery!" makes it all too easy for himself. He lacks a feel for suggestion, an ear for words left unspoken. His brutal simplifications don't do justice to the diversity and elegance of the system.

What, for example, is the significance of the flowers, strawberries, embroidered napkins, and cakes—a whole tableful of offerings—that the wife of a personnel manager, who has moved from Milan to Naples, finds outside her front door the day after her arrival? Who laid all this out? What is the point of this display?

"If you eat even a single cherry from this cake," she explains to me, "then you're in their hands. You've concluded an agreement that lasts a lifetime. Not one but three, four, five large families will demand that you get them work, get them into college, get them pensions . . . What could I do? I had no choice but to go out onto the balcony and proclaim loudly that I don't need anything, don't want anything, can't accept anything."

I have no ready answer to the question of how the unwritten laws of Italy relate to the written ones. The country's legal traditions are impressive, its laws numerous, and its hairsplitting achievements legendary. So there's no shortage of standards, only they're so diverse, complicated, and contradictory that only someone tired of life could dream of observing them all. Their strict application would instantly paralyze Italy.

Why shouldn't a professor be expected to live where he teaches? To achieve this goal, the founders of the University of Cosenza decreed that every teacher they employed was obliged to live within the city. No one took issue with this regulation. The whole faculty solemnly recognized it as binding. Despite that, more than 90 percent of the professors today live in Rome, Naples, or somewhere else outside Cosenza. If they had insisted on fulfilling their obligation, a minor catastrophe would have ensued—for no apartments were available for them. You would have to search with a magnifying glass to find an Italian citizen who lives by the book. Anyone who tried to go by the rules, whether applying for a building license, seeking a residence permit, or trying to exchange currency, would suffocate under a paper mountain of files and official documents. Each new rule breeds new exceptions, new violations, new evasions and deviations.

Extras.   Every Italian, even the poorest wretch, is privileged. Nobody is a nobody. A sober observer might come to the conclusion that often these privileges exist only in the imagination—but subjectively, they are the essence of life. A logician might object that a society consisting exclusively of the advantaged, in which each person is "doing better" than everyone else, as it were, is an impossibility. But the Italians have made this miracle—somewhat akin to the Indian rope trick, or squaring the circle—come to pass.

Five long-distance truckers stand at a bar in Andria, and

each one asks for a coffee: one wants it *molto stretto* (extra strong), another *macchiato* (with just a dash of milk), the next one *con latte caldo* (with warm milk), his colleague asks for a *cappuccino*, but the last one calls triumphantly through the bar: *"Un espresso doppio con latte aparte!"* (a double espresso with the milk on the side). He's known in every truckstop from Verona to Brindisi, and no barkeeper would dare deny him his heart's desire. He's not average, he's someone special. The round of privileges begins harmlessly enough but continues endlessly.

The great strength of this system is that it works not only from the top down but also from the bottom up—because even the poor, the "underprivileged," have their privileges, their consolations and prerogatives. The concierge apportions his favors and his punishments as he pleases, and the doorkeeper enjoys a mysterious power, of which his boss, the minister, is quite ignorant.

The baby-sitter who used to be a nurse laughs and tells stories about the hospital where she used to work. Above separate entrances are the signs "For Paying Patients" and "For Non-Paying Patients." Oh, the privileged private patient certainly has his telephone, his marble tiles, his own bath, all of which he has to pay for through the nose. But is his treatment any better? While the state-insured patient is treated quietly and routinely by the doctor on duty, the rich man has to wait till the big chief, the professor, shows up, because no one else would dare to lay a finger on his spoils. The paying patient lies in his beautiful private room, and sometimes he has to wait until it's too late.

An Extremist. He says: We hate equality. We despise it. We only like distinctions . . . Communism in Italy is a joke. Even the word "comrade" is hyperbole. The egalitarian speeches at the labor union congresses are nothing but rhetoric. No one falls for it, because no one believes in it. We aren't a collective, we're an accumulation of free individuals. We loathe anonymity. No one feels responsible for the "whole," everyone just looks out for himself, for his clan, his clique, his gang . . . The laws are only there for the suckers—that is, other people. Do you think I'd let myself be pushed around like a sheep in a pen? Or that I'd be willing to stand at a counter and wait my turn? Never! Of course, that means we feel total contempt for our neighbors. When it comes right down to it, we dump our garbage on other people's doorsteps. Consideration is unknown. There were two murders in our town this summer because noise became unbearable in the heat. One was right next door. For nights on end the whole street couldn't get a wink of sleep, so one guy drew his gun and shot another who was making a racket . . . That's normal. No one's got a conscience about anything . . . We have left-wing rhetoric but no social superego. We don't need any good shepherds, pastors, or wardens. Too bad for you, you'll say. Maybe you're right. But I also think there's something healthy in all of this. The rest of you always have to stick to the rules, but then you run aground on these rules. We, on the other hand, don't delegate anything to the collective, and that makes us free people. In this country all ideologies founder on that. Fascism was sunk by it too. Every one of us is a chief, a boss, a star, or his cousin has influence somewhere, or he went to school with someone he can call up because he's number one, even if it's only in the fire brigade . . . It also gives us a chance to help out. Not anonymously through regulations, certificates, or computers, but in person, directly, and forcefully. I'm always happy when I can take something in hand myself, do something for my friends, my colleagues, my clients. Because the hospital chief of staff is a friend, I can do something for a sick man who doesn't know which way to turn. I can look after him, even though he hasn't got any insurance, or the right paperwork, or any legal claim . . . Do you understand? And it's the same the other way around:

he looks after me when I need him. That's why social democracy will never happen in Italy, why the laws exist only on paper, and the state is just an abstract glutton, an insatiable chimera. Every man for himself and his own, at any price, whatever the risk—that's our morality.

Attempts at Explanation. Hypotheses. Excuses. It's an old story, a very old story . . . It's a consequence of the late unification of Italy, which never blossomed into true unity . . . It's related to the fact that the state always appeared as an occupying power, so the people resisted it with stubborn antipathy and extreme mistrust . . . It's the Mediterranean character, just like the Spanish, or the Levantine, or the Greek . . . It's a matter of precapitalist attitudes, remnants of feudalism . . . It's a rejection of the "naked cash nexus" Marx talks about, of the impersonal power of money that forces an empty and faceless equality on people . . . It's due to the traditional structure of the family, as it fought for survival in agrarian conditions . . . It's a sign of our backwardness . . . Historically, it's the fault of the Christian Democrats . . . It's because of the paternalism of our parties, which have divided up public life among themselves like bands of robbers . . . It's a matrix of behavior patterns that we've inherited from the Bourbons . . . It's a legacy of the Papal State . . . It's the revenge of the South, a sickness that the Calabrians and Apulians, the Neapolitans and the Sicilians brought with them into the state apparatus and which has now infected the society as a whole . . .

No, says someone else, it's none of these things. I'll tell you what's to blame; particularism, localism. The Venetians force every foreigner to pay for everything through the nose, and a foreigner is anyone who lives on the other side of Mestre. As punishment he pays three to four times as much for the *vaporetto* as a native. Recently the city fathers have suggested charging admission to their island, a toll, as in the Middle

Ages. That's consistent. Because there are no Italians in Italy at all, only natives and newcomers. As in art history, everyone defines himself by where he was born: *il Parmigiano, il Veronese, il Perugino*. And that's how it stays. The man from Turin always remains the man from Turin, even if he's been living in Cagliari for a generation. That explains everything. That's why he's so down-to-earth and meticulous. At the same time, his origin explains why he understands nothing about Sardinia. The poor soul doesn't have a clue! . . . And so the Italians confirm one another's foreignness, particularity, and inequality.

This also means that every other Italian has the status of an ambassador. The Milanese woman born in Giglio has to invite, put up, and protect anyone who comes from the island, even if she left her home forty years ago, even if she goes back there only for three days at Easter to visit her aged mother . . . It's no use. She's still liable. She represents. She's the ambassadress. Giglio will always be her capital, her metropolis. On the other hand, she can't be held responsible for Milan. So privilege begins at birth. It's a distinction to have come into the world in this spot and nowhere else. One may admire other villages, regions, countries, continents—but envy? Or even love? Never! . . . So every Italian town is the best, with perhaps one exception, on which everyone agrees. The exception, and I don't know why, is Rovigo. ("Oh, you're from Rovigo? What a shame.")

An Extremist (continued). He says:

Where does your equality get you? Of all the slogans of 1789, it's the emptiest. The equality you're talking about is a phantom. It has never come even remotely close to realization. Or do you think there's anything in the so-called socialist countries deserving of the name? Don't make me laugh! And what's the situation at home, in the decent, well-protected, orderly North? Is there no selfishness, no muddle, no nepotism, no corruption, no privilege?

I know what your objection will be. I know it by heart! You'll fall back on the formal equality of citizens and praise it to the skies. Equality before the law . . . the fact that even the rich pay taxes . . . the conviction that you have certain rights, just like everyone else, to which you are entitled without a letter of recommendation, without patronage, without a *galoppino*, "without respect of person."

Maybe you will even extol the civil joys of anonymity, the impersonal exchange of services, commodities, ideas, jobs, and administrative documents. You'll tell me that alienation is a pleasure and inconspicuousness is a release, that you live in the best of all possible worlds—a social machine that functions smoothly, hygienically, and without friction.

But you forget one small detail. You forget the price you have to pay for it: conformity, moral stupidity, hypocrisy. Because wherever the struggle of all against all is denied, wherever each self-satisfied bureaucrat can imagine he's good, selfless, and decent, that's where Protestant hypocrisy dominates, and anyone who refuses to share in this self-deception is subjected to sanctimonious indignation.

To me you're like millionaires who don't want to admit they're millionaires, who travel second-class, and run around in shabby jackets, and enjoy all their privileges in secret because they're ashamed of them. When it's a matter of life and death, then everybody, even in Frankfurt and Stockholm, wants the best doctor and the most expensive private hospital he can afford—but discreetly, of course, and without causing a fuss. Even the most radical English trade union boss sends his kids to the public school whose abolition he champions . . . The truth is, you can't bear the truth! I think your social-democratic utopias, your Swedish dreams in which naked power dresses up in angelic white, are bleak and dreary.

The Potentates. No important figure in Italy can be accused of resorting to such disguises. Power, the ultimate privilege, isn't hidden. Invoked and exhibited, displayed and admired, it's an inexhaustible topic of conversation. Its transformation and nuances, its vicissitudes and interconnections are discussed with passion. Intrigue is a pleasure from which no one wishes to be excluded. No one is interested in structural, impersonal, objective, distant forms of the exercise of power. Power is experienced as real, and taken seriously, only when embodied in a person or encountered face to face. One can— one wants to—touch it; something of its *mana*, its electricity, is transferred to anyone who comes in contact with it. It's the most widely used aphrodisiac. In the word *potenza* the political significance merges with the sexual. A famous Sicilian saying expresses duality with matchless precision: "Commandare è meglio di fottere" (Ruling is better than fucking).

A Roman lady, half fascinated, half repelled, summed up her opinion of the newly elected Italian prime minister with the remarkable sentence "He's very phallic." And Andreotti, the widely admired master of Italian politics, who is rumored to be the son of a cardinal, has had the impudence to declare that it's not power that wears a man out but its absence . . .

And what's true of the "Palace" (the name that Pasolini gave the state apparatus, the establishment, of his country, and that's now in everyday use) is also true of the smallest doghouse. For even the artisans' alley in Pavia, the furry-toy business, and the rowing club have their monarchs.

Once, at a party in Milan, a graying, middle-aged, gangling yet slightly stooped gentleman was pointed out to me. Someone whispered, "Take a good look at him. He has incredible power over new Italian poetry." I had never heard of the man, never read a line by him, and no sooner had he passed me with a condescending nod and disappeared behind the door than I forgot his name. Yet the remaining guests, all of whom were in one way or another involved with literature, insisted on discussing his private life, his intrigues, his strategies and defects . . . I asked them if in this case the word "power" was not something of an overstatement. A few slim volumes, which no one reads; invitations to one or two festivals; no money, no career, no politics . . . The whole thing seemed like a tempest in a teapot to me. But no, they said, no one can bypass him. You can't believe how many hours in his antechamber, how many telephone calls, how many recommendations are necessary! . . . And if you make an enemy of him you're a complete outcast, a leper! And you may as well give up!

"I feel sorry for him," said a small, thin, ugly woman poet suddenly. "It can't be fun playing the ringmaster, especially in this circus, where the lions have no teeth and the seals can't balance a ball on their noses. Everyone has to pay for his privileges: the client for a recommendation, the politician for votes, the gangster for protection. Admittedly, poor G. is boss here, he takes pride of place, but in return he owes favors to others. Nothing happens of its own accord. *Bisogna strappare tutto* (everything is a struggle). The emir is not just the emir but the sacrificial lamb too. He has to puff himself up all the time and pretend he's bigger than he really is. Represent, invite, pay, keep up appearances . . . And all that just for the sake of poetry! With printings of twelve hundred! Say what you like, but I think it's heroic!"

She looked around the room and there wasn't a spark of irony in her angry eyes.

The Dream.　I'm sitting on a high, old-fashioned, black-leather barber chair, which is being cranked farther and farther back till I'm almost lying horizontal. In the tall, peeling mirrors I see only familiar faces—the men from the village, sitting on a long wooden bench and waiting: the tobacconist, the priest, the winegrower, the man from the gas station. They talk, they leaf through the newspaper, they smoke. Outside, dogs doze on the piazza in the midday heat. The barber, a toothless old man, has just lathered me. The clock on the wall says a minute before noon.

Then the door flies open and a plump, bald little gentleman enters. A freshly and carefully pressed brown suit, medal ribbons in his buttonhole, a watch chain, pointed shoes brilliantly polished. He stands still and looks around. All conversation immediately ceases. The barber rushes over to the new customer and greets him with every sign of enthusiasm. Astonished, I watch as the tobacconist takes his hat, the priest helps him off with his jacket, and the gas station attendant hands him his newspaper. The fat man doesn't say a word. He only runs his long, pink tongue over his lips and solemnly sits down on the chair beside me. He's quickly rubbed with eau de cologne, tucked up in hot and cold cloths, massaged, powdered, combed. No one bothers about me; I feel the soap slowly drying on my cheeks. I'd like to stand up and protest, but I can't rise from my chair. It's hot. I hear the scraping of the blade, the smacking of fingers on the fat man's skin. A long time passes. Then the fat man jumps up and everyone thanks him. He doesn't leave a tip; in fact, he doesn't pay at all, but the barber's apprentice kisses his hand. I stare at him with utter loathing because I've realized at last who this is before me—this puffed-up zero, this fat little man, is "power."

Hardly has the door closed behind him when they all laugh and slap their thighs, pick up newspapers, and light their cigarettes again. "And why doesn't he pay?" I ask. "Why doesn't he wait until it's his turn, like everyone else?"

The apprentice looks at me with astonishment. "But he comes here every day at twelve on the dot for his shave," says the old barber.

"Why do you put up with it?" I cry angrily. "Why don't you strike the louse dead?"

"It's none of your business," says the tobacconist. "We'll do what we like," says the priest. "Damn foreigner," mutters the gas station attendant.

I jump up and run out of the shop. Suddenly I'm standing in the middle of the street in Milan, opposite San Babila, with the village barber's white bib around my neck. Traffic racing past. A little boy points at me, passersby turn around and laugh. There's still soap on my face.

THE COINS

Chewing gum in one's pockets, nothing but chewing gum, streetcar tickets, broken ballpoints, stamps stuck together, caramels, and soup cubes . . . Does the undersecretary of state still remember? Do my dear friends still remember?

Of course not. They all shrug their shoulders. It's just as if I had asked about King Zog of Albania or the slogan *Tunis—Corsica—Djibouti*, which a couple of million Italians got worked up about at the end of 1938 . . . Total amnesia. And yet the great small-change crisis, the epoch of chewing gum and soup cubes, is only nine, seven, five years ago. The city of Rome, with its twenty-two-hundred-year history of coinage . . . the country to which Europe owes the invention of double-entry bookkeeping . . . Collateral loans and credit, balances and discounts, premiums and balance sheets are all ideas that began their march across the world here. Even the word "bank" comes from the Italian . . . Yet after the greatest boom in its history, richer than ever before, this country, the eighth-largest industrial power in the world, was no longer capable of supplying its inhabitants with those round pieces of metal that have always been essential for the simplest everyday transactions. In those days anyone in Italy who wanted to make a phone call, buy a couple of tomatoes, drink a cup of coffee, or mail a letter had to be ready to accept caramels for change. And it wasn't just for a couple of weeks because of a metalworkers' strike, or for three months because the mint had burned down—chewing gum was legal tender in Italy for five whole years, from A.D. 1975–1979, just as cowrie shells once were in the South Pacific and Africa.

In Switzerland, where the national currency is guarded like the Holy Grail, the government would probably have been brought down within a week. In Japan the minister responsible would have committed seppuku. Even in the sluggish Soviet Union a couple of heads might have rolled. In Italy governments presided over the debacle without losing a moment's sleep. The only people at their wits' end were the tourists. The natives responded with stoic patience and nimble improvisation. After just a few months, the country hit upon a magical solution to the problem—a brilliant trick, the deal of the decade. The Italians let the Finance Ministry go on snoring and printed their own money. A new world, that of the minicheck, came into being.

Immediately millions of little scraps of paper in every color of the rainbow flooded into the cash registers. The face value of these checks is said to have amounted to 30 or 100 or 300 billion lire; every expert names a different figure. And it hardly matters whether an estimate is off by a factor of ten, for of course there was no trace of control over this national game of Monopoly.

Whenever there's an element of doubt, the bank always wins such parlor games, but if the whole thing is to work, ordinary players must have a chance too . . . I enter the bank and deposit a few million lire in cash in my account. After all, there are still enough banknotes available—the printing presses are working tirelessly. In return the bank gives me huge quantities of minichecks, printed on blotting paper, in units of 50 or 100 lire. I put this small change into circulation in the shop, in the payroll, at the ticket office, in the restaurant. The bank is satisfied. It can work with the money I've deposited, in a non-interest-bearing account. A fine piece of business . . . My checks circulate. They're torn, forgotten, thrown away. Perhaps two-thirds are redeemed, perhaps only half . . . It would be impossible to find out exactly how many, because who's going to insist on careful bookkeeping in such chaotic conditions? After a couple of years I go to the bank and ask how much money is in my account. Strictly speaking, no one knows. But somehow we'll manage to reach an agreement. The easiest thing to do is simply split the spoils— I and the bank, the bank and I. During the play-money years, not only did all the country's financial institutions operate according to this system, but so did the co-operatives, the department stores, the highway administrations, the newspaper vendors, the nationalized enterprises, and the chambers of commerce—as well as, presumably, a fair number of bankrupts and bogus companies.

I recall that around that time, on a night flight over Asia, I met an Italian-American banker who was working for the International Monetary Fund. In the dim night lighting—the other passengers had curled up and were asleep—the pale, gaunt, loquacious Genoese, who couldn't stop fidgeting for a second, explained the importance of the Italian billions to me.

"Utterly absurd! The minichecks are a preposterous way of expanding credit, and they have an inflationary effect too, that's obvious. But my countrymen—please don't quote me— like inflation. They complain about it, of course, but you mustn't pay any attention to that. The more zeros the better. Anyone can become a millionaire. Other countries would have revalued long ago, one to a hundred or one to a thousand. But in Rome the so-called *lira pesante*, a lire that would be worth something, doesn't have a chance . . . That would smack of austerity, of restrictions, of doing without! But inflation—that's the miracle of the loaves and fishes, the solution of economic problems by magic . . . It's an irresistible temptation! The truth is, we're living beyond our means, and have been for twenty years."

"An admirable characteristic," I said. "You're just very generous people. Luxury, the good life, where else in Europe can you still find them? Only in Italy . . ."

"Nonsense. It's nothing but vanity. In Italy extravagance is not just a national mania, it's more like a social compulsion. The cars are always a little too large, the restaurant bills always go into the hundred thousands . . . We're all beggars who want to play at being lords."

"But the level of savings," I objected. "More than 12 percent of income! Higher than the Japanese! How do you manage to throw your money out the window and save it at the same time?"

"And that doesn't even include the billions of dollars and francs in the Zürich and New York accounts! It makes no difference—it's all stolen money anyway, black-market money, bribe and drug money . . . You're quite right, the Italians save like maniacs. But they do it secretly. Something that's regarded as a virtue elsewhere, we regard as a secret vice. Any show-off who ruins himself in public can bask in the admiration of his fellow citizens. But someone who doesn't want to throw his money away is virtually a pariah. To us the love of money is a sin that must be kept secret, an obscene perversion to which no one may confess with impunity—which of course only increases the energies applied to crime. No other misers are so dyed-in-the-wool, so shabby, so determined as Italian misers . . . I come from Genoa. I should know."

"And the state?"

"Exactly the same. Just try getting your money out of a government office sometime! The professors' salaries that have 'not yet arrived' . . . The billions of lire that Europe made available to save Venice, what's actually happened to them? No one's been able to find out . . . stuck somewhere . . . blocked . . . going through official channels . . . jurisdictions . . . executive committees. The dead hand of the Finance Ministry! Or these ridiculous currency regulations . . . Pensions and tax refunds—the state holds them back instinctively! An impersonal, abstract miser, suffering from monumental constipation. But just open up any newspaper and you find monstrous deficits, everywhere. IRI, ENI, IMPS, Italy is full of these abbreviations, and each one is a bottomless pit. For them the state suddenly becomes liquid and empties its bowels like a typhus patient. The consistency of the money seems to change instantly. I see it as a kind of ontological diarrhea, an absurd, ostentatious prodigality, and the stink it spreads is far from natural.

"And this tension between holding on and letting go can be resolved in only one way: by the ultimate trick, the magic of multiplication, inflation! The disappearance of metal money is no more than the physical expression of this magical operation. Metal is annoying, it's too hard, too palpable, it has to be dissolved, it becomes blotting paper, chewing gum, the little piece of chocolate that melts in your pocket . . . And what's best of all is that no one's surprised, no one's worried, no one gets excited."

No one, no one at all? On the contrary! I remember years of embittered "discussion," commentaries, parliamentary questions, protests, revelations, editorials, appeals. The small-change scandal was a wonderful opportunity for quarreling, an ideal hotbed of rumors, theories, and jokes. The lawyers set themselves in motion immediately. They subjected the scraps of paper, the rag money, the dwarf checks, to an analysis as thorough as it was boring. Were the banks producing forgeries? Were their bits of paper legal? In the fall of 1976, relying on an ingenious legal argument, a judge in Perugia ordered the seizure of all the minichecks in Italy— an action that, if carried out, would have kept the Italian police busy for months. A few months later a judge in Milan quashed the order with an even more ingenious justification, and the assistant state secretary in charge of the matter, a dentist from Vicenza, explained to Parliament: "With reference to the legality of the minichecks . . . um, um . . . the government has . . . er, er . . . always taken a negative position . . . There are anomalies in their issue . . . mm, mm . . . which, at least in the material sense . . . scrape, scrape . . . represent a clear infringement of current regulations in the area of the circulation of checks . . . ahem, ahem . . . inasmuch as these can in no way serve de facto as substitutes for cash."

This rhetorical gem indicates rather precisely the course the government intended to steer—that is, dull-witted denial of the facts. The public, meanwhile, displayed a quite alarming adaptability. To cope with the shortage of small change, the retail trade simply rounded off its prices up to the nearest zero. On the black market that sprang up overnight, legal coins were traded with a markup of 10 to 15 percent. Of course, that meant that the few coins still remaining disappeared as well. They were hoarded systematically. Public transportation was an especially good source of revenue for the black market. When the company running Venice's buses and *vaporetti* ordered its employees to hand over the change they had taken in rather than sell it, the conductors threatened to strike . . .

People with imagination soon realized that it was child's play to forge minichecks. With over three thousand varieties in circulation, it was hardly noticed. But in fact it wasn't even necessary to compete with the banks, for one could also speculate wonderfully with the official minichecks. Thousands of collectors fell upon each new issue. The freshly printed checks disappeared into specially made albums, more than a million of which are said to have been sold, and were never seen again. A million albums! A simmering mass that drove prices higher and higher, on Turin's Balún, at the Porta Portese in Rome, on the Piazza dei Mercanti in Milan, and at all the other collectors' markets throughout the country.

Especially rare minichecks, with face values of 100 lire, were soon being traded at a thousand, even five thousand times that amount. The intoxication of speculation naturally led to the manufacture of variations, overprints, and off-shades in tiny editions for collectors, and these then surfaced in the albums at fantastic prices.

But how did it all happen? For what reason, in God's name? Had the Italians gone mad? Had they forgotten the art of punching out round pieces of metal and putting inscriptions on them? I assembled a small collection of the most popular explanations, which I can now pass on to the reader:

1. "There was no metal left." (bank employee, Venice, 1977)
2. "In Japan and Singapore they made buttons out of our 50-lira pieces, and that's why the coins disappeared." (theater critic, Rome, 1983)
3. "It's the trade unions' fault. They've ruined the whole country with their demands. That's why the mint doesn't work either . . ." (taxi driver, Milan, 1976)
4. "The foreigners who came for Holy Year took away our small change as souvenirs." (the finance minister of the Italian Republic, 1975)
5. "It's a conspiracy by the banks, which are making a huge profit at the expense of the little man." (Communist trade unionist, 1977)
6. "Coins cost too much, and Parliament didn't want to pay." (assistant in shoe store, Como, 1983)
7. "The 100-lira pieces were taken to Switzerland in huge tank trucks, and the companies there made watchcases out of them." (*La Stampa*, a respected Turin daily, 1976)
8. "The coins are just stuck in the vending machines, which aren't emptied often enough." (waiter, Naples, 1976)
9. "In the mint's present facility it is impossible either to

increase production adequately or to guarantee minimum conditions for the health and safety of the work force." (Senate Committee for Finance and Treasury Affairs, 1976)

10. "What do you expect? That's just how we are . . . *Siamo negati per queste cose* (We're hopeless at things like that) . . . You can't do anything about it . . . It's the system's fault . . . It's all a mess, *un paese di merde* (a shitty country) . . . All these politicians and civil servants from the South . . . Actually, it was a mistake to throw out the Austrians." (vox populi, 1975–1983)

Three things are notable about these remarkable explanations: First, they are, without exception, wrong. Second, they all completely ignore the state of affairs they're supposed to explain. Only one, that of the Senate Committee, says anything about the mint's operation. And third, they're evidence of a rich imagination untroubled by facts. They tend toward either anecdote or abstraction, but in every case toward mythomania. A degree of paranoia is evident in most of these stories. Dark, anonymous forces ("the system," "the banks," "the trade unions," "the civil servants from the South"—i.e., the Mafia) are made responsible for the small-change crisis, or else it's the greedy tourists, the evil Swiss, the inscrutable Malays, the slant-eyed Japanese, who have taken the hard-earned 100-lira coins away from the Italians.

The dull reality, of course, was quite different. Devoid of any such secrets and conspiracies, it centered upon the obvious question: How is it possible to strike more coins? There was no getting around this issue. There was also nothing new about it; the problem had been foreseeable for decades. All that was needed were a few readily available figures, a sheet of paper, and a pencil. In the industrialized countries coins averaged around 8 percent of the money in circulation (6 percent in the Federal Republic of Germany, 8 percent in Great Britain, 10.5 percent in the United States). In Italy the percentage had sunk first to 3, then to 1.8 and finally to 1.2. The catastrophe was entirely predictable. Only the "political forces," blind as moles but lacking the energy and instincts of those remarkable animals, were incapable of such an analysis.

In the faraway year of 1968 it had nevertheless dawned on an unknown civil servant . . . a faint suspicion had arisen in him . . . and he had drawn up a bill. A new mint! Why not? said the M.P.'s, and agreed to make 3 billion lire available for this worthy purpose. Then for eight years nothing happened. In 1976 a further 12 billion was voted for the phantom new mint, and the municipal administration of Rome adopted a new development plan. A piece of land was found on the Via di Grotta Gregna in the eastern part of the city. And in Parliament an undersecretary (not a dentist this time) declared, "We shall now be in a position, taking into account all the limitations I have mentioned, to undertake an examination of the plan for building a new mint."

And there the matter rests: with the examination, the limitations, and a plan gathering dust in the drawers of some ministry or other.

At the time, hundreds upon hundreds of journalists were tirelessly investigating the "phenomenon" of the missing small change, but only two got as far as the actual scene of the crime, even though it is ten minutes by taxi from most Roman newspaper offices. The researches of Aldo Santini and Paolo Guzzanti in 1976/1977 provided the following picture:

The cellar of the old mint, which stands behind the main railway station at 4 Via Principe Umberto, is a relic of an earlier period of industrialization, an inferno of the kind familiar from the novels of Dickens. The ancient presses make a deafening noise, which at ninety-five decibels approaches the threshold of pain. Many workers have gone deaf. The hygienic conditions are indescribable. Everything is covered in dust and cobwebs. Proper ventilation is impossible. The factory council complains about the high levels of cyanide in the atmosphere. There are machines good for nothing but scrap lying around everywhere, including an old press that has completely fallen apart. In these confined, stuffy vaults it's hardly possible to move. Rats scamper along the walls. "Until recently," say the workers, "we had to count the coins by hand, piece by piece. The regulations we have to work by date from 1921. The management is totally incompetent. The mint is entirely neglected."

Five years later there is plenty of small change in Italy, and it would never even occur to anyone to remark upon something so obvious. And as for the minichecks, a Milanese coin dealer in his barred shop in the Via dei Mercanti explains, "Not a soul wants to have them . . . The bottom has fallen out of the market . . . It's completely collapsed! You can get the rarest ones, which used to be worth a million, for 2,000 lire [about $1.20]." The old man smiles contentedly, and the skin on his skull draws up into a thousand little folds. "I always said so! It was all rubbish, a bloom without roots . . . But the little Liebig soup packet pictures, they've retained their value!" It's as if he had invented the Liebig pictures himself.

In Rome I open the telephone book and find that the mint is still at its old address. Nothing seems to have come of the plans, begun fifteen years ago, for the new building. The old place was built in 1911 in the Umbertine wedding-cake style. Painted pink, it's guarded by finance police armed with submachine guns . . . TV monitors in the porters' lodge, grandiose marble stairways, huge old-fashioned desks. Nicola Jelpo, the director of the mint, shows me his plant. We descend to the cellar. We give up keyrings and cigarette lighters at the metal-detector gate. I'm ready for the worst.

What I see, and I'm shown every corner, are light, spacious rooms with excellent air conditioning . . . Clean workshops where work proceeds with great concentration, modern production lines with new presses from Germany. The noise level is no higher than that in an open-plan office. There's more than enough space available; medals, orders, stamps, and memorial coins are being produced as well. The fully automated counting, testing, and packing unit, developed in the mint itself, works without a hitch. And when asked about the mint's capacity, the director calmly explains, "At the moment, we press 1 to 1.5 million pieces daily. That covers demand. But from one day to the next we could expand production by 800 percent without any difficulty at all. It's no problem!"

And that's far from all! The Roman mint is trying to win contracts from abroad and from the private sector. It produces polished silver coins for collectors, so-called "proofs," by hand. It has developed a wholly original bimetallic 500-lira coin for general use. Its outer ring is stainless steel and the rest is an aluminum-bronze alloy. In addition, the director has found time to write a "Brief History of Italian Coinage," renovate the Numismatic Museum, and revive the mint's art school, which has a rich tradition but had long been neglected. All this was carried out with the full cooperation of the trade unions and with hardly any change in the number of employees . . . In other words, it's an Italian miracle just as hard to explain as the decades of disaster that gave the country a chewing-gum currency.

Nicola Jelpo is a polite, reserved gentleman of indeterminate age, with the dark complexion and heavy eyelids of the Southerner. His accent reveals that he comes from Basilicata. He speaks softly, calmly, and thoughtfully. Large Roman head, strong nose, brown suit, immaculate from head to foot . . . His somewhat melancholy eyes light up as soon as he begins to talk about his passion. Mr. Jelpo is—there's no other way to put it—a coin fetishist. He gently strokes an exhibition piece from the workshop of Giuseppe Bianchi, and his gaze rests contentedly on an old screw press dating back to the Papal State, which he has had set up in the entrance hall. An engineer by training, he entered the service of the mint as a technician in 1967, and was appointed its director in June 1978.

"The mint's problems," he says, "were insoluble as long as it was directly dependent on the Finance Ministry and had no freedom of movement of any kind. The state bureaucracy is simply not in a position to manage an industrial enterprise. The regulations were oppressive. A couple of examples: Our workshops were like a junkyard because we weren't allowed either to put the giant old machines in storage or to sell them. Two ministerial officials argued for years about whether they were movables or immovables. Until this dispute was settled, no change could be considered. We had no budget of our own. We could only buy machinery from abroad at a set price. But the decision-making process took years. By the time a purchase was approved, the prices had changed because of inflation and the whole business had to start all over again. In 1976 our stamping machines worked four hours a day; now it's fourteen. At that time the wage agreement with the public-service trade union didn't allow any shift work. There was no money for overtime. On top of that there was the noise level. We knew very well how to solve these problems, but we weren't allowed to. I was often close to resigning . . . You see, at that time it would have been utterly impossible for me to become director of the mint. The regulations explicitly ruled out the appointment of a specialist. The directors had to be civil-service administrators. They came and went, a new one every four or five years. They didn't have a clue about how to strike coins and didn't have the time to learn, because before that could happen they had to retire."

"So who," I asked Engineer Jelpo, "was really responsible for the whole debacle?"

"No one," he replied. "No one or everyone."

* * *

On April 20, 1978, the Italian Parliament passed a law removing the mint from the state apparatus and making it an autonomous section of the state printing press. That sufficed to put an end to institutionalized sabotage, idiotic inefficiency, and endemic incompetence. Within a year the minichecks and the soup cubes had disappeared, and if Engineer Jelpo—who's looking forward to another twenty years at his desk—has his way, they'll never return.

I ask myself whether on that spring day in 1978 the politicians, who for decades had watched the hellish mismanagement in the Via Principe Umberto with the greatest indifference, suddenly experienced a lucid moment, a kind of Zen illumination. Or perhaps, on the contrary, they simply hadn't been paying attention? Perhaps they released the mint from their crippling care *by mistake*, as it were?

Nobody paid for his failure. That much is clear. If they haven't already died, every one of the responsible ministers, state secretaries, undersecretaries, director generals, and directors sits undisturbed in his country house and lives off his pension. Not one has been dismissed, punished, or even called to account. It's unjustly said that the Italians are a spiteful and vindictive people. Quite the contrary. They forgive everything and their good nature knows no bounds.

But ultimately the story I'm telling here is a very edifying parable. It has not just a happy ending but a moral . . . So a new building wasn't even necessary . . . There was no shortage of subsidies, raw materials, or machinery . . . That wasn't the problem . . . Nor were the Swiss or the Japanese to blame for everything, or the banks or the trade unions . . . And the much-cited *paese di merda* was only an excuse too! . . . The mint had everything that was required: skill, intelligence, initiative. Only it was all immobilized, like a Gulliver tied down by the Lilliputians of politics. No sooner had the threads been cut than this Gulliver arose and set to work.

And no Austrian tradition was needed either—yes, it was even possible to manage quite well without the well-known Lombard virtues. For, after all, Engineer Nicola Jelpo comes from the Deep South, from a small town in Lucania. And while a considerable part of Italy's population was busy shooting one another in the knees, cutting off one another's ears, attacking one another with iron bars, bicycle chains, and submachine guns, or at least *discussing* these things, Mr. Jelpo, by no means a representative of the "new dynamic middle class" or a "postindustrial socialization" type but a plump, rather old-fashioned gentleman—perhaps he even votes for the Christian Democrats—calmly pursued his favorite occupation, which consists of striking coins.

Granted, there are more important things than the small change that jingles in a jacket pocket. But as long as Italy has people like Nicola Jelpo, it is not lost.

THE ITALIAN PARADIGM

Headlines of the Week:

Bonn (dpa). ALCOHOL SCANDAL. The President declared on Monday that he did not intend to resign, but also that he had no intention of taking legal action against the news magazine *Der Spiegel*. The magazine has prominently featured an accusation that the President was involved in an international alcohol-smuggling ring, and that in recent years his profits from it have totaled around 180 million marks, said to have been deposited in a Swiss bank account.

Amsterdam (ANP). PENSIONERS RIOT. More than thirty thousand old-age pensioners stormed and wrecked the main office of the state pension fund on Tuesday. The fund has ceased making payments, explaining that the cash due to be paid out at the beginning of the month had "simply not arrived." The Ministry of Social Affairs refused to comment on the incidents.

Hanover (AP). SATISFACTION ALL AROUND AT THE HANOVER FAIR. Following the collapse of several large German companies, there has been a further sensational development. This year Europe's biggest industrial fair was completely dominated by small and medium-sized companies which registered record export successes. Pudding mix, ties, porcelain, and toys were the best sellers. The Internal Revenue Service discovered, to its surprise, that most of the exhibiting companies were unknown to it.

Stockholm (TT). THE POSTAGE STAMP CRISIS. In the future, letters franked with chewing gum will no longer be processed, customers have been informed by the Swedish Post Office. Because postage stamps have been in short supply for years, some companies have begun to print their own. However, the legality of these facsimiles is open to question. The printing press of the Royal Postal Administration is not in a position to produce enough stamps, since its machinery has rusted. Because of trade union resistance, nothing has so far come of a proposal that contracts for the delivery of postage stamps should be placed with the private sector.

London (Reuters). CONSPIRACY UNCOVERED. The British public is being shaken by more and more revelations about the "Association for the Recovery of the Realm." It now seems certain that the Chancellor of the Exchequer, the Defense secretary, the Naval Chief of Staff, the editor of the *Times,* the head of the Security Services, and two hundred leading businessmen belonged to this secret organization, which is believed to have planned a coup d'état. The chairman of the Association is a Mr. Jelly, who owns a jam factory in Macclesfield.

Oslo (NTB). Despite the collapse in oil prices and oil exports, consumption of champagne has increased 500 percent during the last year.

Brussels (AFP). SUICIDE OR MURDER? Bob Kalvén, chairman of the board of directors of Sweden's largest bank, was found dead at four a.m. in the men's room at Brussels' main railway station. The cause of death was listed as poisoning. Kalvén had been serving a three-year sentence for currency exchange fraud but had escaped from the high-security wing of Malmö prison two weeks ago.

Wiesbaden (dpa). A VICTIM OF ANARCHY. The head of the Federal Bureau of Statistics shot himself in his office during the weekend. His farewell letter makes it clear that the civil servant despaired of ever obtaining truthful information from German citizens. "Our figures are in complete chaos," the letter claims. "Everyone is lying. Our statistics are no more reliable than the horoscopes in the tabloid press."

Copenhagen (RB). POLICEMAN DISMISSED. Around 122,000 Danes receive a disability pension because of blindness, yet 84,000 of them also have a driver's license and a car. This was the conclusion of private research conducted by a Danish police officer. The overzealous officer was summarily dismissed for acting without authority and contravening service regulations.

Frankfurt am Main (AP). DOUBTS ABOUT RECOVERY. The German Federal Bank is faced with a puzzle. Although all the statistical data in its latest monthly report point to an economic catastrophe, an optimistic mood prevails in West

German business circles. The President of the Federal Bank explained that the strength of the D-mark and the healthy consumer climate were probably due to the shadow (or black) economy, whose share of the national economy is estimated at 45 percent.

Typically Italian. Which is it, then? The opera or the Mafia? A *cappuccino* or bribery? Macchiavelli or Missoni? Whenever anyone says that something or other is "typically Italian," I want to jump up with impatience, overturn my chair, and run out of the room. Could anything be more barren than the study of "national psychology," that moldy garbage heap of stereotypes, prejudices, and accepted ideas? . . . And yet it is impossible to dislodge these traditional garden gnomes with their naïvely painted faces: the taciturn Scandinavian, blonder than straw; the obstinate German, beer stein in hand; the red-faced, garrulous Irishman, always smelling of whiskey; and, of course, the Italian with his mustache, forever sensual but regrettably unreliable, brilliant but lazy, passionate but scheming . . .

The notion of the typical also seems to be indispensable for home consumption, for the elevated purpose of self-criticism—a genre to which Italian authors have made outstanding contributions. In Alberto Arbasino's furious diatribe *Un paese senza* (Milan, 1980), one can read the following: "It must be recognized that regardless of every kind of survey technique, behavioral pattern or grid, and attempt at explanation, an ancient, archetypal, and cunning meanness predominates in the behavior of the Italian. . . . The anomalies, monstrosities, madness, and outrageous crimes of contemporary Italy—yes, even the 'typically Italian' horror stories— can hardly be said to be anomalous, monstrous, or shocking when considered in their 'normal' context." How did Arbasino's countrymen respond to these three hundred fifty pages of merciless abuse? They elected the author to Parliament three years later!

But the unsuspecting foreigners, on the other hand! As long as a handbag isn't actually snatched or a car broken into, their enthusiasm remains unbounded. Take Gisela G., for example, an unemployed teacher from Münster in West-phalia. She has retired to taste the joys of solitude, i.e., to the obligatory farmhouse in Tuscany. A couple of dropouts from Düsseldorf—former marketing experts—have built an exten-sion on to the nineteenth-century villa on the hill. A commune of hippies from Berlin is living in the old school building amid empty wine bottles and dirty dishes. A mysteriously named "Study Group for Transpersonal Therapy" has in-stalled itself a few doors down; for a weekend fee of 600 marks ($220), tired branch managers and sportswriters can rearm themselves for the struggle for survival in Frankfurt. And a Swiss photographer is said to have recently bought the manor on the other side of the river.

Anyway, Gisela G. writes to me (and I have no idea how to reply): "Dear M., I feel sorry for you! I don't know how you can bear to go on living in those 'well-ordered' German surroundings. I've been unable to cope with them for a long time now. In the North we're constantly being terrorized— by money, by technology, by discipline. Too much property, too many neuroses. Life here is simpler, more natural, more human, not so anonymous and cold—and not just because of the climate. I look after the garden, I meet the people from the village on the piazza . . . I'm simply happier here."

Good for you, dear Gisela! Best of luck. It's just that your ingenuous letter is completely plagiarized, a compendium of platitudes that have figured in European literature for two hundred years . . . Your Tuscan idyll is nothing but a feeble recapitulation. A great love for Italy was first kindled in the sensitive natures of certain visitors in the middle of the eighteenth century. Since then it's become the basis of a billion-dollar industry. It has remained an unrequited love from the start. No Italian would dream of moving voluntarily to Münster in Westphalia or to Trelleborg or the Hook of Holland without a compelling practical reason . . .

At home, dear Gisela, you were always getting worked up about acid rain and the arms race—but in Tuscany you wear rose-colored glasses. Or haven't you noticed that the Italians couldn't give a damn about the environment and think pacifism is a fad? You complain about the wealth and greed of the North—but what would you do if the monthly check from the cold North stopped coming and you had to earn a living in Poggibonsi? The local people are friendly as long as you can pay. They tolerate you, just as the whole country accepts the permanent invasion from the North, and I admire their patience. I don't find it surprising that they pluck you clean as a Christmas goose, charmingly, ruthlessly, and with an irony that escapes you entirely.

In fact, I understand you all too well, because I share your stubborn love of Italy. We can't survive without this refuge. It's our favorite projection, our drive-in movie theater, our all-purpose Arcadia. Now, as two hundred years ago, we can compensate for our defects here, load up with illusions, and dig among the ruins of an ancient, half-forgotten utopia.

Have it your own way. But why must this love be so ignorant, stupid, and narrow-minded? Why does Gisela so persistently overlook everything in Italy that cries to heaven? If she came home to cool, boring Münsterland and found conditions there like those in Mestre or Avellino, she would be outraged by so much cruelty, harshness, and indifference to others.

Every doting love has its reverse side. Tourism can't exist without a double standard. When the visitor from the North has spent his last lira and returned to the German, Belgian, or Swedish autumn, doesn't he after all heave a secret sigh of relief because everything in the North—the central heating, the state, the telphone—works so well? Then when he opens his newspaper and reads the latest horror stories from Italy (chaos, Camorra, corruption) he leans back and thinks, *It can't happen here*. And this pious belief is the final proof that he hasn't understood anything.

The Italianization of Europe. There are symptoms enough, only one must know how to interpret them. Political corruption, for example, has made considerable advances in recent years, especially in West Germany. While preparing their case against the federal minister of economics, the state prosecutor stumbled upon evidence quite tropical in its luxuriance. It's not an isolated case.* The list of those incriminated reads like "an Almanach de Gotha of German politics" (in the respectful tones of the *Frankfurter Allgemeine Zeitung*, the court bulletin of the West German governing parties).

Political parties in the countries of Northern Europe too have shared out the spoils of public life; like real-estate speculators, they parcel out the institutions under their control and install their protégés—from managing directors to garbage collectors. The big television companies in Cologne and Paris, in Mainz and Stockholm have long been a match for RAI, the Italian state broadcasting company, when it comes to opportunism and absenteeism, and the industrial companies wholly or partly owned by the state—the black holes of the Italian economy, notorious for their lethargy and nepotism—have found assiduous pupils throughout Europe. Tax fraud, encouraged, if not wholly caused, by legislation that favors now one special-interest group, now

* *Enzensberger is referring to a string of interrelated cases of corruption and illegal payments to party funds involving ministers, party officials, and industrialists that came before the courts in the early and mid-eighties. (Trans.)*

another, without regard for the consequences, has become a national sport everywhere—even in Scandinavia, where reserves of the traditional virtues of saintly patience and moral conformity are slowly drying up.

It's the same picture everywhere: discredited parties, parasitic administrations, subsidy swindles, Tammanyism, the shadow economy, immobilism . . . But new strategies of survival, of self-help and improvisation are also developing everywhere. From this point of view Italy can no longer be considered an exotic exception. Occasionally it's even quietly suggested that the footsore straggler could turn out to be the forerunner of a risky and problematic future.

There's really not much danger that the Friesians will wake up one fine morning as Sicilians, or the Scots as Venetians, even if there's something to such a notion. The shape taken by the Italian paradigm is not the product of "national character" but rather one conceivable response to a new historical situation, a possible answer to a challenge that affects the whole of Europe. So far no one has managed to address this challenge and no useful theory exists to explain it.

I'll simplify. First of all, I'll count off on the fingers of one hand some of the critical factors involved. Then I want to specify in each case the most obvious indications that the Italians, because of their historical experience, are better prepared than others for our common mess. I see them as old hands: crisis experts, the trouble-shooters of collapse.

1. The Crisis of Sovereignty. The nations of Europe now occupy only a subordinate role in world politics. Sandwiched between the superpowers and pressured by allies as well as adversaries, they can no longer conduct an independent foreign policy. Even if, like the French, they don't want to admit it, their status is no more than that of semicolonial protectorates. In the long term even their economic power

will probably be insufficient to allow them to keep up with the major technologies. They will have to earn their living in the interstices of the world economy and look to softer, smaller, more flexible forms of production. This situation is nothing new for the Italians. Their national ambitions have foundered often enough. At the end of the eighteenth century Pietro Verri was already writing, "For all our astuteness, we are today only the refuse of a Europe we once ruled." Such bitter laments occur throughout Italian literature. Only since the end of the colonial adventure and the defeat of Fascism have the Italians come to accept that the greatness of Rome belongs to the past. Since then the country's foreign policy has been conducted in Washington.

2. The Crisis of Governability. Central political apparatuses have increasingly isolated themselves from society, bureaucracies are preoccupied with their own tumors, and political parties have degenerated into corrupt self-service stores. Society ceases to believe in its ability to solve its own problems. It tries to live by its wits and get around centralized systems. A crazy quilt of quarreling special-interest groups, of disparate cultures and subcultures is forming; underground and shadow economies are beginning to flourish. The Italians learned about this sort of thing very early too. The country was always a polyarchy, "a medley of peoples, of states, of institutions and lordships, thrown together by chance" (Giuseppe Ferrari, 1858). People have always regarded the central government as an exploiter that must itself be exploited wherever possible. Eighty-four percent of all Italians regard politicians and their vassals, the *nomenclatura* of their country, as dishonest and incompetent—a European record. The conclusion they draw is that in case of doubt, you have to look out for yourself. The economic outcome of this strategy is clear. While state activity has left behind nothing but the grand ruins of obsolescent heavy industry, efficient small and medium-sized industrial companies have sprung up sponta-

neously in furniture-making and tourism, fashion and precision engineering. The country's present affluence depends on this swarm of heterogeneous initiatives.

3. The Crisis of Planning. The more complex social and economic processes become, the more difficult it is to predict their outcome. This is not merely a consequence of the ignorance of those in charge. There are also systemic reasons. Under such circumstances global solutions can no longer be either "deduced" or conclusively justified. Action is necessarily taken in an *ad hoc* fashion—bridging gaps, patching holes. Changes can no longer be thoroughly planned and imposed, but can be achieved only through trial and error, in a kind of stochastic process.

This insight too is likely to affect the Italians less than others. Apart from a few professors, they've never believed in the advantages of comprehensive systems anyway, and one hardly needs to commend to them the joys of inconsistency. Their historical experience demonstrates that the larger the apparatus, the less effectively it actually works. They've always preferred to rely on detours, improvisations, and specific, experimental solutions.

4. The Crisis of Work. The shrinking of employment is a traumatic experience for all industrialized societies. Unemployment is not just an economic problem, which could be solved by redistributing profits. Millions of people have internalized the ethic of work, achievement, and discipline to such an extent that they simply can't cope with the loss of the "workplace." For them unemployment is a psychological and cultural catastrophe as well as an economic one.

Such an attitude has never managed to establish itself in Italy, not because the Italians were lazier than anyone else but because the history of the country has not known long periods of full employment. As a result, the Italians possess an extremely rich culture of parasitism. Unproductive "spongers," beggars and prelates, magicians and gangsters, buffoons and barons, swindlers and tourists, whores and bosses, have never really been despised, ostracized, and condemned here. They've always been tolerated, even accepted. This great tradition of *fannulloni* (idlers) seriously handicapped the country's industrialization. But in times of dwindling employment it offers, perhaps, a refuge for those whom the industrial system threatens to make superfluous.

5. The Crisis of Justice. The welfare state's impending bankruptcy, escalating struggles over the distribution of income, spending cuts at the expense of the weak: it very much looks as if "left-wing," "egalitarian," and "moral" conceptions of what a just society should look like are coming under increasing pressure, quite irrespective of the complexion of the parties that constitute particular government majorities. It's not only where neo-Conservatives hold the reins of power that antagonism between rich and poor areas of cities and countries is growing. The idea of solidarity appears to be mere rhetoric. Impoverishment and the consumption of luxury goods, misery and extravagance, combine in obscene symbiosis and form an explosive mixture.

The shock that such a development can produce will remain limited to south of the Alps. In Italy equality was always regarded as unrealizable, if not an illusion. Will the inhabitants of the North too have to accustom themselves to that "everyday coexistence with chaos . . . which has accompanied Italy through so many centuries, and which has never stood in the way of the most sublime expressions of art and of craft, even when, under the indifferent gaze of their contemporaries, people were being massacred in the streets"? (Alberto Arbasino, 1978)

Heads or Tails. Assuming that there is such a thing as an "Italian paradigm," what would that mean? Is it a promise or a threat? A loophole or a dead end? Opinion is divided. The much-quoted Censis Institute in Rome has regularly expressed its views on Italy's prospects. The basic tenor of its reports is radiantly optimistic. Its leading expert, Giuseppe de Rita, never tires of extolling the elasticity of Italian society, its apparently unlimited ability to cope with every shock and handicap—with government mismanagement and terrorism, with inflation and bureaucracy, oil crises, conspiracies, and budget deficits. Indeed, the performance of the Italian economy borders on the miraculous. At any rate, "objective figures" are not sufficient to explain it. Evidently, the average Italian spends more than he earns. He still lives well, God knows how; in fact, he lives better than ever. That is why the apocalyptic warnings and the billion-dollar deficits make no impression on him at all. Arbasino describes this pathological imperturbability with a degree of sarcasm. "One day the country is facing bankruptcy, chaos, and ruin, yet the next morning the word is: 'What's all the fuss about? Everything's booming! Everything's fine!'"

Is Italy really this exceedingly stable roly-poly-man, a "laboratory of the postmodern," which thanks to its relative backwardness and its premodern vestiges, is better able to absorb each future shock? The last shall be the first—anyone who puts his faith in this biblical promise can hardly do without some slight belief in miracles. The learned Marxists have no time for the idea of Italy as a laboratory. Giulio Bollati regards it as an ideological by-product intended for mass consumption: "Natural genius triumphs over a systematic approach, inspiration over the discipline of learning . . . Ultimately it all leads toward the illusion that our culture is the very one that has been called upon to mediate between antiquity and science fiction."

But even if the Italians managed to get by in their own way, with a system that makes a mockery of everything systematic, one question would still remain: At what cost? It's one thing to praise the beneficial effects of the shadow economy; it's quite another to approve of child labor in the cellars of Grumo Nevano in the Campania. (Camilla Cederna has described eight-to-ten-year-olds pulling heavy carts, or bent over sewing machines with no chance of attending school, whose only alternative is a life of crime.)

No, the Italian muddle has as little in common with the gentle dreams of the old Anarchists as it does with the rigid utopias of Social Democracy. Its spontaneous cruelty displays elements of cannibalism. The artistes of crisis sometimes give the impression that they are suffering from a kind of moral insanity.

I have never seen an Italian prison from the inside. What the newspapers report about the administration of justice and the penal system is enough for me. Seventy thousand prisoners vegetate in overcrowded cells. Another forty thousand are arrested every year for some trifle, usually without a magistrate's warrant. After one or two nights they're set free again for lack of space. Anyone held for trial is likely to be forgotten in jail if the judge postpones his case. After four years the prisoner must be released, unsentenced and without compensation, because the statutory period has expired. If a Fascist has been locked up on charges of terrorist activities, no one bothers about his rights anyway—it's his own fault and he doesn't deserve a fair trial. And on the whole, proceedings tend to be judged according to the principle, If it suits me it's just, if it doesn't it's barbaric. Apart from that, the Italian legal system is said to have a backlog of ten million cases, which means that the bourgeois state under rule of law is merely a façade.

In short, Model Italy has its dark side. It can't be put more politely than that. If anyone were to hold up something like it as an example to be followed, I'd cry, "No thanks!"

But history isn't a supermarket, a self-service store in which the public can stock up as it likes. Nor have the Italians freely chosen the society they live in. They've had to get by as best they can. Nobody asked them.

And our own options are perhaps not as varied as we'd like to believe, either. In any case, there's not much room for imitation when it comes to the behavior of a whole society. The Germans, the English, or the Finns could not act like the Italians even if they wanted to. They're not astute enough, not cynical enough, not talented enough; they're too stubborn, too set in their ways, too amateurish, too inhibited. They've invested too much energy in their well-ordered systems, delegated too many resources, responsibilities, and hopes to the state. They're out of practice when it comes to relying on their own initiative and can't say, "Me and my clan, my family, my shop, we'll manage—and all the rest can go to hell." They still believe in the chimera of security, still cling to an order that may already have become an anachronism.

Don't worry: we'll never go as far as the Italians. Not, at least, for the time being. Not in the foreseeable future. No one learns unless he has to. Only when we're left with no other choice will we, somehow or other, borrow this or that number from the Italian repertoire. However, we will continue to regard Model Italy, which is not a model at all but an unpredictable, productive, fantastic tumult, with mixed feelings of fear and admiration, dismay and envy.

HUNGARIAN CONFUSIONS
[1985]

....

AN EIGHTH PART OF PARADISE

"Where my homeland lies," sings György Petri, perhaps the darkest of Hungary's many talented poets, "where my homeland lies, in the Wild East, / on the lovely / glittering / Comecon Islands. / One can breathe the / air! / And what air! . . . / And it really exists! / That is what it looks like! / (Still.) / At home one can / get one's teeth into the air! / This precious compound! / Bewitching Wild East, / starry skies of the / Comecon Islands, / one can never be bored / by you!"

Everybody loves Hungary. The elderly couple from Rapid City, South Dakota, for example. They aren't rich—she was a nursery-school teacher, he was a tennis instructor—and both are retired. But they're enthusiastic, even amazed; this wasn't how they'd imagined Communism. No commissars lurk in long leather coats, no tank rattles across Engels Square, and the visitor's eye searches in vain for worn-out women lining up for a handful of potatoes. The members of the Soviet hockey team at the Golden Bull in Debrecen are in such high spirits that they never want to go to bed again. The table is groaning, the disco music thumps, the plum schnapps flows. And at the currency exchange counter the Swiss photographer happily counts up his forints and concludes that his francs have multiplied themselves miraculously. An easy trick with an exchange rate that doubles, triples, and septuples the purchasing power of anyone coming from the West. The liveried footman at the entrance of the Duna Intercontinental flings open the door for a compatriot who had emigrated in 1956, poor as a church mouse. In California he succeeded in becoming a multimillionaire (records and videos), and now he's taking a sentimental journey by limousine. He stops off at the village on the plain where he was born, and buys himself a villa on the Hill of Roses so that he may die here, in Budapest.

The vegetable importers are content, and so are the visitors to the spas, the film producers, and the International Monetary Fund's watchdogs. Even the Polish women who display a few pathetic towels for sale at the suburban markets under the indifferent glances of the militiamen put a good face on their forlorn trade. And the black marketeers from Kraków, six of whom are living illegally in an unfurnished room in the old ghetto, near Gutenberg Square (specialities: pocket calculators and fake diamonds), don't complain either. The whey-faced Red Army conscripts complain least of all. Evening after evening, just before nine, they heave their enormous cardboard boxes onto the Budapest–Moscow night train. Their weight allowance, their booty, is sixty pounds a month. The elderly married couples from Dessau and Güstrow are just as happy as they climb into their coaches, salamis tucked under their arms, the pinkest frilly blouses hidden under their pullovers, so that nothing goes wrong at Zinnwald on the border.

And I'm no exception. I enjoy being with the Hungarians. I admire them. But I don't really know why. I don't need any pocket calculators or salami, any sulfur baths or Gypsy music; I don't much care for Art Nouveau and I can't stand folklore. There must be some other reason why I can't resist the charm of this eighth part of paradise any more than the millions of others who came to Magyarország, as exploiters and bearers of foreign currency, as occupiers and sightseers. They can't even pronounce the name of the country, and yet they all feel at ease here, all of them, as if they approve of what they find.

But not Sándor. He's the most uncompromising of my Hungarian friends. Not that anyone could tell by looking at him. His laugh is a roar; his heartiness is startling; he pretends to be a *bon vivant*. Only a few know that the Stalinists beat him so badly in prison that his liver was ruined forever. He detects my thoughts even before I've had time to formulate them. I sometimes think he's had too much to do with the police and with censorship, that it has left him with a tendency to see through people. Like the hedgehog in the fable, he is already sitting there, calmly awaiting the latest folly.

"You're just another one!" shouts Sándor. "It's written all over your face! You'll say that Hungary is the happiest barracks in the Eastern Bloc, just like all the others. These journalists from the West are all the same. Shameless idiots. A few café jokes, a little reform goulash, and to finish off they sing their readers the operetta song about cunning Kádár János, who, to the sound of a csárdás, throws dice with the drunken Russian bear for the freedom of the puszta, and wins. And you, my friend, are no better!"

The delicate Biedermeier chair trembles under his weight. Sándor throws himself back and laughs at me.

"I'll quote you," I say. "That repays my debt. And I'll make sure there's no doubt as to who gave me my cues."

He gave me an injured look. This time I was a length ahead of the hedgehog.

"Seriously," he said, "the reputation our regime has gained in the West is unbelievable. I don't think there's a public-relations company between Frankfurt and Los Angeles that could have managed it better."

"Of course not. A good cliché," I contended, getting ready to evade him by taking flight forward, "is a gift from God. Perhaps what we like about Hungary is just the little grain of truth without which the lie can't function."

And to my astonishment my friend Sándor let me have the last word.

THE LAST OF THE MOHICANS

He's been sitting on this chair for twenty-seven years now.
And he looks it too. He's tired, as tired as the doorman
downstairs in his glass box, at the entrance to the newspaper
office, as tired as the creaking paternoster elevator. The same
old desks, the same old coffeepots, the same old typewriters.
A gray film covers the boss's office, just as it does the columns
of the Party newspaper he edits. Different theses, different
programs, but the sentences have remained the same—long,
involved, colorless. Complicated forms of address, tortuous
promises, veiled threats, transparent euphemisms, clumsy
innuendos: we understand one another. The old editor is a
tough nut. I think of the Party sessions he's been through,
the purges, the changes of the Party line, the denunciations
that he's survived. It requires an intelligence as thin, as
smooth, as yielding as the newsprint running through the
machines in the basement. An old fox or an old hare?

It's Saturday morning. He has set aside time for his ignorant
guest, he's well prepared and determined to be pleasant. The
amphibian eyes behind the thick lenses are still lively. He
knows the world, he's well informed, his German is excellent.
He's tough but exhausted. What sustains him? His job? The
daily routine? Power? Of course, he's one of the privileged,
he's used to exerting influence. But something is missing.
The conviction that time is on his side, the confidence that
he will triumph as a result of what he's doing, has gone. He
holds a position, his position, that's all.

Oh, he doesn't expose any weaknesses, not at all. He's not
inquisitive—he knows everything, after all. Yet he doesn't
answer any question directly. He makes lengthy digressions,
avoids the point, refers to "our principles." The first person
plural is his identity, his faith. It is the royal we of the Party.
It's difficult to say whether pomposity or gangsterism dominates this discourse. Still, the discreet request for sympathy
implicit in his reference to "certain external conditions" is

not omitted either. The higher power, Big Brother—in a word, the Russians. Not such a bad thing, this ultimate authority, which can be blamed for everything one doesn't want to take responsibility for. On the one hand, firm principles; on the other, the convenient excuse. Any remaining gap in the explanations is mortared over with self-criticism. My host talks glibly of shortages, failures, mistakes. But his concessionary clauses never lead to any doubt. Quite the reverse: the self-criticism only serves to establish more firmly the indispensability of something that can look back on an unending series of failures.

Yet I only wanted to ask a few simple questions. Why are doctors in Hungary so badly paid that they are forced to accept tips from their patients? What kind of legal security do small businesses have? How much does it cost to maintain the traditional sinecures in the big plants? Can the senseless construction of a power station on the Danube still be stopped? But these concrete questions dissolve like lumps of sugar in a glass of water. My host explains to me how important dialogue, understanding, and peace are. I listen half-dazed, as if in a barber's chair, lost in the fog of these endless, monotonous, complicated elucidations in which everything tangible disappears. An invincible, monstrous patience expresses itself in these communiqués; it is the only thing my host still retains of Bolshevism.

"Please," he says finally, "don't quote me!" No need to worry!—because the confidential government information he is offering me is strictly deadwood. What he is entrusting to me under a vow of silence the birds are already singing from the rooftops. Even the common ground he appeals to exists only in his imagination. "As a leftist, you will understand that . . ." The old conjuror exhausts his bag of tricks for me in vain. The paper flowers are a sticky mass and refuse to open, and the white doves he pulls out of a hat won't rise into the air. I'm close to feeling sorry for the old performer.

Then, just in time, he begins to talk about the scoundrels,

the dark forces sabotaging the country's progress. The opposition are shady, ungrateful riffraff! People who are only out to make names for themselves. Loudmouths with an eye on publicity and dollars. The CIA is behind them, of course. When it comes down to it, the dissidents are criminals fomenting terrorism.

The corridors of the newspaper office are silent. The whole staff, from manager to office boy, has left for the country. We're alone with the ghosts of the past. I'm not surprised to hear my host say that the rebels of 1956 brought Hungary to the brink of fascism. My sympathies for this veteran of the old school remain within bounds.

Not everything he says is wrong. Reasonable arguments also crop up in his Byzantine sentences. It can hardly be avoided. But it's impossible to believe him even where he might be right. Caution, calculation, tactics—if that were all it is! But for this graying editor the lie long ago ceased to be the means to an end; it has become habitual, second nature. What he says is watertight, lifeless, and beyond all hope.

I take my leave. Below, on Blaha-Lujza Square, there are sidewalk vendors and crowds around the entrances to the subway. Perhaps on this Saturday lunch hour I have met the last of the Mohicans. Perhaps this aging bureaucrat personifies a Party that no longer exists. He won't hold on to his position much longer. The loser's fear is written on his brow. He will be sent home with a medal and a good pension. He will keep his villa. The Party doesn't let down its own. Others, more skillful and more up-to-date, will follow him. But I'm grateful to him, because with his transparent lies he has betrayed one simple truth. "We" are prepared to discuss everything, with one exception: power. As many concessions, reforms, compromises as you like, as many as the Russians will swallow, but not one shred of our power will we surrender, not a single inch!

EROSION
....

The ornaments on top of the neo-Gothic spires, the Art Nouveau peacocks and vines: everything is crumbling, cracking, and blackened with soot. The plaster grapes and cornucopias, the harps and the lions' heads are broken; the angels and virgins are only torsos. But they're still there. The great bulldozer of progress hasn't cleared them away. There was no money for it, and it takes a lot of money to devastate the world. The planners have struck elsewhere, far out on the plain, in Pestimre and on Csepel Island, where the gray chessboard blocks for the working class stand, not here in the heart of the city.

Here trees are growing on the roof of the old stock exchange, above the frieze of figures, as if it were a Mayan temple or Angkor Wat. Enormous wooden scaffolds prop up the dilapidated Egyptian towers of the giant building, which is to be resurrected, white as snow, as the "Palace of Television." Diagonally opposite it, lapis lazuli and gold are flaking from the mosaics of the National Bank. Here one can buy shares, people's shares, in socialized factories. But the securities have no market value and yield no dividends; they are phantom shares, the costume jewelry of economic reform.

Only in transience does the ornament show its dignity; only decay discloses its pathos. The star above the police station was once red, before its glass rays were broken, and it shone on the roof in Stalinist splendor until the last lightbulb burned out. No one climbs up to screw in a new one anymore.

For several years now restoration has proceeded diligently in Budapest. The Renaissance courtyards on the castle hill are being painted under the expert guidance of art historians. The late-nineteenth-century bourgeois houses on the broad streets of Pest are also assuming new dignity. But the Hungarian version of architectural conservation bears no similarity to its West German counterpart. It's timid, not radical, a product not of abundance but of shortages. No demolition, only whitewash. What it produces instead of a brand-new past is, at most, yet another provisional arrangement. This half-hearted, careless treatment of the old fabric reveals not only the inefficiency of the authorities or the scarcity of resources but also a conviction that the decrepit lasts longest and that to plaster over the memory of a whole nation would be a futile ambition.

The façades of Budapest do not disavow their scars. No stranger can decipher them. This shattered rosette over here may bear witness to an English air raid. The caryatid over there, with the tip of its nose missing, is a reminder of the siege in the winter of 1944/1945. The marks of a machine gun volley on a balcony parapet—was it an SS man or a Red Army soldier? The submachine gun of a rebel or a Russian tank thirty years ago? It's difficult to decide. And perhaps it was only the rain, the hail, the ice, that loosened the cornice, that attacked the stucco pilaster. Neglect, time . . .

It is this ubiquitous erosion that constitutes the secret, the terror, and the charm of the metropolis on the Danube. An irresistible, spontaneous, higher force: entropy. The painter who dips his brush in the pot knows that his work is futile and that only one thing can be relied on: really existing time, which takes hold of and conserves everything, even as it wears it down. History is a process of erosion. What we call socialism is only its viceroy.

It has been observed often enough that the Western visitor entering eastern Central Europe experiences a journey in a time machine. Regimes that started out determined to liquidate the old now conserve its broken remains. That holds true not only for roofs and walls but also for people and their behavior.

In front of the old market hall on Rákóczi Square, where the flower-sellers are making small talk, beside the fenced-off soccer field with its shouting children, pensioners and workers and idlers in peaked caps sit on the broken benches and skat cards are slammed onto the worn table. All the modest whores with the old-fashioned handbags, who have had their beat here for as long as anyone can remember, are said to have recently become registered members of an agricultural-production cooperative. But otherwise hardly anything has changed. The patched jackets could be from 1932. A half-forgotten category comes to mind at the sight of this gray idyll—"the people." Here it still exists, "like it used to be," quiet, sober, unpretentious, without illusions, prepared for everything and forgetting nothing. At home it has long ago been absorbed into a hodgepodge of conformity, into the melting-pot of some fictitious middle class, but here one bumps into "the people" at every turn, looking like the photographs of August Sander: peasant faces, proletarian faces, the physiognomies of the trades and of the old classes. They are worn but not destroyed.

THE TWO OPPOSITIONS

When it gets dark in Budapest, the hour of the *buli*s has come. A *buli* is an improvised party, loud, chaotic, without extravagance. There are no invitations. A system of noiseless bush drums ensures that everyone who needs to know turns up on time. The furnishings testify to long-faded bourgeois splendor. *Buli*s are usually at a good address, on a Danube embankment or on the hills. An ascetic disorder prevails. Manuscripts, sculptures, junk, cardboard boxes on top of monstrous wardrobes. A 1950s radio with a magic eye on an art nouveau console, a venerable gas cooker in the kitchen, books in five languages on the shelves. Leather jackets, threadbare Sunday suits, punk haircuts. A whiff of Bohemianism, a trace of megalomania, a stupendous scholarliness.

A *buli* is the best way of getting to know the Hungarian opposition from the inside, its norms and its sarcasm, its codes, its solidarity, its gossip, its obsessions, its clichés, self-accusations, quarrels, reconciliations, its triumphs, and its neuroses. Here every comfort is scorned and material success counts for nothing; here only protest, attitude, outsider status, vodka, and integrity count. Only a critical irony fractures the dominant severity.

Strictly speaking, there are two oppositions in Hungary: that of the Central Europeans and that of the Populists. Maybe I just went to the wrong *buli*s, but I find it difficult to do justice to the Populists. Their ideal is "universal Magyardom." Alas, I have never understood what that is supposed to mean. I've been told that I lack the right "roots in the air." Only someone who has spoken Hungarian from childhood can grasp the "Fatherland on high," and with it the Populists' worries about population decline, the swamping of native culture, the decline of folk art, and liberal abortion laws.

Democracy doesn't seem to interest them. They would be prepared to cooperate with any "good Hungarian government" that recognized that the "historic injustice" the world has done to Hungary must be redressed. It is also said that they have a certain aversion to the Jews. Their true *bêtes noires*, however, are the Romanians.

Here their arguments take on a political charge that is not to be underestimated. Two million Hungarians still live under humiliating conditions in Transylvania, which once was a core region of Hungarian culture but fell to Romania in 1919 and 1945. So it's not surprising that the Populists' arguments find resonance among the people as well as in the Party. In addition, the Populists have taken up a number of social problems that the regime would rather have shrouded in silence: the high suicide rate, the abuses in psychiatric treatment, the poverty of pensioners, and the increase in alcoholism.

In this area and on the question of human rights, the red-white-and-green Populist opposition can reach agreement with its traditional adversaries: the "Westerners," the "Cosmopolitans," the "Central Europeans." Otherwise, however, a deep chasm divides the two factions. The urban intelligentsia demands, above all, a radical democratization of Hungarian society. It owes its exceptional strength not least to the fact that Eichmann could effect the "final solution" only in part in Hungary. Today rather more than a hundred thousand Jews once again live in the country. Neither the Party nor the opposition would be conceivable without them. Not only is it thanks to them that Budapest can continue to lay claim to the rank and flair of a metropolis, but without them "universal Magyardom" would certainly look considerably more provincial.

However that may be, it is among the democratic opposition that the unceasing debate about the country's fate is pushed beyond narrow-minded national interest. This discussion is too rich and too contradictory to be reduced to a few simple sentences.

Conversational fragment: "We are not dissidents. We represent normality. We don't have any appetite for power. We have to perform the same role as the media in the West, no more and no less. However, all we have at our disposal is two dozen people and a couple of duplicators. That certainly means that we are irreplaceable—even if only by chance."

"Don't listen to him! We were long ago defeated and split a hundred times by the regime's precision control, which corrupts us with travel privileges, jobs, opportunities to publish. All of us are, directly or indirectly, state parasites. We lack the fanaticism of the Russians."

"Nonsense. There's a kind of division of labor between us and the government. The Party needs us. We say what it can't say. We produce the ideas it doesn't have. If we didn't exist, the Party would have to invent us. And the other way around."

"If that's true, then we have all become Soviet without noticing it, every one of us."

"No wonder, after forty years. The historical capital has been used up, we've lost our identity, and there's no other perspective around."

"There are no irreversible processes—that's superstition. In Hungary being reasonable means accepting blatant unreason; being unreasonable, on the other hand, means repeating what everyone else is demanding, right up to the threshold of pain."

"We've inherited the avant-garde problem of the Party. There's a certain irony in that. We're going forward but no one wants to follow us. The difference is that we have neither the power nor the desire to use the police to give us a helping hand."

"We define ourselves by the regime we're fighting against. If one of us loses his job, we make a problem of national importance out of it. Each of us imagines he's a paradigmatic case."

"Hungary is a laboratory. Each of us faces the same questions: Shall we be reasonable or admirable? Stand apart or cooperate? But what I ask myself is, Who's doing the experimenting? Who *sees* us?"

"That's an unpolitical question. According to its constitution, Hungary is a state under rule of law, not an institute for behavioral research. There are laws that determine what a government department does and doesn't do, or a trade union or a local authority. But what about the Party? It operates in a space outside the law. There's no law that regulates its functions, its duties, its practice. But ultimately that means that the Party is illegal and that we are the guardians of the constitution."

"That's a formalistic argument. I also find it somewhat pretentious. We despise everything official. In our circles a state prize is something to be ashamed of. There's an element of racism in that. We think the bureaucrats are vulgar, clumsy, boring, and stuffy. That's too simple. It doesn't get us anywhere."

"That's not the point. The issue is legality, which also means the rehabilitation of bourgeois ideas. It's our only hope."

"But in Hungary the bourgeoisie was never more than a phantom."

"On the contrary. It was only repressed, and the repressed always return. We have never managed to establish civil society in Hungary. That task still lies before us. We have to study the theorists of civil society. The English of the seventeenth century are extremely relevant. The rehabilitation of the bourgeoisie also means the rehabilitation of private property, within certain limits, of course. In Hungary that's a left-wing demand. Someone who owes everything to the Party or the state is defenseless. He's a serf, even if he lives in a villa."

"Music to the ears of our aspiring young entrepreneurs!"

"That's not an objection. It's demagogy!"

And so on, around the kitchen table, till the early hours of the morning. Till the last bottle is empty.

The practical successes of the Hungarian opposition are by no means negligible: a large *samizdat* literature, the success of ecological demands, the uncovering of scandalous conditions in health care . . . But its real achievement is that it not only has defended the country's moral standard of living but has in fact noticeably raised it. Western observers are seldom in a position to judge what that means. Under the conditions of the occupation and of the one-party state, each step, even the most ordinary, becomes a test. In every transaction with the regime something else, something unspoken, is always at stake. It's no accident that the expression "an honorable man," which has died out in the West, is used all the time in Hungary, and quite unselfconsciously.

"Of course, he is in the Party, but you can talk openly with him—he's an honorable man." "Take care! He pretends to be very understanding, but he's a liar and a thief." No society develops such criteria spontaneously. The greater the confusion, the finer the nuances required for survival. The moral judgments that are won under such circumstances only seem to be simple. In reality they presuppose an extremely subtle ability to make distinctions. The opposition is not the only proprietor of the morality of Hungarian society; nor is it interested in codifying it. But the opposition clarifies that morality anew each day, and uses it with a precision I have not encountered in any Western society.

THE LENIN RING (I)

At about nine every morning, including Sundays, the lottery ticket seller opens out the folding roof over the green-painted iron box that contains his treasures. He unlocks the heavy chain from the chair that stood in the rain overnight, and spreads out his wares on the tabletop of his stand. My lottery seller is not an invalid but a very strongly built man of fifty. The soccer pool coupons are held down by a cast-iron weight so that the wind won't blow them away. Cigarettes are kept in a little box—they can be bought singly here, a sign that there isn't much change in his customers' pockets. Streetcar tickets can also be bought here, for one forint (a few cents) each, and pink lollipops. But these are only extras. The principal business of my acquaintance—for after three days he recognizes me at first glance—consists in selling a cut-rate chance of good luck. This swings in the breeze in the shape of tiny envelopes hoisted up on a string. My lottery seller wears a Norwegian sweater, yellow shoes, and a fat signet ring. He's always ready for a chat. He's never in a hurry. He picks up the big scissors to cut off the ticket the customer is buying. As he does so, he calmly and benignly lets drop in front of the curious, who are intent on learning whether the little envelope contains a first prize, the latest news from the Central Committee. He knows more than the newspapers do. He's an augur, who has already opened many letters. Every morning he draws a ticket for me, one blank after another.

He has put up his stand on the Lenin Ring. A hundred years ago a great boulevard was laid out on the former channel of the Danube that once enclosed old Pest. The great ring was completed in 1896, exactly one thousand years after the foundation of the Hungarian kingdom. It was intended to be a monument to the imperial and royal monarchy, and its segments bore the names Leopold, Theresia, Elisabeth, Joseph, and Franz. However, the jubilee memorial was also meant to turn a profit. This double purpose is still evident in that part of the street which is today called the Lenin Ring: spawned by an orgy of exhibitionism and real-estate speculation, its houses are at once palaces and tenements. There is a fairy-tale quality to the architecture of this loud, common, prosaic boulevard. The reckless poetry of the metropolis depends on such symbioses. On the Lenin Ring the exploitative and the ornamental, the shabby and the sumptuous, the clangorous and the idyllic have entered into a union that is not easily forgotten.

The Palais New York, today the Hungaria, houses a famous, hideous café, and is an example of that architectural megalomania which Budapest's proud citizens called eclecticism. Its tower marks the beginning of the Lenin Ring. It stretches over a mile to the splendid West Station, which was erected to Eiffel's plans, before ending anticlimactically in one of those squares devised by contemporary city planning for the worship of banality. With a contempt that is quite natural in this country, the square, dedicated to the twin deities traffic and consumption—on the left there's a department store of black glass, on the right a highway overpass—has been named for that poor old prophet Dr. Karl Marx.

One could easily walk from one end of the Lenin Ring to the other in fifteen minutes, but only a fool would think of doing so. I've spent whole days reading the wounds and splendors of the city of Budapest from its doors, walls, and nameplates. I think of it as an ambiguous, puzzling, dirty panorama. Every sign in this country seems to promise a secret to the flaneur from abroad and impresses upon him that he is condemned to remain an idiot, an illiterate.

Gyógyszertár, for example. Who could decode such a word? And yet behind the frosted glass and the wood paneling is concealed nothing more than a quite ordinary pharmacy. The Lenin Ring is a street like any other, with cheap restaurants and hardware stores. In small, stuffy offices men in suspenders sit eating in front of some documents. Time has stood still in the street's window displays. The waffles, wrapped in cellophane, look as if they'd been baked thirty years ago. Little pink, gold, and pale-green ribbons are tied around the neck of a bottle of vermouth, paper roses lie on yellowed boxes, and the stationery shop timidly offers a couple of rosy nude photos beside the pencil sharpeners.

But next to this provincial innocence the color blindness of the dictatorship is much in evidence: the Eastern Bloc furnishings of the kiosks, public offices, and hotel lobbies; the brutal substitutes; the guard-room stolidity; the under-developed Soviet aesthetic; the shabbiness of a society in which the new is always born as an already senile decree.

Admittedly, the true life of the Lenin Ring cannot be read from its streetfronts. Anyone who ignores its gateways understands nothing of its seductions. Here every house conceals a dream arcade out of Benjamin's repertoire. Colored lightbulbs glow with promise in foil-lined showcases under archways that lead into the vitals of Budapest. In the evening, when it's getting dark and rain patters on the plane trees of the Ring, these entrances appear both sinister and magical.

They are nothing more than culs-de-sac that lead into back courts, but while one ends in a dark lightwell, the next leads past projecting stairways to the courtyard of a Renaissance palace or a knight's castle. Here one finds platform stages and arcades supported by cast-iron pillars, prison yards, caravanserais, gardens in every state from overbearing pomposity to melancholy wretchedness.

A garbage can smolders in the passageway beside the dusty, empty little office of the concierge. One can hear the creaking elevator. A pile of bricks or a bag of cement waits underneath the fuse boxes. The meter disk turns in a wooden box, which was made to measure ninety years ago and is protected by a padlock. But the pane of glass was smashed years ago, and no glazier has repaired it. Yellowing in the entrance hall are carefully framed public announcements, the "Summary of Relevant Decrees" of 1959, and beside it, dated October 1, 1956, a notice about fire prevention regulations—1956, of all years!

Then the names on the innumerable letter boxes: names crossed out, illegible, smeared in felt-tip, faded, machine-punched, written with a flourish in brown ink. They reveal more than any statistic: there are not enough apartments in Budapest, here every square yard must be conquered with fantastic schemes and defended with dogged skill. The proliferating nameplates speak of exchanges, of allocations, of corruption, of inheritances, dividing walls, divorces, of odysseys of flight from the land and of emigration, of illegal business deals and laborious repairs, of unconquerable desires and of this city's inventive chaos.

THE RULING CLASS

Red Csepel, iron Csepel: the Danube island in the south of Budapest is the birthplace of Hungarian heavy industry. Before the First World War this flat, sooty tract of land was one of the most important armories of the imperial and royal monarchy; today the ironworks of Csepel is one of the dinosaurs of the socialist planned economy.

The green suburban train, on which not a single tourist is to be seen, passes through desolate docks and warehouse streets and runs almost as far as the chimneys out of which red, yellow, gray, and black smoke pours day and night. The soft thunder of the rolling mills can be heard as far as the train stop at Tanácsház Square, where the workers on the late shift climb down. From there it's only a few hundred yards to the great gate of the Csepel Iron and Metal Works. It's decorated with a red star and hammer and sickle, and underneath the insignia of Soviet power is the only Russian inscription I found in Budapest. *Oktyabr'skaya revolyutsiya* (October Revolution), it reads, and a larger-than-life Lenin in jacket and vest, hand outstretched, guards the entrance to the factory area, aided by a white-haired woman who glances suspiciously into the bags of workers coming off their shift. Trust is good, inspection is better.

Red Csepel has played a legendary role in the history of the Hungarian industrial proletariat, from the days of the Council Republic in 1919 to the Budapest uprising of 1956. And today the Danube island remains a proletarian open-air museum that tells more about the realities of that class than the official exhibition high up in the fortress of Buda, which is dedicated to the history of the workers' movement.

To the right of the suburban railway, right up against the factory perimeter, in the stink of the emissions, along pot-holed streets full of puddles, in a huddle of small shops, dirty bars, coal depots, and rented garden plots, there still stand the low, decrepit, jerry-built single-story housing—no more than barracks with lots of doors into which the proletarians fleeing from the land were herded at the turn of the century.

There is no trace of the taste and tastelessness of Budapest. No style or ornament dominates here, there are no currency speculators and no confectioners, only the old misery. Sometimes an old woman can be seen behind grimy curtains, watering the aloes and the busy lizzies on the window ledge— before the bulldozer comes. Often only a clothesline or a sleeping dog reveals whether anyone still lives behind the crumbling wooden walls.

Left of the railway, by contrast, rise the giant ten-story apartment houses that were built in the early sixties, after the uprising: gray and inhospitable but well supplied with elevators, balconies, warm water, and drains. The architecture demonstrates that the hegemonic class is simultaneously a subject one: it displays the cage as an achievement.

Red Csepel is also a symbolic place for the economic reformers. For them this state-owned concern is not the engine of the economy but a brake block, an unprofitable, immovable relic of Stalinism. The machinery still dates, in part, from the forties; the fittings and infrastructure are obsolete. In truth, Hungary's crisis can be read quite literally from the dust in the passageways, from the resignation in the faces, from the rust in the factory halls. The classic proletariat has been forced onto the defensive. Suddenly the unwritten contract between the regime and the workers is not supposed to count anymore. It guarantees them job security, cheap housing, subsidized food, higher education for their children, and tacit toleration of the everday thefts in the factories (the "theft bonus"). But aside from that: as little work discipline, as little effort, as little responsibility as possible. The Party accepted this state of affairs, even though this entailed defending interests that had a negative impact on the economy; in return, the workers put up with the power of the Party bureaucrats. Now the economic reformers want to unilaterally terminate this old compromise, which still embodies aspects of the old class consciousness.

As a first step, the leadership has divided the Csepel concern into more than a dozen smaller units. Voluntary work collectives were set up on a cooperative basis inside the factories. These work on their own account, outside the stipulated working hours, but use the plant's machinery. Some of these teams even have contracts with their own factory, and deliver parts, make urgent repairs, or work overtime at several times the normal rate when there's deadline pressure. This arrangement utilizes capacity more effectively and greatly increases productivity, but also splits the class and leads to the self-exploitation of the most eager of the upwardly mobile. Twelve-hour workdays, even on weekends, are no rarity. The stratum of new top earners can afford everything, but their lives are miserable.

Consequently, resistance to the reform not only comes from dogmatists who still cling to the pro-Stalinist party line—it has deeper causes and strong social roots. The technocrats have carefully but determinedly opened for discussion the question whether unemployment and socialism are really as irreconcilable as orthodox doctrine would have it. They quietly praise the advantages of flexibility, the reduction of subsidies, and labor mobility, and quite openly demand economic sanctions against the old practices in industry.

Old János Kádár, who was a metalworker himself for years, appears on the TV screen, in conversation with a workers' delegation. "Comrade Kádár," says a forty-year-old woman milling machinist, "what's going on? I go to the market to shop. The merchants have plenty of everything, but they want sixty forints [$1.20] for two pounds of tomatoes. I have to work two whole hours for that. If that's reform, then I can do without reform!" The first secretary of the Hungarian Socialist Workers' Party swallows. The logic of a market-oriented economy is clear to him; he has supported it often enough against his opponents. But here, confronted with its costs, he can't rouse himself to its defense. He agrees with the worker. His aide takes down the location of the stand of the greengrocer, who will have to serve as scapegoat. Perhaps he'll escape with a fine. The reform dance will continue, two steps forward, one step back. The workers of Csepel know what they can expect from it: higher prices, falling real wages, more worry, more inequality, and, on top of that, the risk of unemployment.

Nevertheless, their resistance doesn't have a chance. A fossilized industrial structure can't be preserved. And that is precisely the regime's dilemma: economic reform is indispensable, but it can't be achieved without political costs. The managers are demanding a free hand, the workers need free unions. The Party would have to surrender a little bit of its power to each. As long as that thought is unthinkable, Hungarian reform will remain a chimera.

THE HOUSE OF LIES

Here they are again, the Habermans of Rapid City, South Dakota. They're doing the sights. Likable people. Their patience borders on the miraculous. They find the rich Hungarian cuisine fascinating, the manners and customs mysterious, the scramble at the streetcar stops picturesque. But now they're close to despair.

Waiting outside, its engine running, is the bus that's supposed to take them to a first-rate historical sight, and they still haven't got a reservation. There's not a soul in the State Tourist Office who can explain to them why, although the bus is booked up, it is also half empty. The Habermans don't suspect that the ride from the Chain Bridge to the Parliament building, the goal of excursion, will last only five minutes, and that the few hundred yards could be covered just as easily on foot. A couple of dollar bills change hands and the dilemma is satisfactorily resolved. The tourists are thrilled by the Hungarian Parliament. Patiently they let themselves be told, in five languages, that it is 879 feet long, 403 feet wide, and 315 feet high, that it has 10 courtyards and 27 gates, that it contains more than 29 staircases, that its walls are adorned with 233 "Gothic" statues, and that the decorations required 90 pounds of gold leaf. Here even the most rabid Reaganite becomes a meek pilgrim.

The monstrous edifice was built around the turn of the century. A cross between Windsor Castle and St. Peter's, it's a mock feudal-religious stone compendium of Hungarian history, which, if one believes the state artists who were at work here, consists of an endless series of glorious deeds. Here even the revolution of 1848 can be viewed as a brightly painted devotional picture. Lining the corridors are images of the people, a quaint assemblage in folk dress: the post-horse keeper, the blacksmith, the shepherd, each under his own little canopy.

The architecture of this Parliament is dominated by cavernous spaces: functionless stairways, lobbies, chambers, which impress only by their emptiness. The tourists stand respectfully under the seventy-nine-foot-high central dome. An empty golden ashtray standing in front of each of the golden pillars only emphasizes the ban on smoking.

There is no sign of work here. There aren't any offices for the M.P.'s. This shell does contain the first air-conditioning system to be installed in Europe, but it has never housed democratically elected representatives of the Hungarian people. The franchise in force until the First World War withheld the vote from 94 percent of the population and Horthy's authoritarian regime ruled until the Second World War.

Today the guide talks, without batting an eye, about the "free and secret elections" that produce this Parliament. But the representatives of the people meet only four times a year, for two whole days at a time. For fifty-one weeks out of fifty-two the chamber serves the tourist trade. The Parliament's standing orders do not allow for negative votes.

In the foyer a model of the building is on display. For

three years a married couple, who could think of nothing better to do with their lives, toiled to construct it out of a hundred thousand matchsticks. "The House of Lies," as one Hungarian poet has called it, is nothing more than an enlargement of this piece of amateur craftsmanship, a monumental knickknack.

A MEMBER OF THE MANAGEMENT

He received me with open arms in front of the revolving doors of the Duna Intercontinental. He was about fifty, his tie was exquisite, the Armani jacket a trace too tight, the shoulder bag with its many zippers was of the softest leather, and even before we had reached the reserved table he let me know why he was a Party member.

"The Party is our social escalator, better than the Harvard Business School! In this respect the Party has no competition—there are no alternatives. You don't really believe that anyone in the West would even bend a finger for the Hungarians? The day the Americans send their GIs to Budapest, I'll be the first to say to hell with Leninism! But we can wait a long time for that . . ."

I looked around nervously, but he was unconcerned. The thought that he might risk his head or his job by talking too much didn't seem to worry him. His nonchalance was breathtaking. Although he made no claim on my discretion, I do not intend to name him nor even hint at his offices and functions. He was, in his own words, quite simply "a member of the management": intelligent, respected, witty, cynical, and self-confident. An apparatchik? Hardly. An opportunist? Maybe. But this man would also have gone far in Sweden or France, and he would have felt quite at home in Texas.

"But, by and large, you agree with the Party's positions?"

"My dear friend, no one agrees with the Party. The Party is composed entirely of deviationists. We have turned Stalinism upside down. Everyone has a 'personal' opinion of his own but respects the Party line, whose only disadvantage is that no one supports it. It's merely the unstable result of a constant tug of war. That's tactically expedient, since it leaves all options open. Unfortunately, under such conditions any strategy is impossible. The old phrase 'The Party is always right' takes on a very particular meaning for us: it means that whenever the Party makes a decision, it is already supporting the opposite position."

It was difficult to argue with this man. He anticipated every objection. He disarmed me by admitting everything.

"Budapest is full of people who call me an opportunist. But I act out of conviction. I consider myself a radical reformer. And in this respect I'm in agreement with the Party leadership. The difference is that what they think, I say out loud. It's the middle- and lower-level cadres who sabotage reforms, because they fear for their sinecures. At the same time they are the base of the party. It's out of tender regard for these nonentities that the scale of the private economy is played down. The statistics are faked. In reality, more than half the population is involved in the second economy, legally or illegally."

"But it doesn't look as if the hoped-for triggering effect has taken place. One gets an impression, rather, of stagnation."

"Because the Party is afraid to take its courage in both hands, because it doesn't go far enough. For a long time now we've had plans to close down fifty-six of the largest state companies because they're plainly bankrupt. Five thousand managers should be sent home for total incompetence. But who votes on issues like that? The same fools who should be gotten rid of. Everything stays as it is, and we generate more losses. Now the crisis is here, real incomes are going down, our infrastructure is in terrible shape, and it's too late to catch up in, say, electronics. Everyone's complaining about prices, underemployment, overexploitation of plant. No one can bear to admit that these are necessary evils that have to be put up with. Hence the constant policy zigzags and the ambiguity of every economic decision. The results are called transitional problems. But what does that mean? How long can it go on? Everyone wants guarantees—the workers, the Russians, the businessmen; but the plain truth is that in this world there are no guarantees, period!"

"And what do you think of the Russians?"

"Those poor people! One could feel sorry for them. Full of inferiority complexes. And they don't even suspect what's coming to them."

"What do you mean?"

"The satellites, my friend! No, I'm not talking about the military's toys, I mean television. High-frequency transmissions from space that can be received anywhere, without parabola antennas. It's a matter of five or six years, there's no way of stopping it. *Dallas* in Tashkent, the food department of KaDeWe* in Irkutsk! The effect will be absolutely devastating. The isolation of the Soviet population will be over and done with. The Americans can sit back, time's on their side. Don't misunderstand me: I've got nothing against the Russians. They just have to be made into Europeans, that's all."

"And what's your opinion of the opposition?"

"Nothing but dreamers. All this talk about Magyardom only makes me laugh. The way our nationalists whine is unbearable. They always think they're innocent victims. This country has been badly treated for centuries, they say: first the Turks, then the Austrians, then the victorious powers of Versailles, the Germans in the forties, and finally the Russians. Maybe! But what these people don't want to understand is the simple fact that we lost two wars. That has to be paid for.

* *A West Berlin department store with a spectacular food department.* (*Trans.*)

We will never see the lost territories again. The Hungarians in Transylvania are having a bad time. So are the Romanians themselves for that matter. There's no sense in yammering about it. Socialist misery doesn't spare anyone who lives there. Romania is politically and economically bankrupt. We're not. So let's get our industry moving again and offer Ceauşescu a few million! Human rights aren't for free. As a German you should know that!"

"And the so-called democratic opposition? You can't deny that it includes the best brains in the country?"

"If only they weren't so modest! An intellectual must be prepared to face the heat in the kitchen. I have no intention of standing on the sidelines or being one of the losers. I supply work that's useful—useful to Hungary and useful to me. As a result, I'm in a position to set conditions."

"And what if, one day, the government no longer wants to meet your conditions?"

"Quite simple. I'll resign. Anyone who depends on the Party and the state has only himself to blame. I got involved in the second economy early on and set up a limited company to earn dollars—with the help of the Communist youth organization, by the way. Everything's perfectly legal. The contracts are good and production costs are low. With a foreign-currency account behind me I can take more risks than other people. I'll probably be kicked out one day, but I've made sure that I won't land too hard."

He glanced at the clock, excused himself, and disappeared into the darkness with a bounce in his step. For a long time I followed him with my eyes, utterly bewildered.

DISTANT VILLAGES

A late-eighteenth-century manor-house in the interior of the country, off the main roads: Venetian red plasterwork, a giant domed roof, rococo. At the entrance a puffy pensioner leaning on a stick is talking to a small, wiry, mustached man wearing greenish brown riding breeches, who looks like a jockey.

The castle, explains the flabby doorkeeper, is now a home for neglected children. "All Gypsies," he adds contemptuously. "The Hungarians aren't crazy enough to give their children to the state." He can hardly stay on his feet, he stutters, he gives off a smell of schnapps. And what was it like before?

"Oh," says the wiry man, "the count used to live here. He was a real master. Today *everyone* thinks they can give orders." He doesn't mean to say that he misses the old estate—that would be saying too much. But the count was certainly not as dumb as the people in charge today. In 1975 the count and his wife returned for a visit (they live in Austria now). He had had the dilapidated house restored at his own expense—*noblesse oblige*! In the annex, where the horses used to be kept, the mayor put on a banquet to open the building formally, and when he wanted to show the count in, the latter said quite calmly, "After you, my friend! You are my guest! I am at home here."

The small, energetic man with the lively black eyes is over sixty and has been a peasant all his life. "We were always free people." After the war he said to the Communists, "You can take everything away from me, but I'm not joining the collective." They beat him up but he didn't want to give in. After he had been expropriated, he scraped by for a decade as a well-digger. When the reforms came, he gradually bought back his land, one piece at a time. Today he grows corn and wine grapes and raises pigs. He has three horses, he doesn't want a tractor, the work is hard, the fields are small and scattered. He makes the farmer's eternal complaints about rising costs, poor prices, taxes, the officials from the town. "There's no point in asking the people in the Party. I've lived under four regimes. They were all bad, but things were best under Horthy."

Then the ritual invitation. The new, two-story house, the

pride of his life built with his own hands: bath, toilet, cement floors, stuffed full of furniture, mirrors, appliances—a status symbol, a monument to intransigence—feels cold and unlived-in. In fact the peasant and his wife continue to live in the old wooden cottage next door, with the pigs, as they have always done. The tiny kitchen with the coal stove is cozier and more cheerful than all the new alien luxury. Home-distilled schnapps, the old etiquette of hospitality, the trick of hum-bling the guest: he makes me a present of a whole canister of wine. There's no question of paying.

"I save," he says. "I don't go to the bar like the others. I don't drink much, just three or four liters of wine a day, my own." The novelists and journalists are silent about people like him. They are rare but tough, and they survive everything.

In Budapest well-meaning friends had pressed agricultural statistics into my hand; experts had explained to me the labyrinthine history of structural reform in the countryside; a bearded populist got on my nerves for a whole evening, complaining about "the destruction of Hungarian peasant culture." Nor were resentful voices lacking in the capital. Old prejudices resurfaced in the guise of envious stories: fairy tales about a collective farm's chairwoman who flew to Paris to buy her clothes at Dior, about the two pianos that a big earner who was deaf had displayed in his parlor, about the pig farmer said to have built himself a marble crypt in the cemetery. The intoxication with consumption in the country-side was deplored, the building mania of the peasants ridi-culed. Hardly anyone seemed to remember that before the Second World War there had been millions of agrarian proletarians in Hungary living below subsistence level, with-out land or rights. Many emigrated to find salvation; hundreds of thousands wound up as beggars.

* * *

"Empty, desolate, waste," it says in the Hungarian dictionary under the word *puszta*; "heath, desert, estate," and the dictionary is right. The world of the puszta, which no longer exists, bore no resemblance to the backdrops famous from movies, or to the museumlike nature reserve, with its draw wells, Gypsy music, and riding contests, that is shown to tourists today.

Even the books one must turn to for a picture of the puszta are now already half forgotten. The poet Gyula Illyés wrote such a book fifty years ago: autobiography, poetic reportage, political pamphlet, social history—his text is all of that, and at the same time a moving memorial to his birthplace and its inhabitants.

What he describes is a Third World in the heart of Central Europe. A few hours east of Vienna by train, people were living in medieval conditions until the 1930s. There were no free peasants on the puszta. Its inhabitants were practically serfs, at the mercy, for better or worse, of the lord of the manor. They had no plumbing, no postal service, no schools, no electricity, no shops, and no newspapers. I decided to search out the place Illyés had described.

"But what do you want to go there for? It's all been flattened a long time ago," said my Budapest friends. "And anyway, a dump like that can't be reached by car at all."

"Then we'll go on foot," I said.

Rácegrespuszta was not, in fact, marked on any road atlas, and only after a long search did I find a variant of the missing name on a local map, in tiny letters, between the Tolnai Hills and the Sió River.

A fine old sunken road, which really was all but impassable, lined by birches full of larks, led through deep marshes, past beehives and abandoned carts, to a hollow, and there was the old estate I was looking for: the stables built of clay and roofed with straw; the laborers' homes dark holes distinguishable from pigsties only by the many, unhinged doors; in the middle, the steward's ramshackle house.

An almost archaeological search unearths: a well with a rusty wheel, the remains of a latrine, a little iron tower whose missing bell once called the laborers to their work in the fields at daybreak, and finally the lord of the manor's "castle."

In the memory of the writer Illyés the building figures as the seat of a mysterious, absolute power, as unapproachable as Kafka's castle in Bohemia. In reality it is a pitiful, two-story, yellow plastered building with traces of old neoclassical stucco ornamentation; tiny, neglected, indescribably shabby. Broken windows, doors covered in cobwebs, torn mattresses on the floors, broken tile stoves. The castle evidently served as a temporary school after the war. A couple of broken schooldesks bear witness to this use, a battered abacus stands in the corner, and the remains of a shabby little chapel are to be found behind flapping plastic hangings. The "park" is an overgrown, handkerchief-sized patch of ground with a couple of thin robinias. To judge by its legacy, the famous Hungarian gentry, the so-called "seven-plumtree aristocracy," was, even in its prime, an inefficient, corrupt, half-witted class, whose demise is not regretted even by its descendants.

Today the former puszta is a collective. The peasants have built themselves a village on the road, away from the old estate. The houses are well built and clean, the trellis gates lovingly painted; the private gardens bloom; there's a modest, monotonous prosperity.

After bitter conflicts and endless argument, the Kádár regime has definitively closed the gap between town and country and made possible an agricultural specialization that achieves large surpluses. The silence of the villages conceals the fact that here, behind these drowsy fences, where only a dog sometimes disturbs the noonday peace, Hungarian socialism has put an end to misery and servitude and achieved its most revolutionary successes.

THE LENIN RING (II)

Anyone who gives in to the lure of the passageway steps out of the daylight of the boulevards and into the caves and recesses of private initiative. In the gateway of this bourgeois house, in which, according to the inevitable marble plaque, Gustav Mahler lived from 1888 to 1891—or was it in the house next door?—there's an illuminated display case. In it buckles and buttons are laid out: hand-turned, fluted, carved buttons, fifteen to sixty pfennigs each. The "Sports Angler" can supply flies, hooks, and fish food; a stamp dealer advertises his tenacious business; and an "Elektronikus" offers his services on a hand-painted sign. A meager abundance reveals itself in these back courts, an economy that has the vitality of an illness, feverish, extravagant, greedy, a murky productive force that digs its channels and streams where it can.

An advertising agency has opened up on the first floor: "Reklám—Propaganda." It's a travel agency as well, but I can't find the businessman himself. He's there only twice a week, from twelve to three. Where does he sit the rest of the week? In a ministry, a state printing press, a post office?

The "Pop Shop" next door is an illegal construction hammered together out of corrugated iron and concrete slabs that overshadows the inner courtyard. It advertises itself in six languages—Hungarian, Serbo-Croat, English, Polish, German, and Russian—and in fact Saxon accents can be heard in front of the shop window. My compatriots from East Germany are painstakingly comparing prices. The plain brassiere costs only seven marks; the elegantly embroidered model, on the other hand, is twice as much. The Pop Shop also offers girdles and suspenders for customers from Kiev, Dessau, and Łódź.

The black-market economy—underground business—knows no taboos. A masterpiece of unintentional surrealism, a glass sign showing a fleshy red jaw gruesomely sewn up with wire, invites the passerby to consult the master denture-maker, and the feather bed laundry of Imre Elfenbein recommends itself with a yellow, rumpled dead goose hanging from a window.

On the Lenin Ring the flaneur can pursue his pilgrimage for miles, hot on the trail of repressed lusts and questionable desires. The ambiguously flickering little lamps suggest occult sessions, pay-by-the-hour hotels, and opium dens, but in the end it's always the same harmless consolation that's being handed out here: stickers that extol TEXACO or KUNG FU or NINA HAGEN, corsets, videocassettes, Mickey Mouses, candlesticks, jeans, cuckoo clocks, and—terror of terrors—relentless folklore: sweet garbage as opium for the people.

Are these the residues of the past, as the Party still pretends, or is this the new, emerging into the radiance of the colored lightbulbs, at once confused and tentative, cheap and pathetic?

I know that Hungarian economic reform is not a subject for a casual stroller but a chaotic science, a trial of patience for experts. The laws, decrees, and regulations fill whole volumes and are supplemented, withdrawn, altered, and expanded every week. A never-ending dance on uncertain terrain, whose participants call out mysterious abbreviations to one another. GMK,* for example, "economic labor collective," an invention that can make one either a millionaire or a bankrupt within a few months. A foreigner has no right to judge here. Hundreds of thousands participate in this lottery, mustached nomads in leather jackets and Italian shoes, former artists, engineers, amateur craftsmen, civil servants; the cross-overs to profiteer and swindler are fluid.

The new entrepreneurs are viewed with mixed feelings.

* GMKs are worker cooperatives providing goods and services for the private market; they lease state-owned plants and machinery outside normal working hours.

The NEP man encounters envy and admiration but also must learn to put up with a certain amount of contempt. The legal uncertainty is great and there are no long-term guarantees. Consequently, there's a desire for a quick profit. No one wants to invest in expensive capital goods. Who knows how long the state's tolerance will last? A lot of rubbish is produced in this milieu; a whiff of the Orient, of the bazaar, hangs over the scene. Critics on the left talk about a new form of robber capitalism. A Jewish writer says: There's a certain irony in the fact that socialism in Hungary has produced more capitalists than any earlier form of society; there are certainly a couple of hundred thousand; the Hungarians don't notice, but as a result they're taking on certain traits they'd previously ascribed to the Jews.

A therapy for the sclerosis of the planned economy; a light drug to overcome embitterment; a stimulant that mobilizes new forces; a substitute, a hope, a palliative—economic reform is all of these, strangely mixed together. Tolerated, encouraged, slowed down, it has become a giant fact of life affecting every part of the society.

It's in the air on the Lenin Ring. The pilgrim can't touch it, but he can smell it. He stands thoughtfully in the back court and listens: a woman singer practices, a radio plays a tango, a streetcar rattles past outside. Under the supporting beams that prevent a crumbling covered walkway from collapsing are a rusty watertap and potted plants in an abandoned bathtub. Right next to that, Vera Kozmás is selling her charming creations, hats with pea-green veils and embroidered lingerie in a sinfully deep red.

Always the same thing. But then, just before the tired stroller gives up all hope, a cracked and blistered door opens and an old lady appears, leaning on her ivory-colored stick; she pauses, glances down into the courtyard, and a factotum greets her. Or the most elegant blond in Budapest comes down the wide stairway, as if in a prewar movie, smiling majestically, every inch a *grande dame* with her waved hair, moving toward some distant happy ending. She does not notice that everything is crumbling around her.

THE GYPSIES

The little town of Esztergom on the Danube, once also called Gran, is dominated by a single gigantic building: the basilica on the castle hill. The primate of Hungary resides here. The imperial gesture of the dome, which rises two hundred thirty feet into the hazy air, betrays the Church's old greed for power.

The white pillars of the rotunda can be seen from every part of the town, including the factory area on the river flats to the west. The Russians have a gas bottle depot here. Rusty railway sidings, nettles, autumn colors. The footpath leads over a small embankment, a long way from the road, into the copse, to the Gypsy settlement. The low houses form a square, like an encampment. They look abandoned. The latrines stand open, doors banging in the wind, broken windows inadequately covered with plastic sheeting. How could one survive the winter here? The only water is in the yard. The pump will soon freeze up. A soup pot is cooking on an open hearth surrounded by scattered rags. It's the only sign of life.

Leaning on two crutches, a seventy-eight-year-old woman with the face of an American Indian opens the door for us. The house consists of two rooms. No furniture, only dirty straw sacks in the corners. There is not a trace of the Hungarian miracle here. We have arrived in Bhopal, in Luanda, in La Paz.

Gradually the daughters and then the grandchildren crowd in through the door. Not even the grandmother knows how many there are. The first child comes when the girls are fourteen. Contraceptives are unknown. Many children are born deaf and dumb. The old woman was elected chieftain after her husband's death, but she can't cope anymore. She points to the antiquated wheelchair in the yard, in which she is pushed to the doctor's, almost an hour away. She has rheumatism of the joints. She speaks forcefully and confidently. She's not complaining, she's stating facts. It's the floods that make her life difficult, the frosts, the illnesses, the attacks. It's impossible to keep any wood in the shed—it gets stolen. Ever since the windows and the electricity meter were broken in the last fight, there has been no light in the settlement.

The men are working somewhere in the faraway city, or are in jail; the children go to special schools, where instead of toilets there's only a pail. The young people, says the woman chieftain, are no use, the men think only about knife fights and don't know the old rules anymore, and there are no new ones. Where would new rules come from? The authorities? People who believe the authorities have only themselves to blame. She's not asking for money, only for shoes, one should have shoes . . . Three of the six huts are empty: everyone escapes who can.

The Gypsies are by far the largest ethnic and cultural minority in Hungary today. Their number is estimated at 350,000. But while the other minorities, the remaining Germans, the Slovaks, Croats, Serbs, and not least the 37,000 Romanians, enjoy a certain autonomy—they have their own kindergartens and schools and their own newspapers, and at times one almost has the feeling they're being spoiled, presumably for reasons of foreign policy—the Gypsy problem is denied and repressed. After the assimilation projects of the postwar period had failed, policy-makers turned to absurd linguistic regulations. The Sinti and Romani* were redefined as "new citizens" or declared a "special social and ethnic

* *Central and East European Gypsies. (Trans.)*

stratum" and denied every right to form their own associations. However, the resentment of the rest of the population is even more merciless than official discrimination. Most Hungarians are convinced that the Gypsies are dirty, lazy criminals, whom the authorities treat with incomprehensible consideration. The Gypsy question also brings out the moral deficiencies of the Populists, who get worked up over the treatment of the Hungarian minority in Romania but find the complete marginalization of the Sinti, and the economic, cultural, and social gulf that separates them from the majority, quite reasonable.

The Gypsy slum of Esztergom sinks into the twilight. A few hundred yards away lives a rag-and-bone man who has made something of his life. He owns a horse and cart, a couple of pigs, and a house with numerous outbuildings, which he built himself. One of his sons sits in an old easy chair, fat and sickly; a pensioner at twenty-eight, he has leukemia and must be taken to the hospital every month for a complete blood transfusion. Another son is on his way to the disco; he's joined the Esztergom punks. The master of the house hasn't forgotten anything: He talks about the deportation of his parents; in his long Hungarian sentences a single German word occurs: *Gaskammer* (gas chamber). But the ritual of hospitality is sacrosanct. Wine is offered, kisses and cigarettes exchanged. The walls of the living room are covered with pictures from advertisements, family photos, and pinups; a wall cabinet is crammed with plush animals, porcelain figures, and knickknacks. In a glass case lined with gold foil, a crowd of saints surrounds a black plaster madonna. "We believe in God and the Virgin Mary," says the rag-and-bone man's wife. "Maybe we believe too much."

A municipal social worker knocks at the door. She's cool and correct, and doesn't approve of the foreign visitor. She has come, as she says, to "agitate" the rag collector's family, and invites them to a talk on the importance of education. Her words are politely but firmly ignored. She goes, we stay. It gets late. After many embraces the master of the house calls after us, from the doorway, "One must work hard, one must be clean, one must be decent." The son with cancer is silent. The children stare after us. In the dark yard the old Gypsy's litany sounds like a condemned man's cry for mercy.

THE GHOST TRAIN

"Personality cult, offenses against socialist legality, Stalinism: yes, that's what it says in the books. But today no one can understand what these words mean anymore. My grandchildren just shrug their shoulders when talk turns to them, they don't want to know anything about it. Even if the police were everywhere and everything was gray, we were alive. Everyone knew about the interrogations, the deportations, the prisons, but we held on to the fiction that something like normality still existed. We had lost everything: the villa, the silverware, the carpets. Look, for two years I had to dig potatoes and shovel manure on the land with these hands. Today I wouldn't even say it hurt me. Then we were allowed to return to Budapest. We found the old waiters, the old furniture, the old salesgirls everywhere in the city. They didn't have much to sell, but they recognized me. It was peace at last, the retreat into privacy began, a long, laborious, heroic retreat. Every napkin was a silent triumph. People collected stamps, ate cake, played bridge. Sometimes we went to the theater. That candelabrum: the concierge's wife brought it back to me one day, she'd hidden it in the cellar. On Sundays we took the children to the amusement park in the municipal forest.

"Yes, you must go there if you want to feel something of the mood, of the melancholy of the fifties. To me it's a very moving place; I don't know if you can understand that. You turn right at the entrance and keep going to the farthest corner, where the old carousel is. The place is quite dead now. The kiosks with the slanted, silver-glitter fronts are empty, the pink plastic signs don't light up anymore, and the fairy-tale tunnel with the artificial mill, the little boats, and the celluloid swans that used to glide through the dark has been drained. Only the old women still sit there like Cerberuses with knitting needles, and the unsmiling old mechanics, who have nothing to do anymore, guard the ruins in their torn overalls. How pathetic it all is!

"But you won't be able to see the most beautiful thing anymore. That was the ghost train. The children could never get enough of it—they screamed with fear and delight. It was a Marxist-Leninist ghost train, possibly the only one in the whole world. It showed the whole course of world history according to the laws of dialectical materialism, paying particular attention to Hungary, of course. First the apes as they came out of the jungle, then the discovery of fire, then slave society, groaning figures in heavy chains, Spartacus, bloody executions, mocking exploiters. The magnate, the great landowner in his golden tunic, personally swung the whip over the naked backs of the serfs. That was supposed to be us, of course. It was difficult to recognize oneself in those gruesome puppets. Right next to that were the capitalists, fat bankers with top hats and cigars, and the sufferings of the proletariat, all very gory in the darkness, and then the little car rattled out into the open air: the glorious future of socialism shone in the spring sun. It was a triumph, a life of complete luxury, everyone had shoes, washing machines, soap, it was a joy to be alive.

"What a pity—two years ago the ghost train was completely gutted in a fire, the figures destroyed, the machinery ruined, and no one has the slightest intention of rebuilding the thing."

THE SMITH
....

"I didn't know the Smith of Berettyóújfalu myself," says my friend, the novelist György Konrád, who himself comes from Berettyóújfalu, "because the Smith of Berettyóújfalu died a long time ago. His workshop was right back there, not far from my father's hardware store, and behind the synagogue, which is used for storing lawn mowers, sacks, and spare parts now. The windows of the synagogue are smashed, and only a small part of the Star of David can still be seen above the portal. It was a very large synagogue for this remote place, so close to the Romanian border. Berettyóújfalu doesn't need a synagogue anymore, only a large Jewish cemetery behind a wire fence, locked up, overgrown with weeds. Anyway, the smith had his workshop on this small, dusty square behind the synagogue.

"He had a lot of work: the place had twelve thousand inhabitants and was a market town and the county seat, and the horse was the most important means of transport for the peasants, the merchants, and the tradesmen. The forge glowed all day long, the sparks flew. The wagonsmith was a strong, thickset man with a burnt-black face, a giant. He could hardly read or write, but he was his own master. He was older than the century, as old as my father.

"Although the workshop was always full of people, he didn't talk much. He listened to the grooms and the coachmen and heard about everything that was going on, but his only comment was a sarcastic remark between hammerblows. He wasn't friendly, but everyone knew he was the best smith far and wide.

"In 1919, when the old regime collapsed and the Council Republic was declared in Budapest, *Balog kovács* (Balog the Smith), as he was called, took matters in hand, and no one thought of challenging him for the chairmanship of the town soviet. Not only because he was six foot six but also because there was no industry on the plain; the plutonic power of the working class resided solely in the shoulders of the smith.

"As early as the second day of the Council Republic, anything and everything was comprehensively socialized. The big landowners, the cattle merchants, the liquor distillers were all expropriated with a stroke of the pen. But this had no practical consequences: they were immediately appointed provisional administrators of their former property, so everything stayed as it was. Budapest was far away, no one studied the government decrees, the roads were bad, the trains weren't running anymore, and even if, in spite of everything, an emissary from the capital did manage to reach Berettyó-újfalu, it was usually a young coffeehouse dreamer who wore a hat and a suit that was far too light in color. He wouldn't have the faintest idea what he was doing, and would be sent home by Balog the Smith.

"But the goods disappeared from the shop windows almost overnight, and there was hardly a thing to be bought at the weekly markets anymore. The soviets began to ration everything. The result was terrible confusion. If a peasant came into the shop to buy a pound of nails, my grandfather said, 'You need a document from the town hall,' and sent him to the smith. The smith would write on a scrap of paper in a clumsy hand, 'Valid for one pound nails,' and send him back to the shop. But the smith knew the hammer better than the indelible pencil. Writing took him a lot of time, and soon there was a long line outside the town hall. So eventually he wrote a letter that read, 'Dear Konrád, just carry on as before, that is simplest.'

"The Council Republic of Berettyóújfalu lasted only a month. First the Romanians marched in, then the White troops. The police fetched the smith from the town hall. He was beaten, jailed, sentenced, and after serving his sentence he came back and started again where he had left off, in his workshop.

"The Horthy years were quiet. A radio repairman, a doctor, a shoe salesman—that was the 'left' in the town. But the smith wanted nothing to do with this milieu; he had no time for backroom discussions, he kept to himself, remained calmly contemptuous, and was dissatisfied with everything. 'I've done the real work, the others have ruined the country with their stupid talk; let them come here to my smithy and see what it's really like.' That was his attitude.

"In February 1945 I came back home from Budapest. My parents had been deported. The administration had fled, the state had collapsed, a provisional government had formed in Debrecen. Everyone knew: the Red Army will soon be here. Everyone knew too: the smith's hour has come. He took charge of everything, he didn't need any laws, he didn't wait for any instructions. The old Council Communists wanted to introduce the dictatorship of the proletariat immediately; they made him chairman of the local committee and ignored the distant authorities.

"But that was not what the liberation meant. The decisions were made in Moscow and Budapest. Everything had to be approved. The new regime again sent out emissaries. This time they wore no hats and did not lack experience. The smith didn't understand what was happening. He didn't want to know anything about the pamphlets they pulled out, and he refused to read all the way through the decrees they brought. Everywhere in the country the disobedient who resisted normalization were removed; many old Communists were arrested at that time. The smith was lucky. He resigned, he was indignant, he became the smith again, but nothing happened to him.

"Toward the end of October 1956 there were demonstrations everywhere in the Hungarian provinces. Things were happening on the main street of Berettyóújfalu as well. The smith was always in the front row carrying the flag. A revolutionary committee was formed again. And Balog became the chairman again. He was sixty years old by then. But the people in the countryside had become cautious. They didn't take to the streets till four days after the people in Budapest. Furthermore, the border was nearby and the Russian tanks didn't have far to come, so everything was over in five days this time. The secret police came and got him and broke his bones. After a couple of months in the internment camp his health was ruined. He returned, but he never lit the forge in his workshop again. Berettyóújfalu and the district could cope with the loss, because every year there were fewer horses. The smith died in his bed a few years later.

"A legendary figure? That would be claiming too much. His story is an ordinary story, like a thousand others.

"By the way, the smith's son has moved to the city. He studied, joined the Party, and became an engineer. He was never interested in communism."

THE PANOPTICON

"We have no lack of historians," says the historian, "we have all too much material, the interest is enormous. The Hungarians are proud to have been around for such a long time. Whether this high opinion is justified by their history is another matter. At any rate, here nothing and no one is ever forgotten. The walls of our buildings are teeming with statues. Every village commemorates its great sons, even a gymnastics teacher or a chess player if there's nothing else. And if all else fails, then it was Petőfi, our national poet, who spent the night in some hovel or other. He was a stagehand in his youth and got around a lot.

"Yet at the same time it has always been impossible to write history in this country. We have too many skeletons in the closet. Take 1956. One is certainly allowed to talk about it again, but how? Was it a revolution? A counterrevolution?

Was it the people who took to the streets? The mob? The workers? The riffraff? It's best if one simply talks about 'the tragic events.' The past is like a puzzle, one reads into or out of it whatever one wants. One person sees similarities between Deák and Kádár, another between Kádár and Horthy. Some maintain that 1956 was a repeat of 1848, others lump together 1919 and 1945. Even our comparisons are quite arbitrary.

"I was still at primary school when my mother warned me against the labyrinth of the past. She meant the mile-long passages and tunnels in the limestone caverns underneath Buda Castle. The winegrowers used to have their cellars there. At the end of the thirties Horthy had the caves converted into shelters and bunkers, and it was strictly forbidden to enter this subterranean world.

"After the war I once came across an opening in the masonry, in the neglected gardens behind the fortress. I couldn't resist and climbed in, armed only with a couple of boxes of matches. After a few yards I stumbled over a German helmet; then I found skeletons. The walls were black, covered in soot. The passageway opened out into a dripping gallery. Someone coughed. I crept farther and came to an underground lake. An old man in a canoe was drifting on the water. He had a carbide lamp on his head and was poking in the water with a pole. When he saw me, he rowed toward me, cursing. He was a worker who was fishing the corpses of German soldiers out of the water.

"The Russians had occupied Pest in January 1945. The Germans defended Buda until the middle of February. They had set up a hospital in the caverns under the castle. As the Nazi troops prepared to retreat, they killed their men who were too badly wounded to walk, killed them with flame-throwers, instead of surrendering them to the Russians."

Nowadays the caverns under the castle can be reached by comfortable, well-lit stairways—a triumph of Hungarian economic reform, which has made possible the privatization of the nation's history. Entrance Uri utca no. 9, admission seventy forints ($1.25). The *Budavári Panoptikum* is a state-licensed business that also includes a gallery, a mime theater, and a wine cellar. In the cellar boutique, bearded artists sell revolting ceramic vases, art nouveau imitations, figures of medieval saints, and rustic costume jewelry. They belong to a cooperative that has fifty members. Its founder is the actor, businessman, theater director, and lawyer Miklós Köllö, who has succeeded in leasing the subterranean part of the historic old town of Buda. He has made a considerable investment in his business. The underground passages have been drained and paved, and lighting has been installed. Thick cables and timers are everywhere, and loudspeakers fill the whole complex with bells and electronic background music. The decor consists of cast-iron railings, reproduction gaslights, and brand-new escutcheons. Heraldic lettering above the stairs warns (in English) "Mind your head!"

The panopticon displays Hungarian history as a goulash of legendary tidbits. This patriotic Disneyland is populated by sixty homemade figures of wood, plaster, and paint, arranged in twenty-four "compositions." What these are all about is explained relentlessly in broken English by hostesses in woven dresses, who have exchanged some vague college course for this artistic activity: This is the green illuminated tree of life, that is the Tartar horde, here you see the drawn-and-quartered man, over there the flagellant. At the end a leaflet is pushed into the exhausted visitor's hand to remind him of this monstrous outgrowth of the service sector. It sets forth in black and white all that needs to be remembered about Hungarian history:

"The mixing blood had a special significance: it was supposed to have a magical power to the purpose of solidarity. According to the legend, the seven princes of the Hungarian tribes thereby concluded an alliance for the settlement . . . All the prices have let their blood flow into a beaker . . .

According to the chronicle of Anonymous and also according to which legends about the settlement the Hungarians conquered the land of that time with a women . . . The yesterday still blooming kingdom that had created the world famous spiritual life, fell apart . . . The hands which wanted to reach the crone lying on the empty tron already anticipate the subsequent sad future . . ."

ENVOI: FIVE SHORT STORIES

1. The old house on the Hill of Roses, once a banker's residence, is now completely overgrown by wild vines. The high, stuccoed rooms are shared by ten tenants. All day long, music can be heard through the thin dividing walls—the old man next door has only a record player for company. He's ill. He keeps four suitcases of secret papers safe under his bed: Central Committee minutes. He's already somewhat muddled—arteriosclerosis; he stammers; he's treated with forbearance; no one even hates him anymore; let him die in peace. His name is Márton Hórvath. Thirty years ago he was the Stalinist cultural dictator. In those days he banned the music of Béla Bartók; today he tortures his neighbors with it.

2. The successful cameraman, a rather exuberant person of about forty, contemplates himself in the mirror while shaving, stops singing, and after a short pause says,

"The Hungarians, all of us, look five years older than people in the West. Do you know why? It's because of the Russians."

3. György Aczél is a master of many roles: at once the brave pioneer who looks far into the future, the refined cynic, the wise statesman, the workhorse, and the weary traveler who's had enough of wandering in the desert. Above all, though, he is the legendary father-figure of Hungarian

culture, both admired and hated; he is also a member of the Politburo. He quotes half the literatures of the world, he argues well, he knows his trade; but one sentence, which he lets fall quite casually, as if self-evident, I find unforgettable: "I'm in the habit of being in prison."

4. A perceptive friend, who has just helped me to fill in my residence registration form, stands still amid the crowd in front of the post office, and with a look of suspicion on his face says to me,

"Perhaps we've all grown stupid. Are we still capable of thinking at all? The West asked the questions we're squabbling about two hundred years ago. Our battles are anachronistic. At best we're stand-ins. If we came to power, we wouldn't know what to do with it."

5. She's about 33 but looks younger; clever, beautiful, pale, embittered, and with a touch of arrogance, or maybe just self-confidence. One can tell that she'd feel at home in any metropolis in the world. She says:

"We're in the street, my father has picked me up, it's a dull day. A huge, noisy car comes toward us out of the fog. There weren't many cars on the streets of Budapest in those days. I was frightened. The noise was terrible. Perhaps I'm also confusing the rumbling and vibration with the earthquake we had at that time, in the autumn of 1956. But I don't think so. I think it was a tank. That's my first historical memory. It's also my last. Because nothing else has happened since then. Only Kádár, that's all. And the lies, as long as I can remember." With a crooked smile, she quickly adds, "It can stay that way, for all I care. World history and me—we can get along without each other."

PORTUGUESE REVERIES
[1 9 8 6]

....

ROBINSONADE

"**Y**ou can't believe everything you see," said the monsignor. "Facts are all very nice but they won't help you to understand the Portuguese. Very tricky terrain. There is still a great deal of piety, even if it's the superstitious kind. But try doing missionary work among these people! It's like biting on cotton wool."

He knew very well that I had nothing like that in mind, that I was only seeking his advice on worldly matters. When I asked him for permission to tape the interview, he smiled.

"You can throw away your road atlas," he said. "The maps are wrong."

"What do you mean, Your Eminence?"

"Portugal," he said, "like Ireland, with which it has much in common, is an island. Yes, I'm quite serious, an island fading into the western horizon, a remnant of legendary Atlantis. In fact, strictly speaking, it's an archipelago, for in the distance, far beyond the Hesperides, still more Portuguese islands appear. I visited them once, years ago. They were occupied only by bomber squadrons, tour groups, and meteorologists. An ultramarine Europe that delivers Madeira to the hotel chefs and sunny skies to the inhabitants of the mainland."

"And yet I have met people," I objected cautiously, "who claim to have reached Portuguese shores without getting their feet wet, either by train or after harrowing journeys by car." He swept such doubts aside.

"Those are only rumors," he replied. "There is something exaggerated about these fantastic stories of swaying bridges, remote customs posts, and dusty mule trails. Just ask our so-called neighbors! The Spaniards in Andalusia and Estremadura merely shrug their shoulders if you inquire whether there is dry land beyond the mountains, on the other side of the Guadiana River, and whether anyone lives there. Equally, the Portuguese claim to know nothing about the Spanish. If the two countries really had a common border, then surely it would be possible to learn Spanish in a secondary school in Oporto or Lisbon. But such is not the case. English, of course; French too; even German or Latin. But not Spanish.

"Everything that Portugal needs, from peanuts to the brand-new chemical plant, is imported by ship or plane, as is to be expected on an island. The same goes for exports. The continent is far away, as far away as Brazil or India. 'My son studied in Europe.' 'Poor Caetano—he couldn't find any work and had to spend eight years in Europe.' It sounds like an expedition. There's a certain pride there, but the note of complaint is uppermost. Emigration is an old curse of the country, and for most people Europe is a place of exile. After all, who leaves the shores of his homeland of his own free will?

"At any rate, travel costs money. In Lisbon everyone, absolutely everyone, even the most casual acquaintance, will invite you out for a meal, the restaurants are always packed. This is quite deceptive, however, because there is no money around. I read some statistics somewhere recently: only one in three of the Portuguese goes away on holiday, and only 3 percent of the island's inhabitants have set foot on foreign soil in the past year.

"That is more than just a physical fact. This island existence has also shaped the historical consciousness and the mentality of the Portuguese. The isolation produces a preternatural calm that can, however, turn into sleeping sickness, and a patience that can lead to resignation. Old and cherished customs survive longer here than elsewhere. Paganism, for example.

"The islanders are also distinguished by a degree of touchiness and by a healthy mistrust. *'Orgulhosamente sós,'* we stand alone and we're proud of it—virtually no other slogan of the old dictatorship had so much resonance among the Portuguese as this one. It's not surprising; a person without neighbors is prone to monologues. The Portuguese have been accused of being self-righteous and self-forgetful, self-sufficient and self-satisfied . . . This fatal prefix 'self' is always there. Neither their pity nor their torment, their praise nor their contempt, their criticism nor their deception can get by without it."

There was a short pause. The monsignor lit a cigarette and rested his gaze on the oleander blooming in the garden.

"But there are islands not only in space," he said at last. "Time also has its archipelagos."

"What do you mean?"

He picked up a pencil and drew a couple of concentric squiggles on a piece of paper.

"Those lines could be on a relief map or a weather chart," he went on. "Not that I've got anything against geographers. On the contrary, sometimes I dream about timberlines and limits of pack ice, lines of equal precipitation or of equal spring tides—do *you* know what those are? Abstract mountains and valleys emerge, from which it is possible to read how much snow falls in a district, or what proportion of the population is Catholic." The monsignor smiled.

"I have often asked myself what a topography of time would look like. What does the date on the calendar mean, after all? There is a great deal of nonsynchronicity in our world. Why always just isotherms and isobars? It would be much more interesting to find lines that would tell us which time zones we are passing through when we travel . . . lines that show the crevices and faults in history . . . One could call them isochromes. Let us just assume that we are really living in 1986—a bold assumption!—and we visited a small town in Mecklenburg. It might perhaps appear to us that the date there was 1958. A settlement in the Amazon could be dated 1935 and a monastery in Nepal assigned to the Napoleonic period. On such a map, and this is really my point, large parts of Portugal would appear as time-islands.

"I have always had the feeling that it's 'the way it used to be' here. A very ambivalent feeling. Do you know what I mean? A touch of *ancien régime*, a combination of allure and horror. Once upon a time, when people were less demanding, smaller, more silent. Dignity went hand in hand with misery, piety with repression. The old women only five feet tall, dressed completely in black, with their egg baskets . . . The tricycles rattling up steep, narrow alleyways . . . The concertinas that could be out of a Fellini film. In Portugal a supplier or a supplicant still sometimes concludes a letter with the words *com a maior consideração de Vª Exª atto. ven.dor e obgdo.*, which means 'with deepest respect, Your Excellency's attentive and grateful admirer' . . . Threadbare Sunday suits, ancient hats, relics of the old classes. Landlords, stewards, and laborers, who look like landlords, stewards, and laborers . . . Have you noticed the clocks, all the clocks on the towers, covered markets, and shop corners? They date from a time when a clock was something rare and valuable. Only apothecaries, managers, and privy councillors could afford their own clock. You will discover that all these public clocks are wrong, or rather that they have stopped. No one winds them. I am also thinking of the court clerk in his dark office, who holds between his teeth the thread he uses to sew his papers together, so as to leave his ink-stained fingers free, and of the blind violinist on the ferry to Cacilhas. He taps up the gangway with his white stick and has an old camera case hung around his neck, into which the coins rattle while he tunes his violin. In the evening you'll see him again in the Upper Town, outside the nightclubs, and without his instrument. Now he's muttering to himself, he's drunk, he mumbles something about Salazar, and the young girls standing at the entrance to the disco shrink from his sightless eyes.

"In New York I once saw a shop named Second Childhood. Battered lead toys from the thirties were displayed in the window. Yet what the shop was offering its customers, and at exorbitant prices, was not toys but a trip, a journey into the past. Such journeys in time cost nothing in Portugal. Admittedly, the outside world is breaking through in Lisbon, and it does so very brutally and abruptly, but it's difficult to bring the whole island into line, to steamroller it, to rebuild it. Everywhere there are enclaves of silent decay. In grocery stores you can find packages sealed fifteen years ago, on the street you can still see a young man without a job, or an unkempt old man, looking through the trash for something usable. And ideas too have remained behind the times.

"I don't mean to be condescending when I say this. There is a certain innocence in this backwardness. Perhaps even the Church is only a relic in Portugal. Those for whom things were moving too slowly left long ago. The ambitious, the impatient, the greedy have left the country in successive waves. This exodus has been going on for five centuries. One-third of the Portuguese live abroad. The island owes its charm and its misery to those who stayed home . . . Excuse me, I'm beginning to ramble."

The monsignor glanced at his watch. It was exactly right. The audience was over.

ELÉCTRICO

A grooved cable of electrolytic copper strung in a taut crisscross through the blue air, uphill and downhill, is the thread by which the stranger is most safely guided through labyrinthine Lisbon. (I'm speaking of the overhead wire of tramline 28.)

The journey begins in the center of town, not far from the

Rossio, on the Largo Martim Moniz, an ugly, busy, dirty square full of peddlers' stalls, suitcase thieves, and building sites. It costs less than sixty cents and lasts almost an hour.

We entrust ourselves to a marvelous mode of transport: the tram in its original form. Elsewhere it has died out long since and is now to be found only as a treasure in museums. We mount the platform, which is protected by a folding gate, from the running board, and open the sliding door. Incomparable comfort awaits us inside the car: sash windows of honey-colored wood, which can be opened in fine weather; roller shades of brown oilcloth, which one can pull up or down according to the position of the sun; armrests of solid oak; and green-upholstered seats. A leather strap running through brass rings allows us to signal to the tram driver when we want to get off.

Today, as a generation ago, he stands ramrod-straight in front of his controller handle and gazes earnestly at the track ahead, gauge 65 centimeters, and at the cow-catcher, which in an emergency can brush aside unforeseen obstacles and assure the vehicle unimpeded passage. The patents to which we owe this electrical miracle are listed and dated (1889 to 1916) on the chrome cover of the control panel. The manufacturer is also immortalized here: The British Thomsen & Houston Co. Ltd., Rugby, England. Its product has proved indestructible. Its use value has outlived both the empire and the traditional "influence" of the British, who in the nineteenth century treated Portugal like a semicolony.

At last the bell rings. "Turning the controller handle to the right (from neutral) propels the car forward at increasing speed; turning to the left results in electric braking of increasing strength." That's what it says in the operating instructions, in which, besides the drum switch, the auxiliary switch, and the crank handle, considerable space is also devoted to the air brake, the pressure gauge, the headlight dimmer, and the warning bell.

The *eléctrico* sets itself in motion. The shadowy stepped passageways of Mouraria fly past us on the right. Then the driver begins the audacious, steep ascent to the Graça Quarter. He playfully masters hazardous corners, the sharpest turns, and dangerous oblique sections of the roadbed. Then we thunder through the cobblestone alleys of Alfama until an abrupt application of the brake throws us against the back of the seat in front. The car is stopping for a very good reason: two-way traffic is impossible here, where the tram almost touches the balconies. A prudent management has built a little signal tower, from which a hunchbacked veteran keeps watch. As soon as a tram, unseen by us, approached from the opposite direction and threatens to smash us to pieces, he holds out a red signal disk from his shelter to warn our driver.

There's a smell of dried codfish and roasted coffee beans, and one sees, as Neruda once did, ". . . into certain corners, into certain moist houses, / into hospitals where the bones stick out of the windows, / into certain shoe stores with a smell of vinegar, / into streets as frightening as chasms." Sacks full of flour and millet, boxes full of dates, nuts, and olives are piled onto the narrow pavement, and exotic music spills out from the depths of a cavelike grocery store. One could be in Naples, Istanbul, or Jerusalem. The Orient is close. A few houses further on, the tram stops again. The scrupulous driver takes a long steel key out of a kind of umbrella stand to his right, reverses the points, climbs in again, and continues the journey, while the conductor clips the tiny yellow-and-green tickets and lets the well-worn banknotes, which are worth less and less every year, disappear into his money belt.

The division of towns into rich and poor quarters is a ninteenth-century invention. This form of social apartheid did not exist in prebourgeois societies. So in the old heart of Lisbon miserable tenements stand next to magnificent monasteries, aristocratic townhouses next to dingy bars. Line 28 passes prisons, palaces, and slums. But it is impossible to pay attention to the sights. The view over the Terreiro do Paço, with its pink façades lining the broad river, is certainly magnificent, the grocery and hardware stores are remarkable, but again and again we catch ourselves being distracted by the *musique concrète* of the tramway, a performance beside which Honegger's *Pacific 231* sounds like a modest barrel organ. The triumphant singsong of the motor disappears in the clanking, creaking, and rumbling of the undercarriage as it thumps over the intersections; the warning bell clangs, the compressor whines and rattles, the brakes hiss, while the intrepid driver, sometimes cautiously, sometimes with virtuoso brio, climbs astonishing new gradients, passing the old headquarters of the secret police, the faded elegance of Chiado, the Parliament Building, and the luxuriant green of Estrela Park until, after a quieter section, the goal—the terminus—is reached.

The hard-working tram crew do not allow themselves any rest: they take the trolley wheel off the overhead wire, turn it around, let it spring upwards, and fasten it with a halter. Then the green seats have to be reversed, the new destination has to be wound around to show in the little window, the rear-view mirror taken out of its mounting and placed at the front. While all these exercises are being conscientiously carried out, we turn towards a new pleasure, for this is what the terminus of our journey is called: *Prazeres*—pleasures, joys.

The Prazeres Garden, situated high above the Tagus River and surrounded by high white walls, is the necropolis of Lisbon. The cemetery is the scaled-down but precise topological representation of a capital city with all its buildings, streets, churches, squares, and palaces neatly divided into districts, but with hardly any inhabitants. Occasionally there's an old woman, a gardener, or a stray cat. The words *jazigo ossuário* (bone vault) are often inscribed on the front of the houses and mausoleums. They are built of solid, square blocks of stone, clearly for all eternity—at least, they appear more durable than the dilapidated, crumbling homes of the living. The architectural variety is impressive. A pyramid stands next to a chapel, a castle next to a temple, a villa beside a pagoda. Many of these houses of the dead almost look as if they were inhabited. The stained-glass windows are decorated with lace curtains; the bronze, cast-iron, or brass doors have safety locks. Inside, the inquisitive gaze makes out a family altar covered with flower vases standing on little embroidered mats. Sometimes the salon is even provided with chairs for occasional visitors or sympathetic ghosts. But to the right and to the left there are always the marble bunks, one on top of the other as if in a children's bedroom. This is where the magnificently decorated coffins rest. There are still empty places in almost every mausoleum. The older ones are in neo-Gothic, neo-Manueline, or neo-Renaissance style; the newer ones look more like transformer houses or bank vaults. There are hardly any statues to be seen. A kind of ban on images seems to be in force here. The lascivious goddesses, genii, and muses one finds in other cemeteries are completely absent. Instead, the inscriptions speak a passionate rhetoric full of superlatives. I don't know how this place acquired its name, but this community of mortal remains testifies to an extremely lively cult of the dead.

SIGNS AND WONDERS

The doctor died long ago, ninety years ago in fact. But he still has not shut the doors of his poor people's practice.

Dr. José Tomás de Sousa Martins was a man of progress whom the somnambulistic imagination of his countrymen has transformed into a restless, wandering spirit. I came across him for the first time in a shop window on the Rua da Madalena. It's a suitable location for close encounters of the third kind because this street is lined with medical supply shops. Disturbing relics are offered up to the gaze of passersby: Rathgeber's Toe Spreader, for example, a disgusting pink substance something like chewing gum for giants, or a cadaverous wax foot studded with corns and calluses. It would be a bonanza for New York S&M and bondage devotees, except that the chrome-and-rubber dog collars, the corsets and suspensories are dedicated not to pleasure but to the health of suffering humanity.

Amid this fairground of fetishism, this parade of infirmities, a shop has established itself that sells devotional articles: rosaries, neon madonnas, and candles thick as an arm on which the Sacred Heart glows blood-red. And that's where I found the poor doctor, as a plaster bust or a statuette, always copied from the same model. He was wearing a black doublet, its short sleeves folded and puffed, and a fox-red wig. A pencil-thin Mongol mustache hung down to his chin, and he gazed at me with a sorrowful expression. Dr. Sousa Martins, this strange saint, costs 325 escudos (about $2.20*) and up, depending on size.

When I met him again a few days later, he was standing larger than life, in solid bronze, on an enormous pedestal just in front of the entrance to the medical college on the Campo dos Mártires da Pátria. I realized at once that this was no ordinary statue. People were coming and going around the circular flowerbed at the base of the statue, there was a constant throng, an enthusiastic bustle. From his column the doctor looks down on a sea of marble plaques. On some are chiseled only the simple words "Thank you," others bear longer legends and detailed case histories. Passport photos

* *In July 1986 there were 147.53 escudos to the dollar. (Trans.)*

and little dolls testify to his mystic successes, for Dr. Sousa Martins is competent in every branch of medicine and maintains a general practice for hopeless cases. Dozens of candles burn in a tin box at his feet. A pale wax hand, a crutch, a plastic breast, a jar full of kidney stones bear witness to miraculous cures. A robust sixty-year-old woman is carrying on a brisk trade in objects that serve the doctor's cult.

"O spirit of Dr. Sousa Martins," I read on one of the little sacred pictures she sells, "hear my prayer, stand by me, have mercy on me! Blessed be your mother, Mary of the Sorrows, for giving the world such a son!"

No one knew exactly where Barotseland, Matabeleland, and Mashonaland were, but everyone wanted to call these inhospitable regions in the African bush his own, even the poor Portuguese. It was 1890 and the trade in colonial goods was flourishing. Then perfidious Albion presented its most loyal ally, Portugal, with an ultimatum, and when the British fleet weighed anchor at the mouth of the Tagus estuary, it became apparent, alas, that the Portuguese war fleet consisted only of a couple of steamers ready for scrap. An unparalleled humiliation, which did not leave the patriotic Dr. Sousa Martins unmoved. He placed himself at the disposal of a committee collecting donations to have a light cruiser built, and when he went to his reward seven years later the great work had been completed: the *Adamastor*, Portugal's glorious defense, lay slowly rusting in the roads of Lisbon. And so it was not slum-dwellers, cripples, and superstitious peasants from the hinterland who conceived the idea of erecting a memorial to the founder of the Pharmaceutical Society, but gentlemen in frock coats and top hats. It was unveiled on a March day in 1900 by His Majesty King Carlos in person. But what was revealed under the blue-and-white flag brought cries of outrage from the assembled dignitaries.

"For instead of the figure of the eminent professor, they

saw a shape in a quite unacademic, crouching posture, with a beckoning prostitute at its feet. The whole group was framed by a pair of gargoyles, and at the very top was a clumsy coat of arms that resembled a lizard."

Only one thing was clear: this "product of a sick mind" had to be removed. But how? A second Lisbon earthquake was not expected. The suggestion that the "misshapen monstrosity" should be blown up with a charge of dynamite was rejected after furious discussion. Finally it was agreed that the monster should be demolished and the present monument erected in its place; as to the latter, a foreigner is not in a position to pass judgment on its beauty. Common sense had asserted itself. But its victory was to prove illusory. At first surreptitiously and almost unnoticed by the secular and ecclesiastical authorities, but then to their growing annoyance, the statue attracted ever greater crowds—until at last one day the worthy atheist had been transformed into a mystical miracle-worker, the clinician into a shaman, the freemason into a spiritual healer.

I couldn't shake off the suspicion that there must be something peculiarly Portuguese about Dr. Sousa Martins's supernatural medical business, and I decided to question my local acquaintances about it.

"It's really quite simple," said the first, a doctor with a practice in a commuter suburb outside Lisbon. "Of course, I hope that nothing will happen to you here—but if you were ever to get to know a Portuguese hospital from the inside, you would very quickly understand why people flock to Fátima or to Dr. Sousa Martins. They would rather wait for a miracle than die in a corridor."

The second piece of information I came across is of a more general nature. I read it in a book. The historian António José Saraiva says that the Portuguese are convinced "that problems cannot be solved by human or logical means, because there is no reason in things, only chance and miracles."

My third witness laughed at me. "What do you expect? The miraculous is simply our daily bread! Have you never heard of Dona Branca? I wrote a whole series of articles about this lady. Dona Branca dos Santos was already in her late seventies when she opened a bank in her small apartment. She promised the depositors a monthly interest of 10 percent. I don't have a pocket calculator with me, but at compound interest I think that works out to more than 300 percent per annum. The stairs up to her apartment were soon crowded, people came and brought her whole sackfuls of money. The government didn't know what to do, because for months Dona Branca paid on time. By the end of her career, billions of escudos had been deposited with her. But to this day she still doesn't quite understand why her house of cards collapsed, and her customers, thousands of decent Portuguese, are even more in the dark than she is. The billions simply dissolved into thin air.

"Look, I've brought a newspaper with me, one of our competitors. As far as I know, Portugal is the only country with a national newspaper for the miraculous. It costs only 50 escudos, that's 35 cents. 'Earth opens up, demonic dog devours twenty-two workers . . . Proof of the existence of angels found . . . Man kidnapped by spaceship returns eleven years later—not a single day older . . . One-hundred-five-year-old woman, dead three times, enjoys best of health . . . Twenty-seven-foot-high hollow pyramid cures frigidity and impotence . . . Miracle: Chinese mother separates Siamese twins on the kitchen table.'

"As I said, the *Jornal do Incrível* [*Journal of the Incredible*] is our competitor. But I'm addicted to it. I read it every week."

"These marvels that have astonished you are quite small ones," says my friend, the novelist Almeida Faria. "We have much more and much better to offer in this respect. May I remind you of Dom Sebastião, whose ghost still haunts us today?" In such situations the most sensible thing to do is to shamelessly admit one's own ignorance.

"He is the only Portuguese king who still lives on in the memory of the people. The interesting thing is that he owes his popularity not to his successes—he had hardly any successes—but to his failure. Sebastião was completely unlucky: his father died before he was born, his mother never bothered about him, the Jesuits who educated him stuffed his head full of all kinds of medieval ideas, and his marriage plans failed because he suffered from a venereal disease.

"Against the wishes of his counselors, he undertook a belated crusade to North Africa. Unfortunately, the wicked heathens didn't play by the rules. In 1578, in the middle of the desert—his nags were still seasick from the crossing and his knights were frying in their armor—he suffered a catastrophic defeat. Almost all of the Portuguese nobility perished in this battle, and the ransom for the survivors ruined the country. As there was no successor to the throne, the Portuguese crown fell to the Spaniards. The king himself disappeared in some godforsaken wadi—or let us say rather that he has been missing for more than four hundred years.

"For, as every Portuguese knows, he will soon turn up again 'on a misty morning' to obtain justice for his oppressed people and to found the Fifth Monarchy.*"

My astonishment must have been obvious to Almeida Faria, because immediately he came to my aid with a few explanations.

"You evidently don't know that Divine Providence has quite

---

* *The Fifth Monarchy: i.e., the kingdom of Christ on earth after the passing away of the four monarchies of Babylon, Persia, Greece, and Rome. Fifth Monarchism was a prevalent form of millenarianism in the sixteenth and seventeenth centuries. (Trans.)*

a lot in store for Portugal? You see, we are the harbingers of holy tidings and have been chosen to bear a future grail. It's just that word of it hasn't reached everyone else yet.

"I'll be brief. The Fifth Monarchy was promised to us by an illiterate shoemaker in the seventeenth century. Don't worry! We're not going to subdue the rest of the world by force of arms. We are certainly the chosen people, there's no possible doubt about that, but our sole task is the spiritual renewal of the universe. So we don't want to rule over you, we only want you to make your peace with God.

"Don't imagine that this delusion is the exclusive property of provincial crackpots. The coming of the messiah Sebastião was once a popular superstition. In the twentieth century it has become ideology. Fernando Pessoa, the greatest writer of Portuguese modernism, flirted with it. In the fifties the 'Portuguese Philosophy' (a very appropriate name) made the dismal fairy tale of our country's supposed mission respectable, and—you will not believe it possible—it has remained respectable to this day. Not a few intellectuals cling to the hope that someone will actually pull us out of our mess, a mess as old as the legend of Sebastião. The identity of this messiah—Salazar, Otelo, or the Holy Virgin—is not so important. The main thing is that we have someone to turn to."

In the evening I was sitting alone at the bar. Portugal can be very cold. The moisture rises in the old walls, the sheets feel damp, and usually there is no heating. Besides, the strange belief in the return of a royal corpse had depressed me considerably. The bartender, on the other hand, was in a very good mood. He was no older than twenty-five. When he told me he had dropped out of a university program in ethnology, I asked him what he thought of Sebastianism and the Fifth Monarchy. He laughed. "At least this nonsense reveals a vigorous imagination," he said, while continuing to dry his glasses. "After all, we have to compensate for our powerlessness in some way. We have achieved a great deal in this respect. We are never to blame for what happens, it's always someone else—who knows, it might be the stars, God, other countries. That, at any rate, is our historical experience. The higher powers we have to deal with can assume the most incredible forms: an obscure professor of public finance called Salazar, for example. Or take the Common Market, with its incomprehensible escalator clauses and compensation funds. One could call it a Portuguese cargo cult, except that we don't really know what cargo the distant gods will bring us. Because evil as well as good comes from above, from outside. Our bad luck is never homegrown. Someone else is always to blame, the French, the English, but usually the Spanish. It could just as easily be Moscow, or tourism, or the CIA. Presumably, the World Bank is responsible for my standing here and rinsing glasses, but as you see I bear it with a degree of equanimity. Would you like another drink? No? One thing at least is certain: there's no point in trying to take matters into one's own hands."

LOBOTOMY

But something did happen . . . I search, I poke around "in the fog of memory," as the national anthem puts it . . . Didn't something happen then? *"O esplendor de Portugal . . ."* Of course, the television pictures went around the world, the newspaper clippings haven't even faded yet. It was an awakening, an uproar: carnations in rifle muzzles, shattered prison gates, oppressors in flight, tears of joy, peace treaties . . . It all happened not very long ago, less than fifteen years, yet it seems strangely distant, unimaginable, as if it had evaporated and blown away. Something unforgettable that has been forgotten.

I was there, I saw it myself. There was speaking in tongues, a political carnival! The world rubbed its eyes. A dream that many cherished in those days suddenly seemed to have come true, overnight, right where one had least expected it. Backward, isolated Portugal glowed like a *fata morgana*, an island of the future. It looked just as if the eternal losers had overnight become the vanguard, and a stream of onlookers poured in to gaze at this dialectical miracle.

Yes, I remember, it was a different Lisbon. It was as if everything had been blown away at once: the old, mildewed submissiveness, the self-effacing, shabby patience, the wretched fatalism. There were excited crowds on the Rossio until late at night, declarations of brotherhood, demonstrations, rumors, arguments. The whole thing was remarkably peaceful, there was no iron fist, the files of the secret police were overturned onto the streets, the factories were in the hands of the workers, but no weapons were raised; and best of all, the walls of the city were covered with colored signs and pictures overnight. Everyone painted and wrote what he wanted. And it was done without slogans or clichés. The walls were not covered in the stereotyped lies of the bureaucrats, or the dreary graffiti of the illiterate signature-artists of New York, who only ever think of one thing: me, me, me. Instead, painted dreams sprang up, utopias ran wild across the façades as far as hands could reach. It was political intoxication, bright, tropical, psychedelic, uninhibited. Not a monologue but a babble of voices, a delirious abundance of desires: art for everyone, justice for all, the test pattern of a better world projected onto the crumbling plasterwork of an old city . . .

I don't know if gangs of cleaners turned up one day with pails and brushes to remove this total art work, but I doubt it. No such thorough, systematic administration exists in Portugal. I believe the sea of pictures disappeared of its own accord. Indifference, rain, disappointment effaced the writing, washed away the traces.

No one seems to remember anymore what was painted on the walls of Lisbon. Today there are only dull slogans: "Soares out!" "Eanes out!" "Cavaco Silva out!" No one wants to know about the "achievements" of the revolution anymore. The agrarian reforms were buried. In distant Alentejo a few cooperatives still survive, they have no money for machinery, they must fight for loans, and they have taken refuge under the wing of the Communist Party, a party without a project, which has withdrawn into its historic fortresses to await a future that is now only a nostalgic ruin. The nationalized companies stagger on, proletarian enclaves threatened by bankruptcy, controlled by senselessly inflated managements with a reputation for sabotage, corruption, and incompetence.

The small radical parties that in 1974 scattered the confetti of their abbreviations over the political scene can no longer be traced. On a side street of the Campo de Ourique I managed to find a ramshackle house from whose façade a couple of bleached-out banners proclaimed, "All Power to the People!" and "The Rich Must Pay!" But the office had been abandoned, the windows broken, the lightbulbs unscrewed, and the shutters rattled in the wind.

Francisco Veloso, a clever, optimistic banker, told me, "Only someone who was alive before the revolution knows how sweet life can be. Wasn't it Talleyrand who said that? But there had to be a revolution before he was able to say it. At any rate, two minuses certainly don't make a plus. Salazar's dictatorship was only the first crime to afflict us in this century. The second was the famous Revolution of the Carnations. We barely managed to escape. You look at me with such disbelief . . . Do you know what Cunhal, the Communist boss, said in 1975? 'I tell everyone who wants to hear: there will be no parliaments in Portugal.' Thank God that nightmare is over. I'm backing our small and medium-sized industries, the only ones in this country that accomplish anything, and I'm backing democracy."

Then I set out in search of the protagonists of 1974. But that was more difficult than I had thought. Otelo Saraiva de Carvalho, the charismatic veteran, was in the high-security wing of Monsanto Prison and appeared only occasionally before the judges who, in an endlessly protracted trial, were supposed to decide whether or not he was a terrorist. The red generals and admirals had retired to their villas and were not talking to anyone. Some ultraleftists had left for Paris, some Spinolists had gone to Brazil. Eventually I traced one of the student spokesmen of the great uproar, a former Maoist who asked me not to mention his name.

"Yes, of course, I remember our argument in the car, on the way back from Setúbal . . . but I've forgotten what we were arguing about. Those pictures, those words on the wall that you admired so much, were nothing but a starry-eyed painting over of reality, that's obvious. Our revolution was more paint than substance. I painted along with the rest, as you know, and I don't regret it. And, despite everything, the result was an irreversible break with the past. Of course, we didn't create a utopia, didn't abolish capitalism, didn't transform the economic base. But can anyone still imagine what it was like before? A whole country embalmed like a mummy for forty years! That was Salazar's achievement. Time stood still. All the deposed kings of the world found a safe haven here, behind the walls of the regime. It was teeming with servants; pianists were flown in from all over the world for the bourgeoisie's parties. A paradise for parasites, social coma for everyone else. In his own way Salazar was a utopian too. He wanted a world in which nothing moved, total hypnosis.

"And then the abrupt awakening. Suddenly, from one day to the next, everything was supposed to be completely different, and without any real work, without anything really being done. The dictatorship was turned upside down. A miracle. But basically, the whole thing took place *en famille*. The officers made the decisions and the Portuguese people were spectators. The people swallowed the results, just as they had first swallowed the Republic, then the repression, then the colonial war.

"As I said, I'm glad I was there. No one can undo what happened in 1974, even though there's no shortage of people willing to try. But the whole thing wasn't a revolution at all. It was a charade in which the majority of the people played no part. They were simply absent, absent in mind. Their good conscience has never been shaken. First it was the good conscience of the regime, then the good conscience of the revolution, and now it's the good conscience of democracy. As far as the solid majority was concerned, we might as well have been discussing a soccer match on the Rossio as the withering away of the state.

"Apart from that, it's well known that we never complete anything in Portugal. The Memorial to the Discoveries in Belem, a Fascist affair 164 feet high, is one of our megalo-maniac national monuments. But, unfortunately, it's almost impossible to get to the thing, because there's a railway line and a superhighway running in front of it. So a pedestrian underpass had to be built. But it's a risky business to use it, because the steps have never been finished. Who knows whether the workers stole the missing marble steps, or whether the stone has already been worn away? But no one's surprised. After all, the Ajuda Palace is still not finished, although construction was begun in 1802. So our state receptions take place in a ruin. And our revolution too has remained a ruin, a new ruin."

Later, in a dark café, I met a Portuguese who was more concise. He pointed out an old man wearing dark glasses and sitting apathetically with an empty cup in front of him. "That's a former secret policeman, a PIDE man. He doesn't talk to anyone, he has a monthly state pension of forty thousand escudos [$270] like all the others—not bad for Portugal. He arrested and interrogated my father. But my father, who was in prison for three years, said, 'I'm grateful to him, others were tortured, I wasn't, it could have been worse.' You see, we never got rid of these people. We're not very good at hating. We have no memory, we only have daydreams . . ."

Dr. Pereira da Costa is a white-haired gentleman, already slightly bowed by his sixty years, whose energy is not at first sight obvious, unless one were to be impressed by his hawklike nose. Perhaps it's a clue to his origins, for Dr. Pereira was born on the Azores—the Hawk Islands. He is wearing one of those gray suits on which the passage of time has left no trace and which defeat every fashion, because the same tailor has been making them for twenty years.

In 1970, after years of waiting, his life's dream came true. He became director of the Portuguese National Archive, the Torre do Tombo, which had its origin in the Archive of the Royal Household, the first recorded mention of which dates from 1378. Dr. Pereira was confronted by—unfortunately, he cannot express himself more politely—a pigsty. Priceless codices gnawed by rats and worms, documents scattered across dirty cellars, broken boxes, and water-stained fascicles. A whole album of photographs shows how Salazar's rule treated the tradition to which it appealed. We are sitting in the director's office in a side wing of São Bento Palace. Dr. Pereira's glance takes in the magnificent but tasteless throne of Manuel II, the last Portuguese king, and an inlaid pay desk from Goa before coming to rest on an inkwell from the Holy Inquisition that has found its final resting place here.

"Reports, plots, petitions, maneuverings, protests. You can't believe how much persistence and patience was required before the archive was more or less disinfected, arranged, and catalogued. Every shelf, every strongbox, every light-switch was a matter of state. Ministers come and go, but the problems remain. Politics causes nothing but trouble! As you know, we have to share the palace with Parliament. I have nothing against the Parliament, even if it was only a sham for forty years, but they treat us like subtenants. Yet we've been here since 1757, and the politicians didn't move in until 1834. Detestable neighbors! Nothing but trouble as long as I can remember. In 1974 there was even shooting, there were tanks virtually outside the door, can you imagine it! They can have their revolutions, but not here! I spent sleepless nights in the stacks for fear they were going to attack the records."

The archives are vast. They go as far back as the unprecedented voyages of discovery of the Portuguese, as far as their chimeralike world empire. Would I like to see the correspondence of the viceroys of India or the files of the Companhia do Pernambuco? The records of the Portuguese factory in Antwerp? The stud books of the royal cattle herds? The *Books of the Monsoons* or the *Minutes of the Tobacco Consortium*?

I can't make up my mind. But finally I settle for the judicial records of the Holy Office, which are stored in a giant, gloomy room. We leaf through the carefully filed, hand-written reports. They record the statements of forty-four thousand defendants, and in such detail that one can easily reconstruct their lives.

The Church's investigations did not draw the line at its own officers. On the contrary, everyone from the inquisitor to the lowliest scribe was subjected to a formal trial. The archive contains thirteen thousand of these theological security checks. The interrogations were conducted in such an exemplary fashion that they could still, four hundred years later, serve as models for the KGB and the CIA.

I ask my host about the files of the PIDE, the secret police of the Salazar dictatorship. Ah! that's an annoying story, and something of a sore point, because the available material was promised to the National Library and not to the archive. Incomprehensible. On the other hand, it's just a lot of paperwork, because the more sensitive documents aren't there. They're scattered, stolen, gone. It's rumored that the

Communists pilfered some of them for who knows what dark purpose. But the local bosses helped themselves too and destroyed a lot of incriminating material. All very sad.

"But everything will soon be better," says Dr. Pereira, "when we move into our new home—in 1989 perhaps, if nothing intervenes. We're not giving up. We do our work, my friend. Even if only a few scholars make use of it: we shall defend our holdings. We are the memory of Portugal."

As if Dr. Martins, Dr. Salazar, and Dr. Pereira were not enough, I want to mention a fourth and final representative of Portuguese scholarship, a vain, unscrupulous jack-of-all-trades whose name can be found in any encyclopedia. His many publications include *The History of Playing Cards, The Life of John XXI*, and a series of essays about hypnosis. In 1917 he was appointed his country's ambassador in Madrid, and one year later he was even, if only for a few weeks, foreign minister. After his dismissal, he decided to become a neurologist. In 1935 this scholar, Professor António Caetano Egas Moniz, become obsessed by the idea that he had been called upon to put an end to the obsessions of the mentally ill. At first he injected pure alcohol into the cerebrums of his patients to get rid of their delusions. But he soon concluded that this procedure was too mild. He turned to more radical measures to eradicate the complaint root and branch. Although Dr. Moniz had no surgical experience of any kind— he himself could not operate, because both his hands were crippled—he proceeded to saw around at random in the gray matter until the frontal lobes of his patients' brain were destroyed. For this medical feat he received the Nobel Prize in 1949. Tens of thousands throughout the world became victims of his method, lobotomy (also called leucotomy), until word spread that the operation had absolutely no medical justification. The patients' restlessness and anxiety are said to have decreased after this mutilation of the brain. All their aggressions fell away, they became passive and docile. And the surgeons had relieved them of one further burden: their memories had been wiped out.

PHANTOM PAIN

In the gray dawn light the shed where the arriving passengers wait for their luggage appears as dismal and bare as a gym hall. It's almost seven, the New York plane has just arrived. A showing of sneakers and T-shirts from tourist class; the pink pages of the *Financial Times*, Gucci bags, and Rolex watches from first.

Less than ten paces away the conveyor belt brings to light possessions from quite a different world: clumsily tied baskets, rolled-up blankets, nets full of rags, cardboard boxes, diapers, bursting fiber suitcases—like jetsam after a shipwreck. But the wreck has made a safe landing. Its flight number is TM 704, and the castaways come from Maputo. Babies cry, black women wrap themselves in large cloths, a man with a wooden leg rummages in his bag, an old woman hugs to her breast everything she owns, and even the mulatto with the oversized yellow shoes, perhaps a diplomat or a high-ranking bureaucrat, looks dazed, as if he had escaped a disaster. The passengers stranded here all speak Portuguese. The country they have come from, Mozambique, is one of the poorest in the world. Everything is lacking in Maputo, the capital: eggs, drinking water, doctors, bread, electricity, and soap. The arrival hall, which before had looked like a dimly lit tunnel, suddenly appears as inviting as the gates of paradise.

In no other European city does one see as many brown, black, and yellow people as in Lisbon. Nowhere else is the Third World's presence felt so much as a matter of course. The influx from the former colonies has decreased in recent years, but thousands of so-called return migrants still arrive in Portugal. Most now come from the Cape Verde Islands, but stubborn applicants in Angola or Mozambique also manage, again and again, to obtain the sought-after travel documents, whether through bribery or by pulling strings. According to official statements, more than seven hundred thousand *retornados* have come to the motherland since 1974. Asians, Africans, Portuguese? Who could tell them apart? No one seems to worry about it, not even the responsible authorities. The country's immigration policy is a shoulder-shrugging generosity. There seem to be no firm rules and the practice is very relaxed, even though the housing shortage is grave, the crime rate alarming, the unemployment level unbelievable. Nothing is done against the immigrants, but then very little is done for them; for most Portuguese the welfare state exists only on paper anyway. The new arrivals find work on construction sites, many work for extremely low wages on the black market, others become drug dealers or end up in prostitution. But over the years, most have managed to leave behind the corrugated-iron huts on the outskirts of the city. Which is more astonishing, the dogged energy of the *retornados* or the weary tolerance of the Portuguese?

"You're talking like a journalist!" With these words I was rebuked by a German woman friend, who has lived in Lisbon for years and whose advice I always listen to. "What you're saying about the refugee problem is superficial, arrogant, and wrong. The state health service works badly and the pensions are pitifully low. But that certainly doesn't mean that the welfare state exists only on paper! Only a spoiled West German could say such a thing. Before 1974 the Portuguese had no social safety net at all. That makes all the difference in the world! And what on earth does 'weary tolerance' mean?

"In the house directly opposite there were whites and blacks squatting under the same roof for years. I don't remember a single fight. A few streets away there were always long lines at a payout center of the Refugee Commission. I never heard a single malicious remark from the people here in the district, and God knows they're poor enough themselves.

"Portugal spent billions on the maintenance of the *retornados*, as much as 11 percent of the national budget in some years. The people were accommodated in warehouses, vacant apartments, even luxury hotels if there was nothing else. They camped out in the Ritz and the Avenida Palace for months. They were given cheap, long-term loans, clothes were collected for them, and they were given preference for government jobs.

"Sure, some of them brought marijuana with them in their suitcases and boxes and sold it on the Rossio, but who's been telling you that the refugees are responsible for all the crime? What is certain, is that the *retornados* are now no worse off than the rest of the Portuguese and that the poorest of the colonial powers has solved the problem relatively well and astonishingly quickly."

So I let myself be corrected. I even tried to convince the National Guard sergeant I got into conversation with one drowsy Sunday afternoon. Time was dragging in his guardroom on the Largo do Carmo. The flies buzzed and he had nothing to do.

"Seven hundred thousand? That's a joke. Everyone knows it's at least two million. And this crap about coming back home! They aren't really Portuguese. I was a conscript in Angola, I know. And anyway, what decent person ever went overseas voluntarily? From the first there were only convicts, bums, and flunkeys in the colonies. It's not the color of their skin that bothers me—I'm not a racist—it's their culture. They don't want to work, they literally eat garbage, they steal everything they can lay their hands on, bring in diseases, and I know for a fact that some of them eat little children. They're going to give us a lot of problems."

He said all this very candidly and calmly, in quite a rational tone of voice. "Then you're against letting them in?" I asked. "What do you suggest? Should they be thrown out?"

"For God's sake," said the sergeant. "The people can't help it! It's all Salazar's fault. He waged this idiotic war and didn't want to negotiate. Now we have to foot the bill. That's what comes of having colonies. Once they brought gold into the country, now they bring criminals. It's not so easy to get rid of an empire!"

And with that last sentence, at least, the sergeant was speaking nothing but the truth.

The young historian who showed me the wonderful library at Coimbra a week later agreed with him on this point too. "It's not true that we have no memory," she said. "For example, these inlaid tables are made of Indian and Brazilian wood, and the Chinoiserie of the panels is a discreet reminder of our old colony Macao. Of course, every nation edits its own past. But we're not skilled with cosmetics like the Americans, nor in self-censorship like the Russians. The aggressive amnesia of the Germans doesn't appeal to us either. Our specialty is the invocation of shadows. History is a kind of cinema of the soul for us. And it's always the same old film playing: *The Lost Empire*.

"We all know that there is no happy ending for the hero of the film. But we are quite bewildered as we watch. Was that really us? Less than a million peasants, shepherds, and fishermen, it wasn't any more than that, in a remote corner of the world, hardly noticed by anyone—and then, almost from one day to the next, this collective madness, this intoxicating, headlong desire to discover, on our own, everything that could be discovered. The whole thing lasted only fifty or at most a hundred years, but we have never recovered and are unable to forget it.

"Only somehow we can't quite remember the massacres we carried out. Every Portuguese will tell you that we weren't brutal and calculating like the others. No, we always abhorred racism, we always wanted only the best for Brazil and Africa and Asia. We were perfect saints, admirable and unimpeachable. In Timor, for example, the chiefs forbade their followers to tread on the shadow of a Portuguese, on pain of death. You can still hear such stories in this country, and they are widely believed, even by quite intelligent people. We cherish the flattering illusion that we are loved. The revolution of 1974 continued to indulge this dream. It saw Portugal as spokesman for the Third World, called upon to deliver it from its ills. And one still meets people everywhere—economists, politicians, managers—who imagine we have some mysterious know-how, some privileged relationship with the Africans. It's our invisible capital, it's where our future lies. At least it could be our trump card. If we can no longer play a special role in Europe, then we could still take the stage as protector and intermediary for people even worse off than we are. In their eyes we would still be great . . . That's how I explain the sweet phantom pain of the Portuguese that refuses to disappear.

"Or to use another metaphor: if you switch off the light in a room, you see the room once again in the dark, or rather its afterimage on the retina. That is our situation with the lost colonial empire. During the dictatorship there was a map, produced by some propagandist of the regime, that used to hang on every wall. The background was an outline of Europe. Only one country was given firm contours: Portugal, an island. But there were other, much larger islands on the map, superimposed upon the continent. These were our so-called overseas provinces. The faraway tip of this imaginary archipelago stretched deep into the Ukraine. Many of us still have this half-forgotten picture before our eyes. That is how great we once were!"

I don't know who Xavier Pintado is, I have never met him. On the postage-stamp-size photo in the newspaper, he looks like a senior civil servant. But he doesn't write like a technocrat. An article of his, which I found in Lisbon's biggest daily, the *Diario de Noticias*, had the title "The Remnant." No one seems to have paid any attention to it, there was no discussion of it—a bad sign. I shall quote a few passages translated from this text:

"I had been in Geneva, in Switzerland, the country with the highest average income in the world, on official business. When I landed in Lisbon again, Portugal had just formally signed the treaty of accession to the European Economic Community, with considerable ceremony.

"At half past seven I saw an illuminated church in the Lower Town. Two beggars were lying in the porch. One, half cowering away, stretched out his hand; the other, lying on the white stone of the threshold, displayed a wound on his naked leg.

"There were about thirty people, almost all elderly, inside the church. Most were dressed in black. Pensioners, servants, people without jobs—all poor. A small man who was over seventy read out a chapter from the Bible, from Jeremiah, in a weak voice, 'O Lord, save thy people, the remnant of Israel. Behold, I will bring them from the north country, and gather them from the coasts of the earth, and, with them, the blind and the lame, the woman with child and her who travaileth with child together' (Jer. 31:7–8).

"I was not listening anymore, because I had begun to ponder. It was the word 'remnant' that had set me thinking.

"I understood this scene in its historical context. Israel was humbled. The young and the able-bodied men and women had been deported. Only 'the remnant' was left: the old, the blind, the lame, the pregnant. This 'remnant' later acquired a symbolic significance. The poor of Jehovah, the *anawin*, were those who had no voice and no status, and who therefore placed all their hope in the Lord. One day He would free Israel. That was the essence of messianic hope.

"Today, I thought to myself, it is the Portuguese who are

this 'remnant' in the rich Europe that we have just entered, and in which we shall always be the last, no matter what yardstick is used—whether income, productivity, wages. Before our entry the ratio between the poorest and the most affluent in the European Economic Community was one to seven. In the future this ratio will be one to twelve, and two Portuguese districts, Bragança and Beja, will bring up the very rear. There, as in that miserable church in the middle of Lisbon, is concentrated Europe's new poverty, which listens to the pleas of Jeremiah without understanding their meaning. And I asked myself, What does entry into the European Economic Community mean to these people, what relevance does it have to their hopes? I remember a lecture that Michael Emerson, one of the most outstanding economists at the European Commission, gave in Lisbon some years ago. He talked about the various development models found in Europe today. The Portuguese model, he said, only knows short-term measures; it's vague, contradictory, incoherent, and irrational, and ignores every structural problem. Have we been trying at all to achieve stability, efficiency, realistic strategies like the other Europeans, or do we prefer instability, ideology, and a dreamy flight from reality?

"If we make the wrong choice, then Europe can do us only one final service. It will be a bad one. After a transitional period, when full freedom of movement exists within the community, the North will absorb our labor power. Whoever can emigrate will do so. Left behind in a backward country will be 'the remnant.' The Portuguese will be the *anawin* of Europe."

NOISE EXPORT

"The town of Beja," it says in an old travel book, "is a horrible hole in the middle of a plain ravaged by the sun. Its streets lie abandoned; everything sleeps." I wouldn't go that far, though I must admit that the calm of the place is hard to distinguish from despair.

No one goes barefoot, the tiny shop windows are bursting with leather shoes. Like everywhere else in the world, there's an ugly castle with naked walls and dreary cannon. The lonely railway station, built in 1940, looks as if it dated from 1912, as does its dark-green cast-iron clock, made by Paul Garnier, *horloger mécanicien*, rue Taibout 6 et 16, Paris. The municipal park with its bandstand and its duck pond is also straight out of a faded family album. The children, if they are boys, get an ice and are allowed to do anything. Like everywhere else in the world, there are too many banks. An old lady, as small as a child, creeps, stooped down, along a wall. She is dressed in black with a tall, black-felt hat and carries a bundle of brushwood on her head—but her granddaughter wears bright-yellow jeans. In the barbershop there are magnificent shaving brushes and hot and cold facecloths. The chrome of the mechanical chair with its broad projecting footrest gleams as if it were in a dentist's office. A regulation dating from 1954 hangs on the wall of the tax office: "This room may only be entered bare-headed." In an old-fashioned veterinary shop, giant cattle syringes. The monastery's cloisters are a crumbling ruin. A barracks has been established in the central section, the old porter's lodge makes a twilit orderly-room. The plumber sells birds on the side; packets of bird seed are spread out under his pipe wrenches. Like everywhere else in the world, the movies are a last refuge. *Escape from Alcatraz* with Clint Eastwood at the Esplanade, *Throes of Lust* at the Vista Alegre. The unemployed play dominoes in the Beehive Café, founded on July 1, 1951, by Carlos Augusto Lança. But it looks more like 1921. Instead of women here, there is a whirring ventilator, a stuffed falcon, a derelict weighing machine. On a poster announcing a dog race for the May 1st holiday, the greyhounds hang in the air, paws raised. Candy wrappers, breadcrumbs, and peanut shells rustle on the floor. Little snow-white aristocratic palaces house trade union and party offices. The House of the Communist Party is deserted. All the doors are open, Brezhnev's speeches and laughing women tractor drivers are yellowing on the shelves. Eventually an invalid comes shuffling out of a wooden closet. He doesn't know about anything. A donkey trots past a boutique. Occasionally a moped with a tiny engine, deafening noise, silence.

Farther out, near the bypass, behind coils of cable and tumbledown sheds, there's a small, overgrown park. As long as anyone can remember, that's where the Gypsies have stayed. They are too poor even to own tents. They sleep in sacks on the grass, and if it rains they unfurl a piece of canvas. They don't practice any trades either, don't sharpen scissors or mend pots. They have only brought a couple of mules and shaggy ponies with them, because the livestock market will be held in Beja on Monday.

The Federal Republic of Germany begins a few steps behind the camp, in the middle of Alentejo. Brand-new, freshly polished Mercedes limousines and VW buses with surfboards stand in front of bright, new buildings. No wash hangs from these balconies, and a blond woman is taking her dachshund for a walk between flowerbeds neatly framed in concrete.

The German quarter is inhabited by the personnel of DtLwÜbPlKdo Beja. That's how the military, with their age-old taste for tactical abbreviations, designate it. A German air force base has been established in one of the poorest provinces in Portugal. The blond lady, married to a fire marshal serving on the base, quite guilelessly confides her troubles to me in a Swabian accent . . . You can't leave a deck chair or a pair of sneakers outside the door. Everything disappears overnight, even the Flokati rug. The Gypsies take everything that's not nailed down. Then the Portuguese are all so lethargic, you never know what they're up to. The cleaning woman, for instance. She's friendly, one has to grant her that, and cheap, but I've told her a hundred times, you have to dampen the blouse before you iron it—but she always forgets. Then, of course, the sleeves are full of creases. You can imagine what that looks like!

. . . Everyone in the armed forces thinks of Beja as a lousy posting. Where can you go in the evening? The bars are dirty and Germans get funny looks, there's supposed to be lots of Communists here. Then there were the bombs, it still makes me shake when I think of it. A year ago twelve cars were blown up in the middle of the night, totally destroyed. The insurance had to pay. Everyone gets away on weekends and drives down to the Algarve. The hotels are much too expensive, so people prefer to sleep in campers . . . The fire marshal's wife knows the ropes. It's a hot day, the conversation is unhurried, and the dachshund takes its time.

The air base covers almost two thousand acres, and almost nine miles of perimeter fence surrounds an enormous quantity of technology and machinery. The commander, Lieutenant Colonel Michen, an efficient, urbane officer in a pilot's orange-red battle dress, shows me the hangars and test bays, flight control, search-and-rescue service, electronics workshop, hospital, munitions depot, and operational headquarters. There's even a duty-free shop, but a gym and a swimming pool are badly missed. The base gives the impression of a well-managed factory. High tech and specialization instead of military drill. Deterrence as a high-quality product, made in Germany. Beja, the commander explains to me, doesn't serve as a logistic base, its mission is solely low-altitude training, and firing and bombing practice. In Alentejo it's possible to fly as low as 350 feet without any problem; given the German public's lack of understanding of the air force's needs, there's no other choice. He's quite frank about the key purpose of the base: noise export.

No, there are no problems with the Portuguese. Contacts

with the mayor are good, relations with the population by and large positive. After all, the base is the biggest employer far and wide. Unfortunately, there is little private contact with the Portuguese armed forces. Lack of time, stress, and then the language barrier . . . Another officer, obviously a NATO ace, who had been listening to us, interrupted. He knew practically every airfield from Arizona to Anatolia, and all he could say about the Portuguese air force was that it would be worth more as scrap metal, that technologically and aeronautically speaking it was on a kindergarten level, and in an emergency you could forget the Portuguese! The commander's face took on a stony expression. "My colleague, just now," he told me as I was leaving, "is only a guest at this field. Here we . . . how can I put it? In short, we do not approve of such talk."

Then evening in the German House. *Escalopes chasseur* and smoked spareribs on the menu. The Catholic military chaplaincy announces: Holy Mass for the military congregation, 19:00 hours, base chapel, Block 111, Father Dr. F. Hildebrand. Followed by social evening.

After the third beer the stories start. For example, the problem with the black-red-gold German flag. Because the Portuguese flag is the only one allowed to fly on Portuguese soil. At least that was made clear to us very vigorously. Is it written down anywhere? Because formally the base is under Portuguese command. Even the state secretary from Bonn who was here recently couldn't persuade the gentlemen from Lisbon to change their point of view. What were we supposed to do? Finally we just hung our flag out the window. And then the famous incident with the dog. No, it wasn't a dachshund but a neurotic collie. Its mistress, an NCO's wife, was a bit unstable herself. Apparently, she had difficulty adjusting, psychological problems. Anyway, she couldn't stop herself from giving a small Portuguese boy a slap when he hit her darling. You should have seen the parents! They said it was child abuse and the police were called. The trial hasn't been held yet, it can take years before the court reaches a decision, and by that time the culprit will have long since returned home to the Sauerland or the Palatinate. Anyway, it's an unpleasant story. I would call it a cultural conflict: the dog is sacred to the Germans, the child is sacred to the Portuguese. But otherwise we don't have any problems here.

PSYCHOLOGY

The shortest night of the year was almost cloudless. A soft breeze from the river blew across the terrace where we had eaten. "All the existing Wittgenstein interpretations," said Lourenço, my latest acquaintance, "founder on this key point." He was probably right, but unfortunately I can't pass on the proofs he recited. I was much too busy admiring the pink glow that the sun's last rays threw on the wall behind us. There was nothing milky or cloudy about this light. I had liked Lourenço Vaz right away. Wise before his time, shy and nonchalant, not a day over 22, he seemed like a prodigy to me. He was studying mathematics. Although he didn't have a penny—his father was a failed drug company rep and lived on a small pension—Lourenço acted as if Lisbon lay at his feet, he was half dandy, half *enfant terrible*. I asked him to guide me through the city at night.

The tiny tavern behind the National Theatre was packed. The grape brandy knocked back there was strong and cheap. Lourenço spoke perfect German. After the third bagaço I diverted from Gödel, Tarski, and the axiomatic antinomies with a pointed question, and we made our way to the Upper Town. Meanwhile darkness had fallen. He stopped in front of a small house with boarded-up windows. "This," he explained, "is the place one has to have been to—don't ask me why. The young intellectuals are supposed to come here. Take a good look!" The entrance was indeed besieged by fashionably dressed figures, and the door policy was very strict. To my surprise, Lourenço was admitted immediately, and I too was able to enjoy a lukewarm whiskey and booming music. Conversation was impossible. We soon took flight. Outside, old actors, pickpockets, ladies in expensive and badly made clothes, small-time drug dealers, and tourists swarmed through the narrow alleys. Luxury had established itself in the slum.

In the Rua Diário de Notícias the hoarse, moaning voice of a woman could be heard coming from a cellar. "I've never been to a fado bar," I said. "It's really high time I heard it. Would you come with me?"

Lourenço stared at me as if I had threatened him with a knife. "Impossible!" he shouted. "You can't expect that of me. I consider it my duty," he continued solemnly, "to protect you from this repulsive affront. The Portuguese soul," he drawled, changing his accent, "finds its expression in the fado, the music that makes the listener so wonderfully sad. Yes sir! The desire for an inextinguishable pain, the pleasure in an unnameable misfortune, the longing for despair—I'm only quoting what every travel guide ever written about Portugal tells you. And then in the next line comes the famous, untranslatable word *saudade*! The source of the Portuguese soul! The ladies in the Adega Mesquita will close their eyes ecstatically and wail it out for you. Melancholy! Cruel fate! *O gosto de ser triste!* [How pleasant to be sad!] And you have to stay respectfully silent as you listen to it, and cry along with the guitars. What depth! What imbecility! We must drink another one to that." We had ended up in a deserted bar. Besides us there was only a pair of whispering lovers in this dimly lit, red-plush-upholstered cave that felt like a tomb.

Lourenço had still not finished his tirade. "Portugal is the only country in the world in which adults feel uplifted by their own insignificance. I know what you're going to say!

Every country has its own kitsch and celebrates it. But no one believes in the nonsense as passionately as we do. Kitsch is our religion. And why, if one may ask? Because no one needs it more than we do. The fado is the halo around our ignorance, the gloriole we set on our misery. No wonder *suadade* is untranslatable. We're the only people in the world who are proud of having gone down the drain! Cheers!"

He was in full flow now. The cool mathematician was running amok. He had the bottle brought to the table and went on drinking methodically.

"So," I objected cautiously, "what's so unusual about that? There's an element of truth in every illusion."

"That's even worse! If it's true that our soul is nothing but a tear-stained rag, why should I burst into sobs of emotion about it? I don't give a damn about our soul! Any gangster, any speculator or male prostitute is preferable!"

Out of the corner of my eye I saw the lovers in the corner leave hastily. Shy, polite Lourenço was unrecognizable. "Thank God for the multinationals!" He was almost shouting now. "Welcome to Portugal, IBM! Welcome, German brutality and American bulldozers! That's normal! Greed, cancer, exploitation, it's all normal. Or really existing socialism, for all I care! All of it's better than this soap opera that believes itself profound!" He paused and glanced at me contemptuously. I can't vouch for what followed. My own mind was gradually becoming less clear.

"I want to tell you something:"—that's roughly how he began again—"the Portuguese soul never existed. This is something I've studied. It's nothing but the literary invention of foreigners who came here in the nineteenth century to live on their private incomes, people tired of civilization, second-hand Romantics . . . They invented it all. And we fell for it! Even our stupidest ideas are imported. You have progress and money but your lives are cold, empty, and soulless. We have nothing to eat but have laid claim to humane values instead. Poverty lends an inner glow. That's the beauty of Portugal, *saudade*, you can book it in any travel agency. How moving! The very things you avoid like the plague at home, you admire here—our oxcarts, our pottery, our 'primitiveness,' and our lamentations."

Finally I brought him home, on foot, past deserted squares, up steep stairways. Once we had to dodge the spray from a truck that was cleaning the streets, and I think we met the blind violinist in a steep alleyway. I remember how he waved his stick around, and his pale, empty eyesocket—but perhaps I'm only imagining it.

Two very young, childlike Chinese prostitutes stood in front of the entrance to Lourenço's house, snatches of some African music spilled out of the open windows of a shabby pension, the stairway was an endless dark shaft. At last we reached Lourenço's door. He put his forefinger to his lips to show he didn't want his parents awakened. The apartment was like a furniture warehouse, stuffed with enormous cabinets and white-draped easy chairs. Books on symbolic logic lay stacked on a small table in the living room. A grandfatherly smell of floor polish and mothballs hung over everything, and a padded silence prevailed. Patriotic medals were displayed in a cabinet made of glass and elaborately carved dark wood. All of a sudden I felt cold sober. By the light of a porcelain lamp, shaped like a giant owl, that squatted on top of a highboy, I could make out a series of trophies and fetishes from Timor hanging on the walls. Lourenço sat on a wooden bench under them. He had fallen asleep. I left the room on tiptoe.

DEMOLITION

Until well into the twentieth century, roughly speaking until the First World War, the Portuguese master builders were, as far as is humanly possible, infallible. From the capital, which was rebuilt after the earthquake, to the most remote villages, they created an architecture in the eighteenth and nineteenth centuries that was both magnificent and modest, elegant and serviceable. I don't mean the famous architects whose works are awarded the little stars in the travel guides. Anyone able to distinguish between megalomania and greatness will be indifferent to the monstrous sarcophagus of Mafra and the neo-Manueline abominations of Sintra and Buçaco. The country owes its unique architecture to anonymous builders: farms and villas, palaces and tenements of unerring taste, of a craftsmanlike skill and a sureness of proportion not to be found in any other European country.

Whoever spends just a few days on vacation in the paradisiacal garden landscape of the North will not notice the decades of impoverishment in Minho. The small farm economy of the region is based on a partitioning of landed property that has been going on for centuries and has eventually produced fields the size of handkerchiefs. For tens, even hundreds, of thousands of people there was no choice but to emigrate. The evidence of this desperate state of affairs can no longer be overlooked. Over the last twenty years, countless workers have returned to their homeland and have constructed, amid the old farm houses and country seats, settings worthy of a horror movie. The ugliest houses in the world can now be seen in Minho: gaudy huts of lilac, pink, and poison-green tiles with oddly curved cast-iron stairways, squatting on top of huge garages: a spontaneous architecture that, through imitation and self-imitation, has spiraled into a delirious nighmare, far outstripping its models. No new housing project in France or West Germany can compete with this petty-bourgeois example of science fiction. Great sacrifices are made for these constructions. In fact, they have no function. Many of them are too big to be lived in and stand empty. Blinds pulled down, they await owners who will stay in debt far into the future and who serve time in Stuttgart or Amiens for dreams that have turned to stone. They have taken a terrible revenge on the country that could not feed them.

The professional counterpart of this architecture-without-architects can be found in Lisbon. Anyone arriving in the city by ship or ferry sees a row of gigantic cardboard boxes, brutal cubes poorly decorated with candy-pink and sky-blue cutouts, rising above the famous skyline of towers and hills. The Centro Comercical Amoreiras is the pride of Portuguese postmodernism. The terroristic kindergarten uncle who has piled up his building blocks here is named Tomás Taveira. One could safely forget the name if the man, once a well-known left-wing sloganeer, had not become a favorite of the Portuguese New Right.

One should, however, take note of his client's name. Krus Abecasis, a talented demagogue, became mayor of Lisbon in 1979. "At the end of my term of office," he told the citizens, "you will not recognize your city!" As far as was within his power, Abecasis has made this threat reality. The story that he ordered the city parks department not to plant any carnations because he wanted to wipe out every memory of the 1974 revolution is only an anecdote. The transformation of the Rua do Carmo, one of the most elegant streets in Lisbon, into a pedestrian precinct worthy of a small town in the Ruhr or the English midlands is only an error of taste. The fact that he sees no reason to adhere to the existing law of the land is a defect of character. But his central project, the methodical destruction of Lisbon, is a crime that affects not only the Portuguese.

Such an undertaking is made possible by the authoritarian management of local government that is taken for granted in centralist Portugal. Elected councils and citizen involvement in decision making have hardly any historical roots and the local Mafiosi have leapt into the breach. Whole districts along the Tagus River are being given up to demolition by building speculators. The city's main boulevard, the Avenida da Liberdade, conceived in the nineteenth century as a counterpart of the Champs-Elysées, is being surrendered to the barbarism of the banks. Whole streets are falling to the pickax. The mayor's strategy is the pincer attack. On the one hand, the town is left to rot. Here reliance is placed on the rent laws, which make it almost impossible to maintain the historical fabric of the city. But in the long run procrastination is a far more comprehensive weapon than any bulldozer. At the same time, speculation is encouraged by every possible means. The aim of the operation is the enforced modernization of the capital, the aesthetic ideal is slavish imitation, the unattainable model is Houston, Texas.

If architecture were a question of good taste or preservation, and nothing more, one could leave it at that. But the walls within which a society makes itself at home say more about it than their builders ever dream. So what does this spectacular collapse in the craft of building mean, and how is it to be explained? These questions are relevant not only to Lisbon or Minho. Portugal is only an extreme case.

The houses of the Germans display their petty-bourgeois wealth, those of the Swedes the ideology of their welfare state, those of the Italians their productive chaos. Yet the Portuguese lack the paradoxical vitality of the Italians as much as the social-democratic culture of the Swedes, and they can hardly be said to have found their common denominator in consumption. Why is it, then, that their houses grow increasingly uninhabitable?

It's quite obvious, exclaim my clever hosts. Just look at our bourgeoisie! . . . As I don't quite understand, they try to help me out with information, but their explanations sound more like a condemnation . . . It has always been a parasitic class. They just managed to exploit other people, but ultimately a national bourgeoisie is expected to do more than that. The appropriated surplus value has to be saved, accumulated, and put into manufacture. But this class had never even dreamt of doing that. No wonder they haven't gotten very far. First they were ass-lickers to the monarchy, then they were would-be aristocrats. Every grocer bought himself a title, but what was even worse, the whole gang took over the attitudes of the big landowners. The result was nothing but shabby parody, senseless extravagance, and pretension. This lumpen bourgeoisie saw its superiority confirmed by its very idleness. Brokerage, intermediate trade, speculation—anything, so long as it wasn't productive activity! A small, radical minority of eternal social climbers and swindlers—and not just in the figurative sense. They believed competition was a dirty trick, and took protection for granted. They thought performance was superfluous and qualifications were irrelevant. To think of working was the mark of a simpleton.

. . . And it didn't stop there, of course, because just as the bourgeoisie had taken the nobility as its model, so the petty bourgeoisie, in turn, modeled itself on the bourgeoisie. Parasitism was an infectious disease. Living beyond one's means was *de rigueur* in this country. As recently as the sixties, no newly built apartment was without a maid's room, because even the most junior office worker tried to live like a lord. And since 1974 this attitude has taken hold of virtually the whole working population. Where else could you find such a hybrid, useless, and disoriented middle class? The Ministry of Agriculture alone supported eighteen thousand employees, who all lived in Lisbon and invited each other out to dinner at the state's expense—in a country that had to import half of its foodstuffs even though one quarter of its population was employed in agriculture . . .

Yes, to come back to architecture: this is what the buildings revealed. Portugal was a country that was modernizing itself from the outside in rather than from the inside out, through consumption instead of production. It was not the poor of Portugal who were underdeveloped but the rich, from the multimillionaire down to the last little petty bourgeois.

We spoke about this and similar problems for a long time. The pictures on the wall were tastefully framed, the easy chairs were comfortable, and the ice clinked in the whiskey glasses.

AGAINST THE REALITY PRINCIPLE

"I do not know why," Princess Rattazzi wrote in her travel diary a hundred years ago, "but I have the deepest sympathy for this little country that doesn't give up, even though the whole world maintains that it lies deep in sleep, or even on its deathbed."

I don't have the arrogance to contradict the complaints, confessions, and accusations of my hosts. They know Portugal better than any casual visitor. But if they are right, where does their own critical energy come from? What produces their spirit of contradiction? And why is it that, apart from the Portuguese themselves, no one seems to dislike the Portuguese? Whoever gets to know the country wants to come back again. Only a postcard revelation? Nothing but nostalgia, kitsch, mystification? I don't believe it.

The ancient Portuguese art of survival practiced over centuries of decline is sufficient proof that there is more to it. If the statistics were true, then most Portuguese would be dead. Workers whose wages are paid nine, twelve, or fifteen months late, pensioners who have to survive on sixty dollars a month, the unemployed who get no benefits, the peasants who scrape out a miserable livelihood on tiny patches of land: everything points to a wretchedness without parallel in Europe. What do these people live on? Yet no one screams, no one shoots, and no one starves. That is the real Portuguese miracle: a negative miracle.

The statistics are disastrous but beside the point. It appears that the Portuguese sense of the fantastic is not just a romantic aberration. It intervenes powerfully in everyday experience and goes on to become a way of life. The gross national product is an abstract chimera compared to it; the official economy that Brussels or the World Bank believes in, a mere shadow. People live off three and four jobs in the extensive, protean shadow economy, they live off rented garden plots that have never been registered, the bartering of goods, and old-fashioned familial give-and-take. At the same time, it becomes apparent that the reality principle other societies subscribe to heart and soul is not quite so realistic as its faithful servants believe.

The senior European civil servant, a Dutchman I met in Lisbon, seemed to believe you simply need to be patient with the Portuguese, they just haven't grasped everything yet; you only have to praise and encourage them like a good shepherd and they'll see reason soon enough. I think that's unlikely.

Because what the Portuguese set against capitalist rationality is not simply incompetence but resistance. It's certainly difficult to tell one from the other. In any case, the result is a kind of silent sabotage that is not practiced out of anger, conviction, resentment, ideology, or defiance, as it is elsewhere. They don't attack capitalist efficiency, they avoid it, spontaneously, "just like that"; because it's not self-evident to the Portuguese, because the virtues it demands are not theirs.

They stick to their own: to their pathological tolerance, to their skepticism, which only stops short at miracles, to their careless generosity; to virtues that are perhaps utopian, and which, considered deadly sins by a progressive world, bear heavy penalties. But maybe one day they will still be needed? The last word has not yet been spoken. What the Portuguese are defending, sometimes vaguely and instinctively, but always tenaciously, is not their property but their desires—that is, things no one owns. The critique of reason has taken on a material form in this country. Let us assume that politics means something more than armaments and production; let us assume there is a Europe of desires. In *this* Europe, Portugal would no longer be a peripheral appendage but a great power, and like all great powers it would not only weaken its neighbors but fill them with envy.

In Fernando Pessoa's *Book of Unrest* (*Livro do desassossego*), the assistant bookkeeper Bernardo Soares makes the following confession: "Sometimes in the midst of active life, in which of course I am as fully in control of myself as the others, I am overcome by a strange sense of doubt; I don't know whether I exist; I believe it altogether possible that I am the dream of another creature . . . I am almost convinced that I am never awake. I do not know whether I am dreaming when alive, or am alive when dreaming, or whether dream and life do not mingle and overlap in me." (fragment 200)

No one knows whether Soares the assistant bookkeeper is still among the living; at any rate, his inventor and doppelgänger, the poet Fernando Pessoa, has been dead more than fifty years. But even today Soares the engineer lays down the computer printout midway through the meeting, with a little smile, and Soares the textile salesman drops the bolt of material before the big deal has closed. Only a moment ago he was driving a hard bargain—now, suddenly, he seems preoccupied, withdrawn. Is his mind wandering? Is he tired? Absent-minded? What is he thinking about? What reveries has he abandoned himself to? Has he forgotten us?

POLISH INCIDENTS

[1 9 8 6]

....

WARSAW, SATURDAY/SUNDAY

After ten at night, the huge main arteries of the Polish capital are completely deserted, the department store show-cases and the windows in the granite façades are dark. There has been a wooden fence at the intersection of Jerusalem Boulevard and Marszałkowska, in the center of town, for years. The sparse traffic curves around the building site. The needle point of the Palace of Culture disappears into a heavy layer of fog, half haze, half smog, that lies over Warsaw. The sidewalks here are seventy-five feet wide. The few people still out and about look lost on these endless, wet, thoroughfares. Old women, shift workers, pensioners, young people stagger by wrapped in padded jackets, yards apart from each other, stare at the mannequins in the store windows, muttering curses under their breath. An empty bottle smashes on the pavement. No one pays any attention to these isolated ghosts. They waver but don't fall down. Not even the militia is around at this hour.

Where are the 1.6 million inhabitants of the Polish capital hiding? There are not many places of refuge in the city's center. Restaurants are few and they close early. The Shanghai is a drafty, inhospitable hall. The lighting is weak, the food is half cold, and there are no Chinese dishes; the few customers are in a hurry to get home. There's no taxi at the taxi stand. The people in line look resigned. Most of the citizens of Warsaw have stayed home, in the endless highrises that cover the Masovian plain and that are so remote that they're called "the Falklands."

The empty boulevards and squares of the city are built over a necropolis. After the Warsaw Uprising in autumn 1944, more than 150,000 dead were left in the ruins. The survivors were deported. The Germans were already beaten, but they did their utmost to erase every memory of the city from the face of the earth. The remaining ruins were scrupulously and professionally blown up. Almost all the public buildings—the churches, the palaces, the university, what was left of the royal castle—were razed. The electric cables were even torn out of the ground. Hitler seemed to have achieved his goal of making the city uninhabitable forever.

Today the monstrous palaces of Stalinism tower above this *tabula rasa*. Their pasted-on façades proclaim the triumph of yet another foreign power. They cover up the emptiness but the void shines through. The traces of an older settlement can be found only in a few back courts—rotten, dilapidated, cramped tenements, pockmarked by war.

It's almost half a century since this city, this heap of rubble, was liberated. But walking through it, I can still almost feel on my tongue that smell of fire and carbolic acid, soot, and rubble that everyone who lived through 1945 remembers. In Warsaw memory is not repressed. Here destruction and shortages, oppression and self-defense have turned to stone. Forty years after the armistice it is the only city in Europe still living in the postwar period.

When Poles talk about "the war," they don't mean just the German-Soviet attack of 1939 and the years of the occupation, they also mean the course of action their own army took in December 1981. It's difficult to sum up in a single phrase what happened then. State of emergency? But the Jaruzelski government regards the situation that it forcibly brought to an end as the emergency. Martial law? But this coup had nothing to do with law. State of siege? But who was the besieger, if not the Polish people?

The Constitution of the People's Republic did not provide for such an eventuality. It had been unimaginable to the

Stalinists. So in order to give his intervention a constitutional veneer, the general had to fall back on the provisions for defense in wartime. However, this solution had one disadvantage: the regime was forced to formally declare war on its own population. Even though the "state of war" was lifted years ago, the shock can still be felt on the deserted streets at night.

WARSAW, MONDAY

After walking aimlessly through the unfamiliar city for two days, I'm pretty exhausted. I'm living in a district where the ministries are concentrated: heavy industry, energy, mining. This is where the iron men, the party whips of an industrialization that long ago became a nightmare, have their offices. Concentration, centralization. Mountains of paperwork bury the projects of forced accumulation: flooded mines and bankrupt steelworks, monuments to megalomania and wasteful exploitation. The administrators of the catastrophe sit in their honeycombs, breakfast in shirtsleeves, and make phone calls.

The big department stores are a few streets farther on. Shopping is hard, exhausting, boring work. Only someone who is very well informed and has considerable stamina is up to it. The customers, mainly women, give the impression of being highly trained experts. Not poverty but lack dominates life here. Anger or despair would be misplaced. A sharp wit and unflagging patience are the virtues required for survival. The individual counters are either empty or overflowing, depending on what's unavailable and what "*they*'ve thrown down"—an expression imported from the Soviet Union. Scarce consumer goods suddenly appear, no one knows when, where, or why, as if they'd dropped from the sky. People jump on them like a dog on a bone. Today there's dishwashing liquid, which is being poured into canisters and bottles the customers have brought with them, and shapeless balls of toilet paper.

Prices are completely nebulous. The streetcar costs almost nothing, telephone calls just as little, but on the black market the prices are all reckoned in thousands and millions. Presumably the officially controlled prices are supposed to "control" something or to camouflage the frantic inflation of the zloty, but the result is chaotic. A second currency is necessary to fix the real value of a commodity or service. The dollar serves as the economic yardstick in Poland. Regardless of fluctuations, it has assumed the status of an unshakable, almost metaphysical certainty. The state long ago gave up trying to fight its spell and has now become the country's largest black marketeer. Its agencies quite openly advertise luxury tours to Paris, Miami, and Egypt—payable in dollars. The passersby who read these offers are not surprised. They are used to being mocked. Nine million Poles live abroad. Who would want to stop them from helping their friends and relatives at home? Who would cast the first stone? Does the elegant old lady coming out of the PEWEX shop with a heavy shopping bag look like a racketeer? All she has bought is laundry detergent and toothpaste, coffee for her daughter, and chocolate for her nephew. PEWEX is the name of the state's ubiquitous black-market centers. The letters stand for "State Enterprise for Internal Export Trade"—a designation expressive of the madness that has become method here.

If there were no parks, one would have to fear for the mental health of the citizens of Warsaw. But escape from the city's oppressive architecture is never more than ten minutes' walk away. The parks are the city's idyllic side. Time stands still here. Broad avenues, ponds, mossy steps leading down to the river flats, pensioners sunk deep in thought, lots of baby carriages, castles with barred shutters, secluded pavilions, swans, and weeping willows. Urban Warsaw consists not of stone but of vegetation.

The Old Town is another place of refuge. It's not only the largest but also the most marvelous forgery in the world. In 1945 Warsaw was at its lowest point. Everything was lacking, money, materials, food, machinery, and no one even knew what a dollar looked like. Yet the city's inhabitants had nothing better to do than rebuild these seventeenth-, eighteenth-, and nineteenth-century streets with their bare hands on a scale of one to one, a perfect replica down to the last inch. A quixotic venture of heroic dimensions. The Poles anticipated the reconstruction of Europe with their achievement. Its success is demonstrated by the fact that the boldness of the decision has become invisible over the years. Residents and visitors walk across the squares and down the alleyways just as they do in any other Old Town of Europe, whether it's Santiago, Stockholm, or Bergamo. The past seems to have caught up with these walls. They are coated with a secondary patina. Already there's not enough money to repair them. Only someone who looks closely is overcome by a kind of historical vertigo when he asks himself whether this gutter or that door handle is old-old or new-old. Not only did the soaring ambition of the project anticipate all the contradictions of preservation, the Poles also showed a whole continent what it means to reconstruct one's own history.

WARSAW, TUESDAY

"And that broad, flat river is the Vistula. No current: the surface flows smoothly. Yellow sandbars almost break the surface. Small ships wait at the riverbank. The sun throws the pattern of the bridge's ironwork across the water. The far bank is sandy, grass-covered. Laborers idling, railroad tracks, steaming locomotives. It takes a long time to walk across this bridge, which is used by so many poor people . . . Now I have arrived in a humble district that, like all gray, disorderly, lively places, pleases me—I slip past churches and palaces far too easily. This is Praga. Peasant women in loose, floral-pattern linen skirts, dragging baskets . . . There's a broad avenue on the right. Terrible pavement, little houses with dirty fronts. A crack opens up between two houses: the entrance to the market stalls; small, red, wooden booths for fruit, clothes, boots. The vendors are almost all Jews. Sometimes a whole family stands behind a little table . . . So many suffering faces, white-parchment complexions, women with untidy hair, elderly women with thick lips, large eyes, and loose cheeks of a terrible ugliness."

Sixty years later, the suburb on the other bank seems unchanged, poor but alive, just as Alfred Döblin described it. Only the Jews are no longer there. Kreuzberg, Prenzlauer Berg, Wedding, and Lichtenberg—what are these Berlin remnants compared to Praga, the only quarter of Warsaw dominated not by postwar but by prewar times? Faces here are marked by an older vitality, indissolubly mixed with an older misery. On Ząbokowska, where the balconies had already fallen from the façades a generation ago, rusty steel supports protrude from bare brick walls. In the nearby market, old women stand for hours with a cap or a shirt, the only thing they have to sell, pressed to their breast. Proletarian poverty leavened with the criminal energy of the deviant, a terrain of smugglers, whores, and drunks. The tiny shop window of the hatmaker: dust on pastel-colored creations, melancholy reminiscence of the time when Warsaw was known as the Paris of the East. Beside it, a shabby little hairdresser's and a cobbler's. In a back court, among the garbage cans and enclosed by fire walls, a madonna beneath a painted sky-blue canopy. She is wreathed in garlands of little lightbulbs that are left burning night and day. On small lace mats, whole pyramids of tin cans holding fresh flowers. Two mangy cats have settled down in front of this domestic altar.

A couple of streets farther on, an old factory—a sooty brick building with castellated turrets. Over the years, the supporting scaffolding in front of the blank windows has itself become dilapidated. With the help of my pocket dictionary, I decipher the sign at the door, "Warsaw State Plants of the Alcoholic Spirits Industry," as well as the banner hanging across the front of the factory, "The alliance between workers and peasants—foundation of Poland's progress."

At the bus stop on Wileńska, a drunk, a man in his thirties with a mustache and a boxer's build, is blustering with rage. I don't know why, but he's got it in for me. The militia calm him down with difficulty. A student explains to me why he had been shouting, "I'm a worker, I've got a right to make a noise!" It was my red scarf that had provoked his outburst.

There's a pungent smell in the hotel lobby. Coexistence is at its shabbiest in the Eastern Bloc's international hotels. A great effort is made to preserve a semblance of luxury, but the carpets are frayed and the slipcovers of the easy chairs are greasy. Plump little party officials in mouse-gray, baggy suits, their polyester neckties knotted to the point of strangulation, hurry past to the International Meeting of the Socialist Youth Press. In the background, roaring, beery laughter—West German construction engineers. Two women tourists from California search despairingly through the selection at the newspaper kiosk. Not even *L'Humanité* or the *Morning Star* is available here, never mind the *Herald Tribune*. The only product of the foreign press available to the guests is *Pravda*. A black pop musician with tangled Rasta locks guards a tower of speakers, amplifiers, and instrument cases. The man in the moth-eaten fur coat, dozing in a huge armchair, looks like an ambassador of Old Russia. His white, patriarchal beard is yellowing. I already know him. Day and night he guards the hideous oil paintings displayed in a corner of the foyer for any foreign idiot who wants to exchange dollars for Polish kitsch—an altogether legal transaction.

But what ever is the peasant woman in the black headscarf doing here? In her lap she has a pink-plastic bucket filled with fresh mushrooms. Money changers who look like police spies whisper to secret policemen who deal in foreign currency. A compact group of Koreans hurries to the elevator. The members of the delegation look neither right nor left. Actually, they look like Mormons. The morose young Arab constantly running his hand nervously through his pomaded hair is a mystery. He is silent but has ready cash. From time to time he fingers a thick roll of banknotes that he takes out of his hip pocket. An Iraqi embassy employee? A guestworker from Berlin looking for whores? A terrorist waiting for the courier with the detonators? He chews his nails, pulls out a book, reads a couple of sentences, snaps it shut again— Cyrillic letters. Perhaps he's here to study Lenin. Or is he just taking part in a symposium on chemical fertilizers?

I feel just the way he does. I'm nervous, dejected, impatient. The watertap in my room has given up. The room itself is tiny, eight by thirteen feet, and costs nine thousand zlotys* a night—more than half what a teacher earns in a month. The furniture is reminiscent of a student hostel in the early fifties. A mysterious traffic sign is fixed to the inside of the door: a gray, loop-shaped object inside a red circle; a red crossbar indicates that something is forbidden. Illumination comes only after long thought. No immersion heater may be used in my room.

My Viennese friend had seen it all coming. I don't know why, but it always seems to be the Viennese who know their way around this part of the world better than anyone else. "You want to go to Poland?" he had asked me, comfortably

---

*In October 1986, the official exchange rate was just under two hundred zlotys to the dollar; by that reckoning, nine thousand zlotys equals approximately forty-five dollars. (Trans.)

stretched out on his old-fashioned sofa, hands clasped behind his head. "Without any friends, without any contacts, without a single word of Polish? Have fun!"

"But ignorance is my only advantage over people like you," I objected. "You're all experts on Eastern Europe, and that means you already know about everything. That's your problem. I'm just going to let myself be surprised."

"I know you. After three days you'll have blisters on your feet because you want to see everything. But you won't understand a thing."

"So?"

"So you need a guide. A cicerone . . . Don't worry, I don't mean someone from the official travel agency to show you the sights . . . Call it what you like: you need a guardian angel, a bear-trainer, bodyguard, governess . . . I'll give you a couple of phone numbers. When you've had enough, just call them."

I pulled the scrap of paper from my pocket and set to work. It's not easy to find one's way through the Warsaw telephone network. If the line doesn't stay dead, then a multitude of acoustic pleasures are revealed to the caller: dial tones and busy signals in every key, crossed lines, whistling and buzzing, and a strange, regular clicking. I didn't allow myself to be deterred, and after three-quarters of an hour I had reached my goal. I had an appointment with the real Warsaw for the following afternoon.

WARSAW, WEDNESDAY

But before that, I was granted one more look at the realm of fantasy. Chance led me to the Renaissance Castle of the Polish Kings, a new building that had just been completed. There I became a witness to an act of state. Uniformed security guards directed me to a chamber overflowing with gold and purple.

No one asked for my invitation—there doesn't seem to be any private terrorism in Warsaw. Officers in full-dress uniform, civil servants, and party officials—only the clergy was missing—crowded together along the walls under huge, mediocre history paintings. Assembled opposite them, on the windowed side of the room, was a very odd group of people indeed, part bohème, part school staffroom; figures that seemed to come straight out of an old photo album. The visionary with a goatee, the classical fop, the woman piano player in a sky-blue suit, the singer with waved hair who belonged in an operetta—they were all here. A choir of gentlemen in tails and ladies in flowing white dresses had taken up a position at the rear of the chamber. As the last kisses were being bestowed on female hands, the wiry little conductor raised his arm and the hymn *Mater Poloniae* rose from fifty throats.

But why was the desired atmosphere absent? The festive mood failed to materialize. A memory buzzed through the room, as persistent and as hard to pin down as a common housefly. I felt as if I had been transported to a nineteenth-century provincial town. That was it! The arrogant dignitary on the platform, whose eyes radiated a triumphant narrow-mindedness, was none other than the Mayor in Gogol's *The Inspector General*, and the ladies and gentlemen of his entourage all came from the same brilliant play. No one was missing, from the School Superintendent, rubbing his hands, to the anxious Director of Charities—and the police, with their, unchanging faces, had turned out in force too.

They had all assembled to pay homage to Culture. To quote the immortal Khlestakov: "I'm on friendly terms with Pushkin. I often used to say to him, 'Now, Pushkin, old friend, how are things?'—'Well, brother,' he used to answer, 'everything's more or less . . .'" In short, the purpose of the exercise was to shower orders and prizes on the deserving cultural workers who were present in strength. To judge by the profusion of this benediction, a state of warm understanding would appear to exist between regime and intelligentsia.

People who have just been awarded an order of merit seldom look particularly intelligent, so the satisfaction displayed by those who had been decorated was somewhat embarrassing, and their emotions appeared clumsy. The winner of the first-class award, an elderly gentleman in shapeless trousers and dark glasses, was the only one who could hardly suppress his impatience. It was as if the event had been designed to humiliate him. Two gentlemen from the Ministry of Culture set to work together—otherwise, the ceremony would never have come to an end—followed by two secretaries carrying the documents and little dark-red boxes on nickel-plated trays. Throughout the time they pinned, fastened, and tied, throughout the time it rained tin crosses and stars, a strange noise penetrated the silence: an irregular, dull hammering.

Somewhere in the castle perhaps a pipe was being laid bare, or a radiator being repaired, or a wall being knocked down. At least it could safely be assumed that the Polish working class had not chosen this moment to shake the foundations of the state. Everyone pretended not to have heard anything, but even the vice-premier was unable to put a stop to the persistent subterranean knocking.

Late evening. Saved! I didn't realize immediately when she came through the revolving door that this slim, ladylike person, just under thirty, blue hat, blue coat, was indeed my guardian angel. I had pictured—such is blind prejudice!—a fifth-year veterinary student somewhat differently: plain, perhaps wearing thick glasses and galoshes. Jadwiga was blond, matter-of-fact, and aloof, quite the opposite of the saucy Pole of old films and novels. She examined me with her bluish-gray eyes, and my dejected expression seemed to amuse her. A slight squint contributed to this impression.

She had been noncommittal on the phone, no names were mentioned, and she seemed to disapprove of the hotel lobby as well, but we had hardly reached the street when she got down to business.

She passed over the bleak monumental buildings in silence. Her remarks on the problems and misery of everyday life were limited to one sentence. "Funny," she said, "in 1945 we were among the victors. Forty years later we're beggars." She shrugged. What mattered to her and what she wanted to show me was something quite different: the Warsaw inside her head, a symbolic topography. "This is where the riot police vans were parked," she said, "and over there, in front of the wooden fence where the road has been dug up, that's where the big cross of flowers was. This square is called Victory Square, before that it was Adolf Hitler Square, and before that Saxony Square . . . Do you see the sign at the corner? No photographs allowed. Do you know why? This is the headquarters of the army's political section. Jaruzelski planned his coup up there on the third floor."

My companion was guided by a special, invisible map of the city, on which no parking lots or bus stops were marked.

"This monument is supposed to honor the Polish dead of the last war. I think it's hideous. That square over there is named after a bloodsucker called Dzierżyński. You should remember that the founder of the Cheka, now the KGB, was a Pole, the son of a noble landowner." There was no corner that did not remind Jadwiga of an uprising, a crime, a classic writer, a conspiracy, a saint, or an oppressor.

"This is where the Constitution of May 3, 1791, was ratified. You're probably aware that it was the first written constitution in Europe." (I had no idea.) "The Germans shot hundreds of prisoners against this wall. The Confederates of Targowice were hanged over there." (I didn't dare ask why.) "Do you see the cross over there in the park? It marks the place where the members of the National Government were executed."

"By whom?" "By whom? By the Russians, of course, in 1864."

But sometimes it was an unmarked spot that occupied her imagination. It must have been quite near the university that Jadwiga showed me a light-colored patch on the pavement. It was underneath a sandstone portico beside a church. "Until a couple of months ago, the students close to Solidarity gathered here, then the police intervened and removed the candles, the pictures, the flowers, and the slogans. But the militia only created a new problem for themselves. For weeks afterwards two sentries stood on the spot night and day to prevent any recurrence. In our country watch is kept on complete emptiness."

We had ended up in a café in the Old Town. My head was reeling with places, names, and dates: 1768, 1941, 1830, 1981, 1794, 1863, 1944. But months and days are charged with significance as well as years: the 1st of August and November 11th, the 3rd of May and December 13th, the 11th of November and the 24th of March. A calendar shot through with red-letter days, full of echoes, intimations, analogies. Jadwiga was no exception, most Poles have mastered this patriotic cabalistic lore. They are professionals when it comes to remembering. Perhaps Hitler's plan of annihilating Warsaw was ultimately defeated by their obsessive, brooding remembrance. The Nazis were unable to kill the dead.

When we were standing in front of the castle again, I remembered the ceremony at which I had been present earlier. "Oh, those were the martyrs of Polish culture you saw," observed my guardian angel. "It must have been an uplifting sight!"

"Martyrs?"

"I don't mean the housewives. No doubt there were a few housewives there as well. I imagine you were deeply moved by the orders and decorations the government bestowed on them. In this area at least, the supply situation is excellent. I don't begrudge them the pleasure, because no one can doubt their services to Polish culture: washing and ironing, shopping and washing diapers, ironing and darning. It's heroic. Believe me, I speak from experience.—No, I mean the others, the gentlemen in crumpled suits you saw there. Didn't you notice how embittered those cultural workers look? And I can tell you why. These people have sacrificed themselves, they've filled certain posts for the sake of the fatherland—a secretary of some association, chairman of this or that committee—and what thanks do they get? Everyone ignores them. Instead of earning recognition, they're regarded with contempt. People call them boot-lickers and collaborators. The inevitable consequence is that, although their books are published, they're left lying in the bookstores. Fame passes them by, to say nothing of translation. Not a soul outside the country is interested in them. The lackeys of the regime can only explain it as the mischief-making of the opposition or the machinations of the CIA. A regular salary and a tin cross on the lapel is all the thanks they get for their efforts. A rather meager compensation!

"Anyway, that's Polish culture for you. We're all embittered. Polarization is unavoidable—and it's always been like that. I've got a book for you here. Georg Brandes on Poland, in a German translation, Paris, Leipzig, Munich, 1888. You can read it all in there. Either/or. No compromise. Not like your country, where no one cares what intellectuals think."

Bedtime reading. "There is a tale told in Warsaw of a poor schoolteacher who had distinguished himself, and received the order of Stanislaus. He kept it hidden in a case, and used it only to punish his children with. When the youngest was naughty, he said, 'If you cry again, you shall wear the order of Stanislaus about your neck at dinner.' That was enough . . . Perhaps, after all, there is no condition more elevating for a race than one in which no distinguished man ever receives any external distinction, title, or decoration, and where the official tinsel of honor is regarded as a disgrace, while on the other hand the official garb of disgrace, the political prison blouse, is regarded as honorable . . . Every child who daily . . . sees the names of traitors encircled by garlands on the obelisks is from a tender age familiar with the thought that those whom the authorities honor are not as a rule the best men, and that those whom they persecute are not as a rule the worst."*

ŁOMŻA, THURSDAY

The smoke of potato fires across an endless plain, no tractor, no machine anywhere. Occasionally peasants ploughing in the fields, women loading sacks onto carts, geese marching across the highway, isolated farmsteads, small vegetable patches, piles of coal behind the houses, rowan trees in brilliant cinnamon, flocks of magpies.

It's perhaps another sixty miles to the Russian frontier. I feel that I'm far away, at the end of the world—or, rather, at the end of our world. We stop at the roadside to eat a couple of apples, alone among the fields. The problems of Warsaw lie behind us in the dusk: the currency shortages, planning failures, debt conversion negotiations, underground newspapers, demoralization, legitimation crises. I can't imagine that such phrases are worth much in this countryside. I began to daydream a little—if one were ever fed up with everything, exhausted by the political misery of the country, if one let oneself fall, it would be possible to dream life away in one of these low houses, because here there is no news, no outside world, no events . . .

* *I have slightly emended the 1903 English translation (from the Danish) of Georg Brandes,* Poland. *(Trans.)*

Jadwiga, apple core in hand, gave me a sidelong glance. "That's what happens when you get too involved with literature! Haven't you noticed the television aerials on the roofs? There's not much chance of an idyll out here in the country . . . We'd better start driving again before it gets dark. These carts don't have any lights, and the peasants don't even bother to put a reflector on the back. It's pure suicide driving on these roads at night."

"I'd like to see a place," I had told Jadwiga in Warsaw, "where nothing happens. A completely ordinary small town, far away from the capital, deep in the provinces."

Jadwiga thought this wish very strange, but she was ready to fulfill it. For dollars it would be possible to get hold of a Fiat Polski. The gas, a rare, strictly rationed liquid, was provided by PEWEX, the official black-market dealer of the People's Republic. We let chance decide the destination of the journey.

ŁOMŻA, FRIDAY

There must have been a shakeup in the Municipal Parks Department this spring. A few remnants of that enthusiasm can still be discerned. However, in time, empty cigarette packs and old newspapers have overwhelmed the pathetic flowerbeds. Yet the benches are used a lot. Men of indeterminate age hang about here, a couple of empty bottles beside them. They give the impression of being carefree and having plenty of time. People call them "blue birds." Idlers? Unemployed? Bums? Perhaps a little bit of each, yet none of these words really fits. They seem like people beyond any punishment or admonition. If reality comes too close, they simply wave it away.

Their turf lies right in the middle of the former marketplace, a square surrounded by low houses of indeterminate age. The market hall, or rather, a big shed built for this purpose at some time in the past—1930? 1948? 1960?—stands at the edge of the dusty park. The skylights have been painted over, perhaps to black them out against air attack, but most of the panes are broken. A red banner hangs across the front of the building. I ask my guide what it says: "The most important task of civil defense is to protect the population." Jadwiga fails to understand what I find so funny about that. But I have decided to explore the whole square like an ethnologist. I want to understand what's happening here, and I have high hopes that a careful on-the-spot investigation will dispel my ignorance.

A few booths nailed over with wooden boards lean against the outside of the building. "Closed for repairs," says a notice, which is itself in need of repair. But a creaking door is still open, and inside, an old woman reigns behind a counter. The shadowy hall is empty except for some furniture made of bits of ready-molded plastic stuck together—brand-new junk, straight from the factory, that nobody wants to buy.

We make a careful circuit of the square. The pensioners' and invalids' association is shut for the day. There's no sign on the shop next door to indicate what it sells, but the housewives are packed together behind the drawn curtains. It's 11 o'clock and meat has just gone on sale. An hour later the shop will be empty and the gray-haired woman butcher will be sitting all alone under a salami. The travel agency in the next building is advertising holidays in the High Tatra Mountains. A paper model airplane that has lost its left engine hangs among the potted plants. First prize for the best essay in Esperanto is a trip to the World Esperanto Congress in Peking. Pity we're too late, the entry deadline was a year ago.

Next, "Services." Broken refrigerators rest behind frosted-glass panes and wait for new motors. No one's around. In the public library two women librarians are knitting furiously, as if in a race. A stone plaque on the town hall reveals that our old friend Feliks Dzierżyński was active here in 1920.

The nature of his activities is not elucidated. Jadwiga shrugs her shoulders.

In the fishmonger's the only sign of fish is a rotten smell. No one wants the cans piled up on the shelves. Are they old, bad, too expensive? Next door, on the other hand, you can buy as many flowers as you want. There are flowers everywhere in Poland, even here. Flowers for the churches, for the poets, for the Madonna, flowers for the graves. There's a souvenir shop too. Though who on earth would have such a strong desire to be reminded of Łomża with plaster vases, embroidered mats, and spinning wheels? Objects arranged in display cases apparently out of a *horror vacui*. It is an abundance born of shortages, but instead of alleviation it produces only greater sadness. The shops smell strongly of valerian, dying cyclamen, and leatherette. In fact, the smells here are altogether very strange. Disinfectant, cabbage, and urine predominate in the lobbies of the tenements.

Five men's tailors are busy around the square. You can see them from outside, working with their big scissors and measuring tape while their wives sit at the antiquated Singer sewing machines with their golden ornamental lettering. Dead wasps and faded color photographs from dated fashion magazines decorate the windows. The workshops look wretched, but the tailors earn a lot: a suit costs at least fifteen thousand zlotys.

In an alleyway a few houses farther on is a ramshackle garage occupied by the State Purchasing Office for Poultry, Eggs, and Feathers, but the shutters have been lowered as if it had abandoned all hope of ever doing business. Beside it, in a yard overgrown with grass, is a hut decorated with a six-foot painting of a shaving brush, although that is not what's on sale here. The word REKLAM (advertising) indicates that the sign-painter himself must live here—the man who has adorned the marketplace of Łomża and has perhaps supplied the whole region with beautiful make-believe.

The square's leading shop for devotional objects offers what he can't provide: transcendent consolation and supernatural grace. The local branch of a Catholic business, it's always open and has a large stock. It sells plump, grinning plaster angels with mouths rounded in song, baptismal robes, brightly painted candles as thick as an arm, the Polish pope in every size, color, and price range, brand-new icons, vestments, golden monstrances, and in the shop window there's a plastic suckling madonna. It has begun to drizzle. Shivering, the schoolchildren lick their ice cream, the drunks in the bar begin to bawl beneath the numerous signs warning of the dangers of vodka, and the "blue birds" in the marketplace cover themselves with some old editions of the *People's Tribune*.

What does this little town with its fifty-two thousand inhabitants live on? Perhaps it's best not to ask a question to which even Jadwiga didn't have an answer. If one scratches the peeling layers of paint on the façades, more and more layers of repression and apathy appear—the Tsarist regime, the rule of the landowners, the murderous attacks of the Germans, Stalinism . . . The region was repeatedly renamed: Podlachia, New East Prussia, the Russian Empire, the General Government of Warsaw, the Soviet Union, the Greater German Reich. Armies marched through here again and again, burning and looting Łomża—as if there had ever been anything worth taking here. That the place still exists at all, as humble and enduring as the grass, is a superhuman achievement.

WARSAW, SATURDAY

An embarrassing story: I've had an argument with my guardian angel. The cause was rather strange. Someone had told me that three-quarters of all Polish couples have a church wedding. Was it true? And was it true that the Church imposed all sorts of conditions? Confirmation and confessional certificates were demanded, and even that wasn't the end of the gauntlet the candidates had to run. They had to take a course of ten lectures, their attendance was checked, and they had to pass a test. On top of that there were two embarrassing visits to the doctor entailing thorough instruction in acceptable means of contraception. Didn't the Poles already have their fill of the state bureaucracy? Why did they willingly submit to domination by the priests as well?

"What's wrong with that?" asked Jadwiga.

I explained that in Germany, on the whole, people did not regard Woytila as a competent counselor on gynecological matters. Apart from that, as far as I knew, abortion was still the most common method of birth control in Poland.

Somewhat reluctantly, Jadwiga agreed.

"But then I don't understand . . . The political hypocrisy of the Communists and the sexual hypocrisy of the Catholics—they're like two sides of the same coin!"

I was talking to the wrong person. Jadwiga's nostrils quivered, her mockery turned to fiery indignation. It turned out that my provisional guardian angel was an ardent daughter of the Church. I was foolish enough to pour oil on the flames. I asked her why, when every Western fad from computer games to New Age workshops was greedily absorbed, there was no women's movement to speak of in Poland.

"Feminism is a detestable aberration!" she exclaimed. "We will be spared this misfortune at least. Because in this country women are too emancipated and self-confident to fall for anything so nasty. Our men worship us—it's true! They worship us, and that's the source of our power."

"You value tradition."

"We respect one another. It's probably different with German men. They lost their honor to Hitler. The Poles may have been beaten, but they fought on the right side. It's not victory or defeat that counts in history but honor or disgrace."

I was too astonished to contradict her.

* * *

Bedtime reading. "In Poland, Catholicism in this century has always been in opposition, in constant, restless conflict with the power of the State, frequently blended with that love for the truth which emancipates, and with that enthusiasm which exposes to martyrdom . . . People close their eyes to infringements of the Catholic ritual by priests, and even at a probable disbelief in certain dogmas, because they know them to be zealous supporters of Catholicism as the intellectual Polish national power. The stamp of comparatively innocent hypocrisy, which unquestionably adheres to them, injures them only among the few. General opinion regards them favorably.

"The point of view for the appraisement of the different parties and intellectual powers, which the foreigner feels himself compelled to adopt, is this: how far do they offer a greater or lesser power of resistance to the principle which aims by all means at breaking down the individuality of the people, the coarse and fearful principle of Asiatic absolute monarchy? It will be only when the danger which is threatened herefrom is removed that Poland can afford the luxury of measuring the different aims of the times by a new and sounder standard." Georg Brandes, *Poland* (1888).

WARSAW, SUNDAY

The Church of Saint Stanisław Kostka in Żoliborz, a district in the north of the capital, is an ugly concrete building dating from the thirties. The priest Jerzy Popiełuszko held mass here for years until, in October 1984, he was tortured and murdered by three officers of the State Security Service. Since then the church has become a place of pilgrimage. In 1985 two and a half million people flocked to the grave of the martyr. The church nave is decorated with flags displaying the holy numbers of the nation's history: 1569, 1830, 1863,

1914, 1985. The information office organizes film showings in the crypt and offers printed material in five languages. Warnings about alcoholism, dates for marriage courses, and appeals by ecological groups hang in glass cases beside the entrance. The stations of the Cross have been laid out in the little cemetery to lead pilgrims to the priest's grave. The whole area feels like an extraterritorial enclave to which the forces of the state are refused entry.

The "mass for the fatherland" takes place here on the last Sunday of every month. Ten to fifteen thousand people stand tightly pressed together in semidarkness in the big square in front of the church—men and women, children and pensioners, steelworkers and university professors. It's seven in the evening. The balcony and porch of the church are brightly illuminated, as is the priest's house next door. A crowd of nuns in white stands on the terrace. There's a tense, expectant silence.

Surprisingly, the mass begins with a political speech. An elderly gentleman with the face of a scholar translates the most important sentences for me in a whisper. "Poland must take the lead and show the way," says the priest, "then other nations too will see the light . . . Let us give thanks to our prisoners for the sufferings they have taken upon themselves." Now some leading men from the banned Solidarity union, who have been released because of the amnesty, appear on the balcony. They are greeted with applause. The photographers' flashlights and the Western television spotlights don't seem to disturb anyone. The rite of the mass is frequently interrupted by storms of applause and by interludes. Actors recite patriotic poems with tearful pathos. A little band performs some hits on drums and electric guitar. One can't accuse this Church of being afraid of kitsch. The atmosphere is that of a political rally. Patriotism and religion enter a mystic union here. A feverish, ecstatic tone dominates the sermons. The lost eastern territories are invoked between offertory and sanctus: "We pray for our brothers in Vilnius and L'wow."—"The Polish nation, crucified by a godless power, follows Christ's path." The outside world is not mentioned in any of the long speeches. It's impossible to imagine a single word being spoken here about Chile, South Africa, or Guatemala.

The Church's sense of power is unbroken. It is not afraid. Its monopoly position is quite clear. It commands the only public space into which the power of the state cannot penetrate. The flight from the loneliness of the suburbs ends here in national communion. "Holy Fatherland"—no one in this square flinches at such a phrase. After one and a half hours in the cold, the communion host is passed into the crowd. No one moves from the spot. The singing congregation holds out thousands of little crucifixes toward the priest, countless hands form a *V* as a sign of victory over the Empire of Evil and Darkness. Emotion, a sense of mission, tear-filled eyes. After the mass, delegations from dozens of factories, mines, and cooperatives march around the church in a long procession with their rebellious slogans. As in old Jerusalem, even the cleverest governor would be hard pressed to distinguish between a pilgrimage and a demonstration. When the crowd scatters peacefully around ten, there isn't a policeman in sight.

A bare apartment in an old building in Praga repaired in a makeshift way by the tenant himself. Only an elegant but battered bureau piled with manuscripts and leaflets, and the library of books in several languages that cover the walls on roughhewn shelves, point to a middle-class past. We sit around a paraffin heater and drink tea. We are in that imaginary place called *Mitteleuropa*, which consists of only a few thousand such apartments scattered across the map: Zagreb, Brno, Budapest, Vienna, Kraków, Trieste, Berlin. Even the hospitality here is colored by this iridescent past, by its agreements and disputes. I've simply been taken along, a stranger who an hour before was still standing in the dark, in the crowd in front of the church. Someone who couldn't understand what everyone else there understood. One had to whisper what everyone else knew into his ear, and then invite him home in order to argue with him.

My host, the interpreter, really was a scholar. He lost his professorship some time ago, but this has only increased his authority. He lives from hand to mouth, like his students assembled here. There is an air of conspiracy about the little meeting, half salon, half seminar. They talk about Berdyayev and Buber, Nietzsche and Dostoyevsky. To my astonishment, they also appear to think highly of Klages and Ernst Jünger. "Rationalism is finished."—"Perhaps the turning point, the metaphysical reversal that is being signaled everywhere in the world, will begin here. This is the opportunity presented by Poland's misfortune, it is concealed within it like the kernel in the nut. The pope is the symbol of this hope."—"There are already clear signs of a spiritual rebirth in America, but a civilization built on material values will find it difficult to take the necessary steps."

I listen patiently, but eventually I risk putting in a word for common sense. I find the whole discussion pretty eccentric, I assert that, leaving ideology aside, Soviet power isn't going to be expelled either by prayer or by conspiracies. "If you were in Jaruzelski's shoes," I ask, "what kind of compromise would you aim for?"

It was as if, with this modest question, I had stirred up a hornet's nest. "What you call common sense is capitulation, the surrender of every value. Going by that principle, the Poles would have ceased to exist a hundred and fifty years ago! If we had compromised we wouldn't be here anymore. Do you know what the official Russian position is? They distinguish three pillars of counterrevolution in Poland: the Church, agriculture, and the intelligentsia. Converted into strategic terms, that means the intellectuals, the peasants, and the Catholics have to be exterminated in order to achieve communism in Poland. Don't you think that's pretty close to Hitler's program?"

I give up trying to argue. The conversation turns to Heidegger's relationship to Christianity. I'm dead tired.

A very young student accompanies me on the way home. Dressed in black, mustached, and pale with ardor, he looks like a nineteenth-century Polish conspirator.

"Imagine, just for the sake of discussion, that the Soviet occupation had disappeared overnight: what should a free Poland, if it were up to you, do with the people you call collaborators and traitors?" He stops—we're in the middle of the bridge across the Vistula, the moon is shining on the river—and shouts, "Hang them!"—"That's not a very Christian thought," I remark. "After all, you're talking about millions of people."—"But the Communist Party is a criminal organization! It must be eliminated. We will have to do here what you failed to do in Germany." We continue walking. I'm silent. After a long pause, my companion admits, "Well, that's what I say now . . . But if it ever really happened . . . I can't even imagine it . . . There would be such confusion . . . Everybody trying to make themselves heard . . . Everything would be turned upside down, but in the end we would probably get along with one another again."

WARSAW, TUESDAY/WEDNESDAY

The people of this city are always looking for something: a watertap, a book, an apartment, a couple of pints of gas. I'm looking for a rare commodity too. I need a small grain of common sense. Or is the phrase "reasonable Pole" an oxymoron, a chimera?

"Nonsense," says a Scandinavian friend I have turned to in this moment of need. "In my job"—he's a foreign correspondent—"I meet quite a varied cross-section of people, from bureaucrats to fanatics, businessmen and poets, fellow travelers and prophets, to say nothing of the silent majority. I probably don't need to tell you that I love this country— after all, I've been living here for twenty-five years—though what's much worse is that I can't live without it. It gives me my daily dose of adrenalin. The West is too sleepy, too self-satisfied for me. But there's also something I hate about the Poles, and that's their endless posing and their constant emotionalism. This habit of posturing, it doesn't just get on my nerves, it's also politically disastrous. The worst thing is that this defect has always afflicted the opposition above all. Terrible!"

"But aren't there very good grounds for having such an attitude? Do you know what my unreasonable acquaintances said? 'Had we, as decent pragmatists, submitted to the reality of power, then the Poles would have disappeared a hundred years ago.' Don't you think there's something to that?"

"No. Those are historical projections. I don't want to come across as a friend of the Soviet Union, but I don't believe that anyone today wants to exterminate the Poles. It's just nonsense! The Russians long ago accepted the fact that socialism doesn't have a chance in Poland, and that they have to put up with a traditionalist, conservative, clerical neighbor. They have accepted that freedom of opinion exists here to a degree which is unparalleled in the Eastern Bloc, including Hungary. Never have so many Poles traveled abroad as in the last few years, and that means to the West.

"And, God knows, the dictatorship is hardly effective. The Jaruzelski government isn't even capable of controlling the Scouts. It's careful, clever, and on the defensive. Just don't offend the peasants! That would mean trouble. Subsidized prices have to be treated like an unexploded bomb. Any thought of fundamental economic reform is impossible under these circumstances. And as for the Church! For heaven's sake, just leave it alone! The dissidents aren't being imprisoned, they're being released. Since the last political amnesty there have been fewer political prisoners in this country than in France, Italy, or West Germany. But don't imagine that anyone is grateful to the government. Quite the reverse, the opposition is reacting by sheltering behind boycotts and verbal radicalism—sometimes there are even extreme-right-wing undertones. Anyone who doesn't go along with this polarization is ostracized."

My Norwegian friend's bare but comfortable bachelor apartment is as busy as a railroad station. One of those who come to visit him, drink a cup of Nescafé, and smoke a pipe while I'm sitting there is the journalist Adam Krzemiński. He belongs to the minority that advocates a realistic relationship between the conflicting interests. Consequently, he has fallen between two stools, a position he finds altogether reasonable, given the existing seating arrangements.

According to him, martial law was not really necessary. "The mass movement of opposition would have run aground on its own mistakes, it never had any realistic, long-term plans. Workers' control is an honorable aim, but the Gdansk shipyards would have been bankrupt long ago without huge state subsidies. Yet no one in the opposition wants to think about productivity and international competition. It makes demands, but the thought of giving anything in return never occurs to it. It never asks itself what consequences an action has. In a word, they're in cloud-cuckoo-land. More than anything else this country needs to get rid of its illusions, but I don't see it happening."

In a gloomy café in the Old Town I meet a young critic. He lost his job with a publisher after failing some loyalty test, and now he's getting by, with some difficulty, as a translator. But P. refuses to play the victim of political persecution. He considers himself an outsider for quite different reasons.

"The Party can't stand the intellectuals, and vice versa, that's quite normal. Communism is ideologically bankrupt. In this country a bus conductor earns three times as much as a doctor or an academic. The regime's motto is: 'If little Jack is nice to God, God will be nice to little Jack.' If you don't behave yourself, you won't eat. It's idiotic and it doesn't work. Personally I'm more bothered by the Poles' religious paranoia. If things keep going the way they are now, the Church will soon have gathered all the intellectuals in the country around it. Anyone who dares to criticize Woytila is already treated like a pariah. The opposition seems to believe that there is no intellectual bliss outside the Church. When you also remember that the clergy is incapable of self-criticism—the Church has never come to terms with its anti-Semitic past— you'll realize that prospects don't look very rosy for people like me. I admit that such a situation is unlikely, but if Poland were ever ruled by the Church instead of the Party, emigration would be the only choice."

"So you believe that secularization has definitively failed in your country?"

"I wouldn't say that. I can't conceive of a theocracy in Europe. 'In Poland everyone believes in God, but only to spite the Reds.' I'm quoting Marek Edelman, an old Bundist.* He's the last survivor of the Warsaw Ghetto Uprising. I think he's right. But there's something else. In the last forty years people have gotten used to their lack of responsibility. They need a roof over their heads. The more water comes through the ceiling of the Communist barracks, the more determined they are to find some other shelter. At least you don't get wet under the dome of the Church! But perhaps my point of view is too subjective . . ."

* Bund (union): Abbreviation for the General Jewish Workers' Union of Russia and Poland, i.e., Jewish Socialist Party. Active in the Jewish Pale of Settlement from the 1890s to the 1920s. (Trans.)

P. is one of the few Jewish intellectuals who have remained in Poland.

Finally, Ryszard Kapuściński. Masterly and outstandingly intelligent, he is a poet who disguises himself as a reporter and has seen the whole world. His theme is power. His most important books deal with Poland, but by distancing themselves from Poland as much as possible. (The subject of his best book, *King of Kings*, is the reign of Haile Selassie.) Kapuściński is a man in middle age, a hard worker, an observer who misses little, is untiring and ready to help. He wears faded jeans or old battle fatigues and is always in a hurry.

"Sorry I'm late."

"I know. Work . . . I know all about it."

"If it were only work! The excessive demands are much worse. What I mean is more embarrassing. I feel like a con man. In this country the intellectual, especially the writer, is considered a kind of moral court of appeal, an adviser on every one of life's problems. I think it's terrible that such authority is simply attributed to one, but it's impossible to get rid of. It has very little to do with the quality of work anyone produces. It's enough not to allow yourself to be bought— and in next to no time you've been transformed into a father confessor, a guru, a prophet. The Poles regard their intelligentsia as a substitute for their absent sovereignty. Of course, it's all a mystification, because it's completely impossible to fulfill such expectations. It's an anachronism! An impossibility! Purely nineteenth-century. Many of my colleagues come to believe in the role they're assigned. In fact, we're alarmingly provincial. That's also true of the opposition. It believes in miracles. It underestimates not only the Russians but its own country's ruling class as well."

Silently I swore never again to doubt Polish reason. "There is one question in particular that I would like to ask you because until now I have found no one able to answer it: What do those in power think? I try to understand the measures they take, but I'm unable to recognize any strategy. What kind of future does the government expect? What is its agenda?"

He smiled mirthlessly. "It doesn't have an agenda. It's the same situation everywhere—in society, in politics, in culture, in the economy. A state of absolute stalemate, of total blockage."

We were sitting in the coffee shop of the Forum Hotel. America on the cheap, furniture as if from Swedish do-it-yourself kits, fast food Polish-style. In my excitement I let the meal get cold.

"But that's impossible. Economically at least, no government, whatever else it's up to, can get by without long-term planning."

"Since Gierek's failure it has been impossible to talk about economic thinking. Productivity doesn't count in Poland. Government, trade unions, and the opposition are all agreed on that point. Heavy industry operates without consideration for costs—partly under direct Russian control. Of course, we have four or five economies apart from the state sector: a private economy, a black-market economy, a mixed sector, and on top of that a subsistence economy and a dollar-based economy. Heavy industry keeps on producing but it has no future. The infrastructure is breaking down, the coal mines are caving in, the environment is being destroyed, and there's no money for new investments. Every reform the system can conceive of has either been tried already, in which case it didn't work, or else been blocked, by the Russians, the bureaucracy, or the organized interest groups. We've got our backs against the wall. The managers of the big plants are working two or three months ahead at most, and sometimes just from week to week. People are already lining up now, in September, for coal. Everyone agrees that winter is coming, but the system is not in a position to prepare for this contingency. An energy crisis is inevitable.

"What all of this means for the mood of the people is obvious. They're embittered, worn out, anxious. Even the workers feel they've come down in the world. The Poles used to be considered courteous. If that was ever true, it isn't anymore. In such conditions it's impossible to motivate anyone to any effort that goes beyond individual self-preservation. I don't believe that the government set collective depression as its political goal, but that's what the result comes to."

"To self-destruction?"

"To self-preservation at any price. If one's capable of thinking only a few weeks ahead, one can hardly tell the difference."

"And who is to blame for the whole mess?"

"Well, that's a good question. Everyone you ask will suggest a different scapegoat. Usually it's the Party or the Soviet Union. But the economic catastrophe has deeper roots. I don't want to bore you with a summary of historical facts, but I can't avoid mentioning the partition of Poland in the nineteenth century, because one consequence was that a Polish bourgeoisie was unable to develop. It was German and Jewish entrepreneurs who introduced capitalism to Poland. And the Second Republic had too little time and too many conflicts to catch up. You know what happened next: the Polish bourgeoisie, which included the relatively small Polish intelligentsia, was liquidated by the Germans and the Russians. You only need to look at the statistics: the urban population was reduced by 40 percent in the forties, that of the countryside by only 5 percent. The Jews were almost completely exterminated. It's a wonder that there's anything like a Polish intelligentsia today at all. In short, what we lack is not factories or even capital but a leadership stratum in the European sense of the term."

"Nevertheless, the regime has had forty years to train its own cadres."

"But our ruling class has come straight from the Third World! You don't know the dumps in the east where the children went barefoot until not so long ago and the teachers were illiterate! A purely agrarian society. By the way, that also explains the cultural hegemony of the Church. The information medium of the peasants is the sermon, they don't have anything else. And as for our so-called cadres, it must be obvious that they have no ideas, perspectives, or aspirations whatsoever, apart from careerism. They're ignorant and brutal. At best, they possess a degree of cunning."

"If we go back a couple of generations, we all come from some village or other. In that sense we're all backwoodsmen."

"Look. I come from a remote little hole in White Russia. I always feel ill at ease in Paris or London. I *am* the Third World. My work depends on it. I understand what's happening in San Salvador, in Iran, or Ethiopia, because I'm a Pole."

Bedtime reading. "How easy it is to subdue this country, which is constantly being alarmed by domestic and foreign conspiracies. All that's required is a temperature of twenty degrees centigrade and twenty inches of snow and there are already problems with the bread supply. But where are the causes of all this to be sought? Who is to be blamed? The government? The system? Russia? Ourselves? This winter has revealed something—not only the weakness of the economy and the administration but something considerably more important: namely, the lack of clarity about who is trying to frustrate a diagnosis of our social reality. For years now we have not known what we are capable of and who we really are: a country without freedom or a nation of alcoholics, a leading industrial power or an exploited colony or the eternal Polish shambles. Are we martyrs, anti-Semites, or a society that has not adapted to modern civilization? . . . And so we live somewhere between servitude and fiction, in conditions that persist whether we accept them or not, and that are constantly working on us and changing us. Until finally one winter we discover that it has snowed. Then we ask ourselves, Is this our snow? Is it our job to clear it away? Because possibly it's their snow, forced upon us by the Russians within the framework of friendship, and so shouldn't they remove it themselves? We are being asked to volunteer to clear the snow. But we don't know who is appealing to us: civil society or the authorities we want to get rid of but can't.

"Still, we look around for shovels, we have to dig ourselves out somehow, we have to get going. And then it turns out that there are no shovels. So then we ask ourselves, Who is supposed to provide the shovels—the government or the people? *Them* or us? We stand in the snow, deep in thought yet incapable of drawing any conclusions. The lack of shovels not only demobilizes our energies, it paralyzes our minds."*

WARSAW, THURSDAY

Don't feel like going out.

In the afternoon I force myself to call up Jadwiga and apologize. One can't survive here without a guardian angel. We assure each other that our argument was only a misunderstanding. The reconciliation is sealed over tea and tarts. If everything goes well, then the day after tomorrow we shall drive south in the Polski Fiat.

WARSAW, FRIDAY

Surprising turn of events: I've been invited on an excursion into the past, or was what I saw today the future? In this part of Europe it's not always easy to tell the difference.

"If you can't cope with all the consonants in my name,"

---

* *Kazimierz Brandys; I have slightly altered Richard Lourie's English translation of Brandys'* A Warsaw Diary, 1978–1981 *(New York, 1984). (Trans.)*

said Grzegorz in faultless English, "just call me Gregory. I've been told that you want to write something about Poland. Not a simple business. If you've got nothing special to do this afternoon, forget your work for a couple of hours. I'd be very happy to show you my collection."

His riding breeches were as perfect as his accent and his manners. He was almost sixty, at once languid and wiry, and his bushy, reddish, carefully plucked eyebrows reminded me of those prewar cavalry officers of Polish legend. But I knew that his military career had been short and had ended in prison. As a young man, he had fought in the Home Army.* He was arrested after the Soviet troops had marched in. When he came home, his parents were dead and the family possessions had been expropriated. Hard times for the rural nobility. But there was no mention of such memories as we drove out of the city in Gregory's car. We went south along the Vistula for just under an hour. Once we had left the obligatory small talk behind us, I cautiously asked about his computers.

"Ah, you've heard about my sideline? Don't tell anyone, but basically I don't know a thing about computers. I find them boring."

I didn't believe a word, but I thought it best to remain silent.

"Pure chance that I got involved with the things. It could just as easily have been cotton or excavators. Only those useful objects don't have the same aura or, let's say, the same ideological sex appeal. People are mad about computers in this country. The things are being torn out of my hands. I haven't the faintest idea why every screw factory and every district administration absolutely must have a computer. But the bureaucrats expect miracles from them. And of course

* The Polish underground forces that obeyed the command of the Polish government in exile in London. (Trans.)

everything has to come from the West, hardware, software, peripherals . . ."

"Nevertheless, I assume the business is not entirely without risk. A small shakeup in the Party apparatus, one of the regular changes of course, and before you know it there are accusations of economic crimes and the black market . . ."

"Ugly words," said Gregory. "You're right, of course. But bear in mind that some branches of the administration are among my best customers, to say nothing of the state enterprises."

"And what about problems with the customs, the American embargo provisions, currency controls?"

"True," sighed Gregory. "All in all, it's a tedious profession. But we've arrived."

The avenue led straight to the main building, an extensive early-nineteenth-century wooden house that glowed snow-white in the dusk. The first guests were already waiting for us in the hall, a stage designer and his wife, an actor, a woman gallery owner—not a soul who could understand even the first principles of Basic or Fortran. But the most remarkable thing about the long room with its high, paneled ceiling were the walls. Gregory's collection of Polish painters from the turn of the century was overpowering. City night scenes, "nocturnes," blurred landscapes, coloristic, shimmering portraits—an art movement I knew nothing about. They could probably be placed somewhere between Symbolism, Art Nouveau, and Late Impressionism, but to my eyes these pictures were very autonomous, very distinctive. I asked my host about the history of his collection.

"All acquired in the last twelve years," he said. "Before that I had my hands full with the house. When I managed, after a lot of wrangling, to buy the house back, it was in a terrible mess. After the expropriation it had been taken over by some state organization, but the rooms proved unsuitable and so it was left empty for a long time. The roof had nearly caved in. Of course, I only acquired the house, the land is farmed by other people. I don't care about the furniture, as you can see it's all just thrown together. Instead, I began to be interested in these painters. There are a couple of famous names among them, but most were undervalued or forgotten. However, that has certainly changed in the last few years . . . What do you want to drink? Vodka? Port? Sherry?"

"The pictures in your house are dark, but the atmosphere is cheerful," I said. He laughed.

"You've been infected, haven't you? Poland is a tragic country, the situation is hopeless . . . Or something like it. The usual depressing phrases. It's difficult to avoid the national clichés, especially for a foreigner. I'm afraid there is even a certain kind of tourist who is enthusiastic about it. They look here for what they miss at home: drama, faith, despair, perhaps even heroism. And there are all too many of my countrymen who are ready to oblige with these doubtful virtues."

"But Polish history provides good cause for them."

"Maybe. But people also put together the past that suits them. The pale, suffering Pole, this tragic sacrificial lamb is a fairly recent figure, historically speaking. Don't forget that from the sixteenth century on we were notorious throughout Europe for our dissipation and frivolity. The Poles were thought to be a merry, extravagant nation, lurching from one banquet to the next. The songs of our Renaissance poets are evidence of that. In times of peace these propensities always come to the surface again, even in the nineteenth century. Or just think of the years between the wars.

"You must admit that it's also a question of what possibilities the economy allows, and of wealth."

"That's very true! Yes, hatred of the rich is our specialty. But it's a recent achievement. The only area in which socialism has been victorious! Envious puritans were rare in old Poland. All this talk about corruption—it's pure demagogy. Poor

Gierek! If you had actually seen his famous villas—with their gilt watertaps and all—you would feel sorry for him. They are about as luxurious as a terrace house in Liverpool or Bochum. No German greengrocer would think of moving into something like it.

"But enough of that. In the end, each of us invents his own Poland. We have no choice. We have to do things ourselves, without waiting for the Russians, the Americans, the Party, the Church, or the world market. If I had waited for the Landmarks Commission to do anything, this house would now be in ruins."

"It's easy for you to talk, Gregory."

"Do you think so? Then you should take a look at my neighbor. He farms the land that used to belong to us, and I must admit he does it better. He delivers fresh vegetables to Warsaw every day. Of course, it's making him rich. It's unavoidable. He's investing, every year he builds a couple of new greenhouses, the temperature is regulated automatically. I supplied him with the necessary computer system."

"So, despite everything, things are getting better."

"I tend not to be optimistic. It doesn't seem very helpful. We don't need prophets. The Polish situation is unpredictable. Only the provisional is true. It's quite possible—" he indicated his house and his pictures with a vague gesture—"that one day I'll lose all of this. But as long as it lasts, I feel I'm a custodian. The provisional is our strength, we've had lots of practice. And if worst comes to worst, we just have to start all over again." He turned to his friends and called, "Would you be kind enough to bring in a couple of baskets of firewood? And you could help me pull out the big table. The others should be here soon. An even dozen! Tonight we're having a party. A provisional party! I hope you'll enjoy yourself."

KATOWICE, SATURDAY

If one looks more closely, the old divisions of the country are still quite noticeable. Warsaw centralism has never quite succeeded in leveling out the differences they left behind—differences in customs, in architecture, in the appearance of the towns. Katowice (Kattowitz) is a Prussian industrial hell—Duisburg is idyllic by comparison. Kraków, humiliatingly neglected but still glorious, is, by contrast, an ancient Central European city: Polish Renaissance, Austrian Baroque, Viennese nineteenth-century.

The small towns we drive through are also reminders of lost times. The country road lined by autumnal chestnuts crosses a vast plain. We often have to pull over for horse-drawn carts loaded with coal. An old marshaling yard, rusting switch towers, grade-crossing barriers. The next town lies on the far bank of a small river. The anglers observe their silent devotions under the willows. A couple of gray geese waddle through the bushes.

In the old center of town on the other side of the bridge, there's a lively Saturday bustle. In the waiting room of the typewriting bureau—half living room, half office—are customers who want to fill out an application or hand in a petition. Lining the wall: stag antlers, dusty accordion files, and a portrait of the pope, decorated with wilted flowers. The owner smiles with restraint. He can't quite decide whether he should try to look like a lawyer or a hairdresser. The cactuses on the flower stand are a domestic touch, but the many framed diplomas lend his shop an official air, and to leave no doubt that he is on the best of terms with the authorities, he has hung up a sign that reads, "The socialist state is the most precious achievement of the Polish people."

I doubt that the women doing their weekend shopping share that view. In front of them they push their most precious achievement—the place is full of strollers. The neo-

Gothic brick church displays competing values: the Don Bosco Vocational College of the Salesians, but also the representative of the "Patriotic Movement for the Reconstruction of the Nation," founded in 1982, who is available for consultation in a crooked brick villa. And in the spirit of coexistence even the ideological enemy can offer his most precious achievements—*Once Upon a Time in America*, directed by Sergio Leone and starring Robert De Niro, is showing at the Luna cinema.

The perfume shop at the corner is selling a toilet water called Lady Day, but glass beads, plastic bags printed with Western ads, and rubber enema bags are also on sale. The gift shop displays just as comprehensive a stock: the sword of the first Polish king, Bolesław I Chobry, with a colored coat of arms, suitable for use as a letter-opener (1000 zlotys); a solid-brass truck filled with coal on an anthracite base, suitable as an ornament (350 zlotys); and, as the ultimate luxury item, an imitation Art Nouveau brass pendulum clock (10,000 zlotys).

Yes, I think I'm something of an expert on Polish marketplaces. The differences between here and Łomża, the little town in the distant northeast, stare one in the face. The park in the middle of the square had already made way for progress in the seventies. Gierek, whose power base was in the Upper Silesian coalfields, had the "Rainbow" department store built for his clientele where the park benches used to be. The late functionalist building is brutally out of place beside the old town houses, but the women's clothing department has a good selection. Only the colored-neon flicker of hope has been extinguished—the sign hasn't been working for a long time. But another achievement, the underground toilet in front of the police station, is enjoying a brisk trade.

The Party Headquarters next door seems all the sleepier by comparison. It's a venerable yellow building dating from the Austro-Hungarian Empire. If one half-closes one's eyes in the midday sun, it's possible to imagine District Commissioner von Trotta in residence and to hear the faint strains of the Radetzky March.

But the smell is disturbing. Joseph Roth could have had no inkling of such a smell. It's not just the lignite soot that covers the town. Something else, sweet and pungent, mingles with it, like the smell of gas. It must be the chemical industry, whose chimneys are visible behind the roofs of the town.

To conclude our sightseeing tour, we make a short visit to the Central Scout Store. The Scouts play an important role in Poland. Their emblem, many times enlarged, hangs on the building—a painted cardboard Maltese cross, a lily at its center, oak leaves in the background, with the motto "Be vigilant!" on the horizontal wings of the cross. In the hobby department there's a large selection of model kits for paper airplanes and tanks, but also adhesives and welding equipment. The textile department's stock is even more varied: woolen underpants, caps, uniforms, but, above all, every possible kind of badge, chevron, standard, braid, and mark of rank.

The local Scouts can also buy a shield with the name of their hometown. But who would voluntarily sew these eight red-rubber letters welded onto a green felt background onto their sleeves? The little town we visited is called OŚWIECIM— in German, Auschwitz.

WROCŁAW (BRESLAU), MONDAY

He loves Beckett, he admires him "because he breathes so calmly / in anticipation of the end of the world / but he too begins to be boring."—"He remembers while / eating sausage with sauerkraut / that poetry is dead." Title: "Poetry Has Rosy Cheeks." He's troublesome, he's famous, he's withdrawn, he sabotages every kind of approval. Tadeusz Różewicz does not draw attention to himself. You can spend the whole day with him without remembering what he was wearing. His ambition is to achieve complete inconspicuousness. I have known him for twenty years, and he surprises me again and again.

Suddenly he stops in front of the "Dragonfly" department store in the center of Wrocław. "Not bad at all," he claims. "Don't you want to go in?"

The display windows don't look very enticing. "You can really buy everything here," says Tadeusz. "This shirt, for example. Don't you need a shirt?" He holds a gray checked short-sleeved shirt under my nose as if he were trying to sell it to me. "In Germany you would have to pay thirty marks for a shirt like this. Here you can have it for three marks. A bargain!" Jadwiga, cool and distant as usual, doesn't feel like buying anything either. Am I imagining it, or did she really wink at me? It would have been the first time.

"People complain about the food supply, about prices, about their everyday troubles. And they're right, it's good to make noise, but people here live better than you think! The so-called ordinary people are very clever, they manage to find everything. The Poles are a little like the Italians, they can wangle their way through things. We're the stupid ones, the so-called intelligentsia. My son, for instance, he's a junior lecturer at the university and earns all of seven thousand zlotys [$35] a month. It's his own fault! Why didn't he become a garbage collector?"

"And you," I ask him, "don't you ever complain?"

"I don't have any time," he replies. "Gas, for example. People get upset if there isn't any gas. Then they should sell their car! I haven't had one for a year now. I walk. That's nice too."

We make for the nearest bar and allow ourselves a first beer.

"Why don't you have any time?" I ask.

"Everybody calls me up. Old ladies who write poems are unbelievably persistent. Recently a surgeon even came to me with his manuscript. Why can't he leave poetry alone? After all, I don't cut people up. Or I'm supposed to sign something, some appeal for or against something. But I'm too old, I can't be bothered. It used to take me two hours to write a poem, now it takes two months. I work a lot, but I write almost nothing."

But then he pulls a little colored booklet out of his pocket and smiles happily. It's a cheap paperback with old-fashioned illustrations, published in German in Moscow a generation ago—Grimm's Fairy Tales. "Do you know 'Clever Elsie'?" he asks. "I always read it when I can't sleep." Amidst the noise of the bar, he slowly reads out a few sentences for us in his heavy accent. " 'Clever Elsie began to doubt whether she was really Clever Elsie, and said to herself, "Am I she, or am I not?" This question she could not answer, and she stood still a long while considering. At last she thought she would go home and ask whether she was really herself—supposing they would be able to tell. When she came to the house door, it was shut; so she tapped at the window, and asked, "Hans, is Elsie inside?" "Yes," he replied, "she is." Now she was really terrified, and exclaimed, "Ah heaven, then I am not Elsie!" ' "
Tadeusz laughed. We finished our beers and left.

"Yes," he continued, "I've got problems with my apartment. They want to build another story above me, that means a whole year of noise. After a while I'll feel like poor Elsie."

"You should live on Sand Island, there are beautiful houses there."

"Yes, that's where the cardinal lives."

"You chose the wrong profession."

"Don't say that, I'm a cardinal too, only no one knows, thank God. Otherwise, even more people would call me up."

"An atheist cardinal," I said. His smile was inscrutable.

"Yes, you know, suddenly the Poles are all getting mystical again. It's an old story. Mickiewicz, Słowacki, our best writers, smart people, but suddenly one day they become mystics. It's an occupational hazard, like silicosis for miners."

"People need a roof when it rains."

"Yes, yes, I understand that . . . But must they all write in Church newspapers? The same people who used to look at me suspiciously because I wasn't a proper Marxist . . . What Różewicz writes is nothing but petty-bourgeois nihilism, they used to say! And now they've all gone pious."

I glanced uneasily at Jadwiga, but my guardian angel didn't move a muscle.

"Well," said my friend the poet eventually, "there's no need to be frightened, this isn't Paraguay, Poland isn't going to become a Jesuit state . . . I'm the last rationalist in this country. You can have my autograph."

Meanwhile we'd arrived at the next bar. I told Tadeusz about the awards ceremony I had attended in Warsaw Castle. "Decorations and orders are nice too," he said, "why not, and they're inexpensive. We've got a new minister of culture now. He's a classicist and is supposed to be a man of some wit. Everything's bound to get better again, it's not impossible, I'm an optimist. But that's for my grandchildren. I'm sixty-five. I don't need any more ministers."

The last flies buzzed around the table. We drank.

"Medals are very nice," said Tadeusz, "but we have to try and see what's underneath"—he pointed under the table—"and that's very difficult." His voice was very quiet, as if he had eaten a mouthful of chalk. There's nothing you can do to get around people like that, I thought. Neither pressure nor seduction works. He's small, white-haired, and pigheaded. He sees through everything. Every government is powerless against him.

ŁÓDŹ, WEDNESDAY

An involuntary stop. The Polski Fiat has shaken us along almost twelve hundred fifty miles of Polish country road without complaining—apart from a little difficulty with windshield wipers. These are attached to their mounting by just a loose prong. We soon discovered how the owner had solved the problem: he wrapped old newspapers around the fitting to reinforce it. But this solution worked only in good weather. As soon as it began to rain, the mass of paper turned soggy and the wipers threatened to fly off the windshield. We didn't take offense at this small shortcoming. But now, just as we had crossed the bridge on the Warta in the direction of Warsaw, the engine began to make highly disturbing noises. So chance has brought us to Łódź. The first gas station attendant we could find diagnosed transmission failure. This brought our pleasure trip to an end.

Undaunted, Jadwiga promises to make a virtue of necessity. She has friends everywhere, so she has friends here too. Tomorrow they will show us "the ugliest city in Europe." Łódź, which Poles also call "the unloved one," has a promising reputation.

ŁÓDŹ, THURSDAY

Woke up with symptoms of an impending flu. No wonder, when I think of my coal-black handkerchiefs and the stabbing bronchial pains that attacked me, unused as I was to breathing under such adverse conditions, in the Silesian coalfields.

The city is demonic. Esthetic judgments are irrelevant. Its chaotic topography would be the despair of any town planner. Łódź is the Wild East made stone: there are traces of past greed and exploitation everywhere. The place grew in such a violent and uncontrolled manner that without our local guides—J. is an unemployed journalist who writes for the underground press, Sława is a gentle, plump graphic artist— we would not even have found the center of town. The inhabitants crowd through this muddle as if trying to clear up after an earthquake or an air raid. And yet, except for the ghetto area that was reduced to rubble by the Germans, the war spared the city. The decisive blows had already been struck a century before—the city's heyday was also an earthquake, an early capitalist catastrophe.

The factory is the heart of this community. One stands in front of the gigantic old brick fortresses in which the looms throb and the spinning machines hum today, just as they did fifty or a hundred years ago. Dreadfully little has changed here since Reymont and Israel Joshua Singer wrote their breathless novels *The Promised Land* and *The Brothers Ashkenazi.* Even the main railroad station in Łódź bears the name Fabryczna (factory).

Nowhere in the world is the machinery of exploitation so openly displayed. Right next to the machine hall rises the palace of the manufacturer, a shameless, megalomaniac, and gruesome neo-baroque edifice "in the French style." In the enormous, icy ballroom the letter *P* in the cartouches beneath the naked youths and women immortalizes the name of Poznański, who began as a ragman and ended as a textile magnate. You can see him, a plaster Bacchus garlanded with vines, grinning down from the twenty-foot-high ceiling of the hall of mirrors. And a stone's throw away, on the other side of the street, stands the company housing he had built between 1880 and 1890. The façades are blackened as if by fire, the stairways are damp, the rooms tiny, dark, and low. There are two wooden chests secured with padlocks in front of the door to each apartment, one for coal, one for sauerkraut. J.'s father lived here. The son knows the place, he knows the old stories of rickets and tuberculosis, strikes and police raids, and of the barricades erected again and again in the back courts.

But the miserable history of the Łódź proletariat is not yet over. The future of the textile industry looks gloomy, the factories are out of date, and little money is invested—the situation of the women workers is correspondingly hopeless. Nowhere are wages so low as in Łódź, nowhere is infant mortality so high, nowhere do people live in worse conditions.

* * *

In the monstrous brick castle that once belonged to Poznański—it is still the largest cotton mill in Europe—five thousand women on piecework rates toil around the clock in three shifts. A trade union investigation showed that a woman textile worker who has to provide for a family must make do with an average of five and a half hours of sleep a night. During one of the big strikes of the seventies, the women occupied the factory. They demanded that the Party and government leader of the time negotiate with them personally. When he appeared, after days of hesitation, there were explosive scenes. The women pelted him with dry rolls and moldy sausages. If the security police had not rescued Gierek by helicopter, he could hardly have escaped in one piece.

J. tells me this story over lunch. We are in a pub on the Street of the Siege of Stalingrad, only no one calls it that. Its old patriotic name, Street of the Eleventh of November, has withstood every rebaptism. It commemorates the prewar Second Republic. When the early shift goes home in the morning, the vodka is already flowing freely at the widow Szmidtowa's, Category III. The food is cheap and good. Szmidtowa herself died a year ago, but the whole quarter pays its respects to her memory. Stalin always had to take second place in her bar, even in the early fifties, because she refused to take the religious picture down from the wall. The toughest characters became as gentle as lambs under her maternal gaze and quietly went home when she showed them the door after their tenth glass. The old waiter who serves us shows not a trace of interest, but the whole place pricks up its ears. We appear suspicious to the regulars. "It's a good thing it's still so early," says J. quietly. "There could be trouble when those guys get more than a glassful inside them. The older ones don't like to hear anyone speaking German here."

In the afternoon we went to the bazaar at the end of Petrowka Street, which was once called the "Red Market." As is to be expected in this town, it outdoes everything else I've seen of Polish markets. Here too the long hall reminiscent of a Zeppelin hangar is "closed for repairs." The sign with the word *remont* (repairs), ubiquitous in Poland, tells passersby: Abandon all hope. Instead, the open-air market offers an overpowering sight. There are swarms of fortune-tellers who for two hundred zlotys, for twenty zlotys, or for a cigarette, will reveal all the secrets of the future; cripples who doggedly haggle over a parcel of lingerie; shapeless, prematurely aged women crowded around a barrel of pickled cucumbers; a crippled veteran in a wheelchair who lurches through the crowd busily operating his controls. I feel as if I'd stumbled into a Neapolitan freak show, I rub my eyes and, feeling quite bewildered, look at what's for sale: computer programs among the brussels sprouts, *samizdat* porn, "sweet bars" from the GDR—a kind of chocolate substitute that makes a profit of 400 percent for the smuggler. Also, a black-plastic devil that sticks out an obscene rosy-rubber tongue when you squash its head, and a live rooster. "Too bad for you, my beauty," murmurs the peasant woman, stroking him.

A few rows farther on, "industry"—stalls on which spare parts, smashed appliances, scrap from a hundred car wrecks overflow. An archeologist could reconstruct our technological civilization from these remains, piece together a complete television or a whole Mercedes from the parts, just as a Greek amphora is reconstructed from its fragments . . . And behind the market is the massive, threatening silhouette of a power station that, rammed right into the heart of the city, emits hissing, evil-smelling, poisonous clouds.

ŁÓDŹ, FRIDAY

In this town even the cemeteries seem to be without shape or plan. They sprawl, as if even death were unable to rein in the energy of the founding fathers buried here. The Protestant cemetery shows the part played by German entrepreneurs in the rise and the shaping of Łódź's industry. "Their whole life through / They were hard-working, charitable, and true." One of the textile millionaires, a certain Scheibler, had the replica of a neo-Gothic church built for himself in the middle of the necropolis, on a scale of one to one. The sarcophagus in which he was interred at the turn of the century acts as the altar. The pointed Gothic windows have been bricked up, and the iron gates are rusty. Broken-off spirelets and finials lie smashed on the ground and overgrown with weeds. But Scheibler—"who faithfully fulfilled his duty"—built for the Day of Judgment, and so his cathedral-mausoleum survived even the shells of the Red Army with only a few scratches.

But what does the German cemetery amount to compared to that other necropolis which, hidden behind high walls, spreads across a huge area in the north of the city! The place is difficult to find. You walk for almost a quarter of an hour along an old, mossy cart path to a tiny entry, step through a rusted door, and find yourself in a yard where goats graze and hens scratch the ground. Two barking dogs bare their teeth. A man is hammering away at an old, battered car; a second man fidgeting with a cement mixer glances suspiciously at us. Above the ruined consecration hall is the Star of David.

Before the Second World War, one-third of Łódź's inhabitants were Jewish. Now only the cemetery still bears witness to the dominant role that Jews once played in this city. After decades of neglect the whole expanse has become a second Angkor Wat. The mausoleums stand among giant weeds like lost temples in the jungle. Trees have split open the stones, marble plaques and cast-iron railings have fallen victim to grave robbers. A metal plaque, placed here in 1970 and already almost illegible, commemorates the hostages shot by the SS here in 1944.

A hundred paces farther on, the grave of Ładysław Goldberg, who died on March 15, 1908, displays an allegory of mortality: a broken column. But more recently it fell over.

What was already broken, broke a second time. So the whole cemetery has become a memorial twice over, a palimpsest of death.

The flu has reached my sinuses, and I wonder if I haven't taken the wrong pills. I stagger through the undergrowth. A domed Egyptian building emerges out of the wilderness like a hallucination. It's the temple of the ragman Poznański. The interior of the building is boarded up, but the mosaics have disappeared and the gold leaf has been scratched off the pillars. A five-pointed star flanked by two inverted crosses with the number 666 above it has been clumsily painted on the marble. The accompanying words read, "Satan is our love, Lucifer our guide." It's the motto of a Satanist sect that has spread throughout the city's secondary schools in recent years, worrying both Church and Party.

In the evening, a big farewell dinner at Sława's. She lives with her husband and two children in a two-room apartment on Wschodnia Street. The house is in an old slum area. Vodka can be bought here at any time of the day or night. The bootleggers hide their stock in the hydrants and meter boxes at the house entrances. The oldest and cheapest whores in the city have their beat here too. The dark tenement block was built in 1905 and looks as if no one has since lifted a finger to repair it. The narrow inner courtyard reminds me of a prison. A cheap, private workingman's café has established itself under the stairs. But today a festive table awaits us, abundance instead of shortage. Not only has Sława's husband, a delicate-looking man with the large, dark eyes of a prophet, managed to found a private publishing company that operates in the narrow gray zone between censorship and *samizdat* and publishes exquisite bibliophile editions in tiny numbers—he is also an outstanding cook. He bustles about in the kitchen, where toys, brooms, and boxes are piled up beside Sława's desk, and creates a wonderful dinner amidst the chaos. Except I was unable to appreciate the aroma that filled the apartment. I was firmly in the grip of the virus, and a hot fog was rising in my brain.

"Assuming," I said, before the soup had arrived on the table, "assuming the first free elections to the Polish Parliament took place tomorrow . . ." I don't know what devil had gotten into me to suggest such a game.

"A silly idea," said Sława. "You know what things are like here."

"But just suppose, for the sake of argument," I responded lamely.

"Who's going to run?"

"No idea. But for a start, there absolutely has to be a Catholic Party."

"Forty percent," J. called out. "Assuming it includes the peasants."

"Don't be silly, thirty at most," said Sława's husband, holding the soup tureen.

"Then the Social Democrats," I continued.

The numbers came promptly and firmly, like auction bids: "Twenty-five!"—"Thirty-six!"—"And the right?" I asked.

"National Democrats and Piłsudski supporters, ten percent. That leaves the right-wing extremists. There'll always be eight percent who are Fascists."—"Eight percent? Impossible!"

"And what about the Communists?" I asked.

"The Communists will be banned, of course."

"Are you crazy? That would be the biggest mistake possible. I say five percent."—"Nonsense! At least twice as much. All the people who are scared of losing their jobs, their country houses, their pensions. The riot police alone. That's millions of people!"

After a long, fierce argument, the dinner party agreed on the following result: Social Democrats 32 percent, Christian Socials 36 percent, Peasants' Party 7 percent, National Democrats 9 percent, right-wing extremists 5 percent, Communists 11 percent.

"But that's sensational!" I cried. "Do you know what that

means? First, forty years of party propaganda was a waste of time. Second, Poland is, politically speaking, a quite normal European country. Just like France or Italy!"

They didn't want to accept that. "Just imagine how chaotic it would be!"—"Splits, brawls, street fights!"—"It would be madness, all our faults would come to the surface!" They laughed. I had infected them. They were bubbling over with self-critical excitement.

"Apart from that, it's fantasy to think of the Poles as good Europeans. We don't have a clue about what you call normality. We're not ready for it. Hasn't anyone told you how vain and self-centered we are? We're a backward nation obsessed by our own problems."

"And you've forgotten something else. We don't know how to get along with our neighbors. Because for as long as we can remember, these neighbors have always had only one idea: to attack us. We've gotten used to that. I'm not at all sure that we can manage without enemies. At any rate, we'd drive you all crazy with our special demands and our touchiness."

Shaken by attacks of coughing, I contradicted them. I assured them that Europe needed Poland. "Even your mistakes are badly needed," I said. "What else is Europe but a conglomeration of mistakes? Mistakes that are so diverse that they complement and balance one another. Taken separately, we're each unbearable in our own way. Just look at the Swiss or the Greeks! To say nothing of the Germans."

Then Sława's husband brought in the roast hare, and a long, respectful silence settled over the table.

A few glasses later, J. asked me what I had thought of Łódź. "Unforgettable," I replied. "A brutal marvel. But one should . . ." I paused.

"One should what?"

"It should be possible to do something . . . develop a project, make proposals . . . One can't just let a town like this go to the dogs! The textile industry is a monoculture, a dying monster . . . You must think of something! For example . . . The film studios. Yes, of course! Munk, Polański, Wajda. You've got this famous film school here, and a lot of theater. People like you, journalists, musicians, directors, graphic artists, writers . . . That would be the solution! Łódź must become the media metropolis of the East. Television studios, printing presses, record companies, editorial offices, data banks, publishers, satellite stations . . . An industry of the future. Any number of jobs. As many jobs as you like." There was no stopping me.

"Get rid of the noise and dirt, the antediluvian looms and Warsaw regimentation! A great debate on the future of the city. A project. Why don't you propose it?"

I stopped, fork in hand. The circle of my friends stared at me as if I were mad. Jadwiga laid a cool hand on my forehead. "He's got a temperature," she said. Her gray eyes examined me with a mixture of mockery and sympathy.

We turned our attention to the dessert. After a long pause Sława asked me, "How much longer are you staying in Poland?"

"I'm leaving tomorrow."

"In your condition? Out of the question."

She was right. I couldn't get another mouthful down.

"Please forgive me," I said. "What I was saying before was really naïve. I know very well that things aren't so simple."

"Don't worry," said Jadwiga. "We don't even understand ourselves." She spoke so quietly that I had trouble hearing her. "You already know that we are more pious, brave, and clever than all the rest. But you don't seriously believe that we can be saved, do you?"

Her voice sounded strangely soothing. The tiled stove glowed. I wanted to contradict her, but I could feel my eyes closing and only managed to mumble something feebly and gratefully.

SPANISH SHARDS

[1 9 8 5]

*"From the shards one knows the pot,
and from the chaff the grain."*

....

THE PALACE AND THE SOUK

"**T**he city has a festive atmosphere." That's what it says, in black and white, in Europe's stupidest travel guide. The Madrileños have no reason to open the book, but if they saw this sentence they would feel insulted. They are proud of the unpleasantness of their metropolis, its rush, its noise, the rapid turnover of ideas. Madrid's population can't explode fast enough for them. They can hardly wait for it to pass the five million mark, and they feel flattered if foreign visitors recklessly compare Madrid to New York. They love their fourteen-lane boulevard, the Paseo de la Castellana. Only someone weary of life could think of going for a walk on this promenade. The Madrileños will even boast a little about their crime rate. The word *chulo* is seldom mentioned without a note of admiration. The dictionary says: "a vain, impudent, rude fellow; a tough; a crook, pimp, or thief; child of Madrid, typical representative of Madrid's working class."

Madrid is about as festive as Moscow or Houston. From the start everything was always one size too big, even when the capital was still a sleepy hole on the bleak Castilian plateau. Its architecture is monumental and tasteless—power and repression have always been at home here. In this city it's not easy to tell a ministry from a bank, or a bank from a barracks. Their portals are all so enormous that the general, the president, the minister would all have to stand on tiptoe just to reach the door handles.

The overbearing gesture is as old as the place itself. A good three hundred years ago a Spanish king took a look at his country, and behold!—the periphery was blooming and full of life, but the center was waste and empty, so he pointed his finger at the map and spoke: Here let us build palaces. And it came to pass, and ever since then Madrid has been designed to impress the periphery. However, the charm and the vitality of the city lie not in its façade of power but in its underside. Anarchy lurks behind the ceremonial bureaucracy. Hundreds of thousands of adventurers have moved to Madrid, and it is to them that the city owes its uncurbed and plebeian spirit.

At night the downtown is like an anthill. It's impossible to think of sleeping. If the infernal traffic on the Gran Vía pauses at the lights for a moment, then the oriental singsong of the lottery ticket sellers can be heard, promising passersby the joys of paradise like muezzins. Flanked by their two children sleeping on the pavement, a ragged couple has unrolled their mattress in front of a movie theater. The family drama and the story of their homelessness are told on a giant hand-painted poster. The board is protected against rain by a plastic sheet. No one stops to study the endless correspondence with officials and courts, the photocopied documents and eviction notices. There are only five coins in the tin plate. The Madrileños don't believe a word. They say, "You can write anything you like on paper. They're professionals; they've been here for weeks already. Only foreigners fall for it."

The Rastro is the souk, the grand bazaar, of the capital. This is where Europe ends. Forty-five pesetas gets you there. That's the cost of the subway, which runs from the Spanish capital to the Orient in a matter of minutes. Even buying a dog on a Sunday morning is no problem in Madrid. You can have a boxer out of a cardboard box or a chow out of a beer crate. Right next to the dogs there are oil paintings—hundreds, thousands of oil paintings, a whole street is covered with them.

The range of skeleton keys is fantastic. Even the lover of

used nail scissors can be satisfied here. And as for Che Guevara, whose posters the left of both hemispheres took down from their walls fifteen years ago—here he can still be found hanging above a pile of genuine fake furniture. Anything that can't be nailed down is sold here: girdles, pacifism, noise, sunglasses, goldfish. In less than five minutes you can purchase the gratitude of the People's Mujaheddin with a small donation, or buy a heavy-metal outfit or a crocodile skin once owned by the Duchess of Marlborough.

Here even politics takes on the character of the fairground. All the Communist parties of Spain—I counted seven or eight—are present. The Anarchists, whose rich tradition otherwise seems to have been swallowed up by the soil of Spain, can still be found, alongside stacks of underpants and garlands of Fascist insignia. And relics of its heroic age are going cheap too. For example, *La Voz de la Sangre* (*The Cry of Blood*) by Vicente Ballester, a novella with inky red-and-black illustrations, foreword by Federica Montseny, the grand old lady of Anarchism, published in Toulouse, 1946. It's a little yellowed but otherwise as good as new, and costs just 50 pesetas—30 cents. Not a purchaser in sight. The old man at the stall, a veteran of the movement, stoically rolls himself a cigarette.

Spot-removing liquids, creams, and powders of every kind are among the articles most in demand on the Rastro. Holding a bottle high in the air, a bearded salesman preaches his everyday miracle, surrounded by a dense crowd. The old spot, the old dirt, the old shame disappear in a flash of magic that holds the audience spellbound again and again.

The upper ranks of Madrid society practice their own magic arts. Their workday doesn't end at nightfall. In fact it really begins at eight and lasts until daybreak. The famous *movida* consists of a nonstop pilgrimage from one bar to the next. An implacable rigor governs the sequence of bars, restaurants, and nightclubs; it's absolutely necessary to be seated just where there's no chance of getting a table. Here jobs are bestowed and intrigues spun, coups planned, markets divided up, and alliances forged. This society in which politicians and landowners, officers and journalists, artists and bankers meet has something oriental about it. It is generous and gossipy, vindictive and indiscreet, secretive and unpredictable.

A few years ago the "Danes"—in the shape of the decent, liberal men of the future—moved into this "Arab" world. The Socialists under Felipe González came from the provinces. They came as victors, representing the better Spain. Have they turned Madrid inside out? Or has Madrid swallowed them up?

A foreigner can't answer this question, even if, as custom demands, he has done the rounds for a couple of nights. Who knows whether he went to the right bars, sat at the right tables? He became a party to countless secrets. Whether they were of any importance is another matter. The only thing that's certain is that they are all firsthand.

"The minister of the interior asked me out onto the fire escape to tell me how matters really stand. He can't speak freely in his office. He knows very well that he's being bugged by his own security service."

"What do you expect? Not a soul in Madrid works. Everybody takes long weekends. I tried to call the Foreign Ministry on Friday morning. There wasn't even a receptionist there to answer the phone."

"Felipe is a *caudillo*. No one dares to contradict him. The people around him are complete cowards. The state does what it likes. The Socialists don't even know what separation of powers means—and they're the very ones who want to simplify the administration! I can only laugh. We're not ruled by a party but by a gravy train. The Socialists have eighty thousand members, most of whom only joined one or two years ago, and forty-nine thousand of them have already managed to grab civil-service jobs!"

"I know him, I used to play football with him in Seville, when he was still a student. Felipe's an ultraleftist in private. He treats the capitalists as if they were decent people, but among close friends he says the members of the Spanish Employers' Association are all absolute criminals. There's only one exception, and he's an idiot."

"I assure you the next coup is already planned—for mid-October, but it's certain to fail. I've looked at the Air Force's operational plans. If it comes down to it, their planes will bomb the barracks."

"The Socialists? Of course they're sons of whores, but they're *our* sons of whores, and that, my friend, is what counts!"

THE ORACLE

There are no tourists on the suburban train from Madrid to Aranjuez, just ordinary housewives, tired commuters, and high-spirited schoolkids. The train passes the brick-red battlements of Madrid's outer suburbs. Then the line crosses the devastated approaches to the city: wrecked warehouses and ruined factories, scrap metal dumps and railroad sheds. No one pokes his head out the window to look at the gigantic Christ of Cerro de los Angeles. With outstretched arms the huge concrete figure blesses the whole of Spain. It stands in the dead center of the country as a reminder that Spain is dedicated to the Sacred Heart of Jesus. In 1936 the statue was "executed" by a group of Anarchists; the bullet holes of this symbolic murder are still supposed to be visible today. A television broadcast tower now overlooks the savior. The slow train climbs chains of stony hills. Under the power lines sheep graze in the Castilian dust. At last the train stops at Ciempozuelos.

* * *

I have come to this small place not as a harmless visitor but with the deceitful intention of spying on my hosts. The ugly mistrust that persuaded me to do so had been planted by a Latin American friend who spent years in exile in Spain, barely scraping by.

He often told me: In Madrid you'll meet the usual editorial writers, a state secretary, a trade union boss, and of course a few dozen authors. They'll all be very friendly and present you with their books. But what will they tell you? That the old Spain is dead, that there are only a few people left who won't change, who still cling to their old delusions, that everything is quite, quite different, that Spain is part of Europe. They believe it themselves. They admire their own achievements. Modernization, the famous transformation. Unfortunately, they're living in make-believe, in a country that doesn't exist! As if centuries of sclerosis could be gotten rid of just like that, with a little bit of good will and optimism. In reality everything is still the same. Only the packaging has changed."

"And where can I find this reality?" I asked him.

"I can tell you that: in Ciempozuelos."

My friend had lived there for a couple of months in 1978. I, however, had never heard of the place.

"That's just it! In Madrid they don't even know where Ciempozuelos is. But this dump and thousands like it are the real Spain, not the pink tea rooms of Barcelona and the computer shops of Madrid!

"Imagine a couple of streets of wretched ugliness, twelve thousand inhabitants, four cheerless cafés, and the principal industry of the place is insanity. Every time I went to the station I passed the long walls and the barred windows of the lunatic asylum. One in three of the population is a patient. I never went inside, but even a blind man could tell it was a snake pit. And whoever's not inside is under the thumb of the Guardia Civil.

"The only person I could occasionally have a decent conversation with was the local trade union leader. He tried to find an office and a meeting room for months. The Guardia Civil went to the landlords and warned them not to harbor this Communist. He also told me how the police in Ciempozuelos regulate the labor market. Anyone who's looking for work must register with the police and have his impeccable life and good conduct certified. No testimonial, no work. Every morning, the hired hands go to the marketplace to sell their labor. A policeman stands behind each landowner. The Guardia Civil decides who gets work and who doesn't.

"There's also a factory in Ciempozuelos that produces plastic tubing. Any worker who contradicts the foreman or demands higher wages is summoned within twenty-four hours to the police barracks. Then he's thrashed with leather belts or bare fists. No one talks about it. They're frightened. One hour from Madrid and that's the end of Spanish democracy!"

As though I had flipped a coin, I resolved to make Ciempozuelos, this insignificant little dot on the map, my oracle and test case.

At first sight everything seemed to confirm what my embittered friend had said. The train station lay deserted in the brooding heat. I found the first of the four dreary cafés on an empty street. A dried-up fountain, the remains of a park overgrown with weeds, the ruins of unfinished buildings ... And the prisonlike building over there must be the mental hospital. However, the doors were nailed shut, and the windowpanes behind the iron bars were broken. The snake pit was empty.

By contrast, the old main square with its arcades presented a surprising picture. The town hall had been restored and was resplendent in fresh whitewash; the balconies had been repaired, and there were new paneled doors and posts of light-colored oak on many houses as well. The square had been renamed; now it was called Plaza de la Constitución, Constitution Square. I found a newly opened municipal library and a small hall for cultural events.

Then I set out to visit the Guardia Civil. The station house was very close, and on the way I discovered two video stores (*Gandhi*, *Ben Hur*, *Tortures of the Inquisition*, and *Deep Throat* were among the specials). Sprayed on a wall: "The people of Ciempozuelos support the just struggle of the Palestinian people." I also found the Kingdom Hall of the Jehovah's Witnesses, which was next to a small discotheque. On an adjacent house wall someone demanded the immediate dissolution of all organs of repression, and directly opposite was the station house, an old, oversized, yellow building. A flock of sheep moved down the street, and four giggling nuns in the habit of their order struggled to pass through it. They were carrying electric guitars and a drum set.

The gate stood open. A red-faced sergeant greeted me, rubbing his hands. He didn't ask for any identification, led me into a small office, and offered me a cigarillo. He seemed really pleased by the unexpected visit. Above his desk the monarch showed a restrained smile. The sergeant—forty-five years old, with two children, eighteen years' service, and a salary of 80,000 pesetas ($488) a month—emulated his supreme commander. I asked him how the garrison, which consisted of eleven men, passed the time. "We keep the peace," he replied. He admitted, however, that there were no threats anywhere in sight. Now and then trouble broke out over hunting and fishing rights. "Last month we even had a theft: a couple of shirts and a portable radio. We were able to solve the case."

"What about the trade unions, the strikes, the labor conflicts? I've been told the Guardia interfere in everything."

"Those days are gone. It used to happen. What do you expect? That's democracy. There's less work for us. We have to make the best of it. Take our mayor, for example. If you had told me five years ago that we were going to get a Communist mayor, I wouldn't have believed you. Anyway, he's a very good man. People voted for him not because of his party but because of his ability. The election was very close. If he hadn't been such a strong candidate, the druggist would probably have won. He's in the Alianza Popular, the right-wing party. You must have come past his house; the shop is on the left, at the corner, if you go toward the town hall."

I asked the sergeant what had happened to the mental hospital. "What? You haven't seen the new building yet? The hospital's name is San Juan de Dios, two streets from here, it's impossible to miss it."

True enough. A few hundred yards from the old snake pit I came upon a Christian social utopia. A complex of white buildings and pavilions scattered across a large park. The hospital gates were wide open. There was no check on people going in or out. Patients sat dozing beside a pond, played cards in the open air, asked me for a cigarette. There were hardly any staff to be seen. I had a look at a carpentry workshop, a bar, a swimming pool. Gardeners were busy in the greenhouse. Children played on the swings. Music could be heard coming from the chapel. Here I found the four little nuns again. They had set up their drums in front of the altar and were playing a couple of mildly political rock songs. One was about Nicaragua, another about world hunger. A small audience, mostly elderly, listened attentively. I met a young psychiatrist who told me that the founder of the hospital, Pater Menni, was soon to be canonized—an idea that seemed altogether reasonable to me. I have never seen a mental hospital of comparable quality in West Germany.

On the way back to Madrid I began to brood about my experience. I had pursued a vague suspicion. Reality had proved me wrong. I was pleased about that. In less than eight years this insignificant place had changed radically. The miracle of Ciempozuelos wasn't a trick of propaganda. But was what I had seen the exception or the rule? How many Ciempozueloses are there in Spain? I don't know. I only know that the inhabitants of this small town see nothing remarkable in their fate. The most beautiful thing about their miracle is that they think it's quite normal.

THE ANALOGY

"The political and social backwardness of Spain when compared to its neighbors remains a permanent theme in Spaniards' reflections about themselves well into the twentieth century. If ever there was something like a Spanish ideology, the last thing inherent in it was any exploration of the causes of this backwardness, or any attempt to consider remedies. Instead, combining defiance and regret, it valued a society of estates over industrial society, the Middle Ages over the modern era, culture over civilization, introspection over the outside world, and community over society. Above all, it glorified a special Spanish path and celebrated the Spanish soul . . . It mixed a kind of proud melancholy with a commitment to the role of outsider, with which it was all too easily satisfied."

This quote is from a recent book by the German sociologist Wolfgang Lepenies (*Die drei Kulturen*, Munich, 1985). I have, however, taken the liberty of tampering wth the quotation. Wherever "Spain" now appears, Lepenies wrote "Germany." Who is right? The author? The forger? Neither? Or both?

"You're puzzled? You don't understand what's happened here? That does you credit. I feel the same way—despite the fact that I've been living here for fifty years and feel completely Spanish."

We were sitting in the smoking room of an old villa in Chamartín, to the north of Madrid. It was a miracle that the house, with its yellow plaster façade, had survived the frenzy of the real-estate boom, the rapid proliferation of expressways, highrises, and shopping centers. My host was an elegant, elderly gentleman who had emigrated from Germany just in time and managed to become a successful fur dealer in Spain.

"Many foreigners still go into raptures over the Franco years, even now. In those days you had only to clap your hands in the evening and the night watchman came running to unlock the front door. The servants were grateful and docile. Anyone who ate meat three times a week was considered a rich man. But it was a suffocating, lifeless time. I'm glad it's gone. And the ideological glue that cemented the Spanish consciousness—honor, soul, loyalty, race, pride, fatherland, glory, etc.—has dissolved into nothing. Virtually overnight. Gone without a trace."

"That's exactly what I don't understand," I said.

The traffic in front of the little garden was infernal. The neon lights of the new hotel opposite threw reddish reflections onto the polished surfaces of the old furniture. My host sat in semidarkness.

"Just imagine," he said quietly, "if Hitler had lost the most important thing he possessed, his delusions, and become a cold-blooded, rational, calculating dictator."

"I can't imagine that."

"I emigrated in 1935 because I realized that something of that kind was out of the question. But let's just suppose that he had limited himself to oppressing only his own people, jailing and killing them. You will concede that the alarm displayed by the rest of the world would have remained within bounds. The Nazi regime would have been unassailable. Sooner or later the Germans would have attained a degree of affluence. One day, in the middle of the boom, Hitler would have died in bed of old age. And his successor, an extremely talented technocrat by the name of Speer, would have become the administrator of his estate. What would

Speer have done? He would have skillfully, tenaciously, and cautiously initiated the dismantling of the regime. Naturally, he would have met embittered resistance from the gentlemen of the Gestapo and the military high command. But perhaps he could have pulled it off. And now let me ask you this: What then would the Germans have done with their collective madness? With their Nordic soul? With their Aryan obsession? With the whole distasteful ideology? Chucked it all away and thrown it in the garbage can!"

"I understand what you're getting at."

"Of course the comparison is faulty. The Falange, after all, were mere children compared with the Nazis."

"But the crucial difference is that the Spanish liquidated their dictatorship themselves. The Germans defended Fascism to the last ditch. The Allies had to demolish our cities and partition our country; only then could democracy be introduced, by decree of the military government."

"Yes, but the result is quite similar, is it not? Model pupils in Bonn, model pupils in Madrid. Enlightened, liberal people, dedicated Europeans, freedom of the press, full shop windows and empty churches. Here and there a few dark spots that no one wants to know about. But otherwise? The old vices, the old virtues, the old convictions—all down the drain! Well, it's no loss as far as I'm concerned. And in only ten years! First the boom, the 'miracle.' Then the 'transition,' euphoria, the 'change.' Finally compromise, disenchantment, crisis, exhaustion, cynicism. I'm talking about Spain now.

"You see a country that is utterly reasonable, boringly normal, just like West Germany. There are, of course, plenty of people, who complain that Christianity is irrelevant and that Marxism is old hat. And I admit, the result is loud, corrupt, and vulgar. Take a look at my garden—nothing grows in it anymore. Spain has completely lost its charm. The unemployment, terrorism, crime, the coup threats—they all get on my nerves. And the mess and the ugliness . . . But I don't long to be back in the thirties, forties, or fifties. Today in Spain you will find at least ten completely normal people for every fanatic. After centuries of imbecility that is indeed a triumph. A triumph!"

The old gentleman glanced at his cigar, which had gone out, and added, "As a German you should appreciate that."

THE MUSEUM OF DELUSIONS

Under glass and on red velvet, exhibit number 25,775: the plate from which the first Marquis del Duero, Captain-General Manuel Gutiérrez de la Concha, breakfasted a quarter of an hour before his death; also the cup from which he drank. Beside it in a glass case: a wooden doll with bulging blue eyes, dressed in colored rags and resting on a ramrod—this is what a fifteenth-century gunner looked like. Without a number: the gilded, pearl-handled pistol that the notorious Fascist Queipo de Llano left behind, as well as the microphone he used for delivering his daily inflammatory tirades on Radio Seville.

"In the Army Museum the history of our Fatherland is quite tangible. So strong is the spiritual power it radiates, so powerful and deep the admiration it awakens, that the material objects in its collections seem to be transformed into a hymn of glory, a heroic poem. The emotions they arouse are comparable to those felt by a Christian who lifts his thoughts to God in the solemnity of one of our great cathedrals." That's what it says in the official guidebook to the Army Museum in Madrid.

History has been abolished in this palace on the Calle de Méndez Núñez. Everything is synchronous: the Middle Ages and the Civil War, Pizarro and Napoleon, the Berbers and the Indios. An ossified eternity rules in this glorious panopticon. Hundreds of muskets, medals, busts, swords, flags, and suits of armor in hallucinatory confusion. No crimes or defeats ever took place. War is a single, total work of art touched by magic and mildew, a fantastic reliquary pieced together out of a thousand fragments.

"See the fascinating tableaux of soldiers of the twentieth century," tempts the leaflet set out in the entrance hall. "Soldiers of the Motherland, from overseas, from our protectorate, from the last civil war, and the figures of famous men, such as Alfonso XIII, Juan Carlos I, Hitler, Mussolini, Eisenhower, Göring, de Gaulle, Franco . . . The Museum is so beautiful, so precious, so important, so interesting!"

Under an oil painting of the Immaculate Conception of Our Lady, patron saint of the infantry, two recruits from Jaen are busy polishing one of countless swords. There is devotion in their faces. A battle that will never end is being fought by 13,700 tin soldiers. The office of Colonel Moscardo is a tiny room furnished with matchstick-size chairs, tables, and sofas, decorated with a gallery of passport photos of yellowing officers. The wall they hang on is made of paper, the building is made of plaster and plywood, and the ceiling, which allows the visitor to look in, is a sheet of clear plastic. The commander of the Alcazar is a Lilliputian put together by an army that for forty years has had, thank God, nothing to kill but time.

There are some second-rate museums whose most important exhibit the curators are quite unaware of—for it is the mentality of the exhibitors themselves. Such museums are self-portraits. There is something innocent about them. To Lieutenant-General Varela, the director of the museum, everything must appear equally valuable: the Filipino kris and the Caudillo's briefcase. Mass murders are collected here with the same impartiality as postage stamps in the schoolyard. Only the most recent exhibit seems somewhat out of place. It's a battered American limousine, a black Dodge, registration number PMM 16416, which on December 20, 1973, was hurled forty feet into the air by the force of a bomb explosion.

The occupant was Franco's last regent, Luis Carrero Blanco. The unsmiling attendant probably does not suspect with what inward joy some visitors regard this battered coffin.

THE TROUBLEMAKER

"You're going to laugh," says Juan Cueto Alas, "but it really is a pleasure to be a Spanish intellectual. You can say anything you think, you get printed, and you even get paid for it. A wonderful situation! It's never happened before in this country."

"And what," I ask politely, "did Spanish writers and thinkers live on before?"

"Tradition presented them with two possibilities: either the slow and servile path of advancement—at court, in the academy, in the civil service—or a life of poverty and hunger in the provinces. For anyone who could not reconcile himself to these alternatives, there was always a third possibility: prison. Don't forget that although the Enlightenment may have had its advocates in this country, we had no Enlightenment."

With a casual movement of the hand, Cueto points to the collected works of Don Gaspar Melchor de Jovellanos, a famous eighteenth-century friend of the people, who personally experienced all three options available to a Spanish intellectual.

"Presumably you have acquired some new hazards in place of the old."

"Of course. Overproduction, the star system, quick money, and fashionable nonsense. At last we're responsible for our own mess. The days when we could go around feeling like martyrs are gone. I know many who still mourn them, especially on the left. They miss Franco; they're annoyed because they're doing so well. They're the widowers of the dictatorship. I know all about it. I've been through it all, the

Resistance, Communism, the Algerian revolution. I'm glad it's behind me. It's a marvelous luxury to be able to laugh about politics. Unfortunately, no one else is laughing, at least not in public. Our humor has remained clandestine. That too is inherited from the Franco period. Public discussion still frightens us. You might make a fool of yourself if you go too far. So we prefer to make dignified speeches. The appearance of conviction is what counts in our debates. Actually, 'debates' sounds far too grand—it's a chorale of monologues. No one listens to anyone else, no one argues against anyone else. The Spanish intelligentsia is rhetorical and literary. It's never heard of microelectronics and molecular biology. The intellectual's greatest ambition is to write one of those mindless novels that are full of tragic figures, even though our reality, thank goodness, has become banal and prosaic. The novel has become a spectator sport. Personally I prefer soccer."

Cueto lives on the periphery of the Spanish periphery. The city of Gijon was once an important coal and ore port and a thriving center of heavy industry. Today it bears the marks of postindustrial poverty. Anyone who lives there by choice is considered eccentric. A considerable distance to the northeast of the town, opposite a run-down Moorish-style discotheque, stands a solitary house—half Mexico, half Berlin-Grunewald—from which the mortar is crumbling. The rooms are packed with the heavy "Renaissance" furniture left behind by the builder, an old Nazi, along with the swastika pattern mosaic on the bathroom floor. The writer lives alone with his dog in this house, which he likes precisely because it's not what one expects—he loves incongruity, confusion, risk. Everything he writes his Apple computer passes on to the Madrid media. Cueto sits on a worn-out old swivel chair and talks. He talks so much that his cigar keeps going out; so many things occur to him that he doesn't have time to offer his guest coffee. It is a sign of his generosity, for what is a cup of coffee compared to an argument? Cueto is not one to resist the provocation of a catchword.

"Consumerism! Everybody's against consumerism as if it were something new in our country. In fact we've been virtuosos of consumerism for centuries. It's the medium and the measure of our progress. What did we do with our empire? We consumed it! When it was finished, foreign capital came and turned us from colonizers into the colonized. Our modernization was the result of the massive import of capital goods and luxury commodities. We weren't interested in manufacturing; that came later, chaotically, in fits and starts, without any economic logic. It was tourism, imitation, and consumerism running wild that triggered the boom, not production. And now? You can buy the latest products of information technology at any kiosk. The kids don't swap stamps in the playground anymore, they swap computer disks. All imported, all in English—intelligence on credit. It's easier than inventing something ourselves. The state limps along behind. The police don't know how to use computers; they prefer truncheons. There are no laws on data processing or data protection, and because it's less effort to link up to foreign networks, there aren't any Spanish data banks worth mentioning.

"Its an old pattern, and the result is always the same: dependence. Dependence has become second nature to us. Administrative, corporatist attitudes still dominate in Spain. Protection is our ideal, protection against the summary eviction of thoughts, tenants, feelings, businesses. 'Life' isn't a sentence to us, but a promise. I see it as the secularization of our famous, holy, inviolable 'values'—their petty-bourgeois version, as it were. Eternal Spain has shrunk to the size of a chair: everyone clings to his own seat. The industrialists are incompetent and cowardly. They let themselves be subsidized by the state. Just like the trade unions, which never tire of demanding safe jobs for life, plus pensions guaranteed by the government. Their only strategy is to block things. And private life is no different. No one wants to move. No one wants a rented apartment. Even people without money buy one and immure themselves for life if they can. I know people who don't get divorced, simply because they own an apartment. They separate but don't move out! They'll do anything—just as long as nothing changes!"

"I have to disagree. I find that Spain has changed at a furious rate."

"Yes, yes, yes! You're right. The speed is dizzying. We tumble from one phase to the next without any transition. Everything happens in a hurry. Do you know what we've got in Spain? Galloping immobilism!"

Now that he was unleashed, there was no stopping him.

"Dynamics without change, lethargic recklessness, nothing is digested. Before a problem is solved, it's already out of date. The result is a very specific form of amnesia. Take the Civil War, for example! Of course, in reality it's anything but forgotten. But the memory has been put in deep freeze. All the difficult problems are shelved. *Por ahora no*—not just now, please. That's the watchword. It's still too soon to think about it, it's too dangerous, later maybe! And so yesterday's problems are swallowed up by today's, and today's by tomorrow's. *Somos todos amigos!* We'll work things out. Cease-fire agreements everywhere . . ."

"I can hardly believe that. When I look at the Spanish media I get an impression of enormous disorder, a racket in which you can't hear yourself speak anymore, a Babel of voices."

"Nothing but froth. Our pluralism is nothing but a parti-colored mask on the surface of things. Underneath you find a terrifying degree of conformity. A consensus approaching total capitulation. The right is bankrupt and the left has given up. The result is a tacit ideological treaty that everyone abides by. The aim of the agreement is comfort, consolidation, security."

"And you're the troublemaker?"

"Don't worry. No one's losing any sleep over me. The only risk I run, as a professional prophet, is that events will prove me right."

"You're much too unfair for anyone to agree with you. If I look at your government's policies, where's your consensus, your cease-fire agreement? The Socialists are risking one battle after another."

"You're right! The Socialist Party is doing capitalism's dirty work for it. It's a pity our Socialists aren't more cynical. But no, they suffer like dogs—their moral worries aren't an act. And they've got plenty to worry about: unemployment, pension cuts, NATO, the losses made by the state-owned companies, inflation . . . *Pobrecitos*! The poor guys!"

He really does feel sorry for them. But now Juan Cueto Alas has to pack his bag quickly or he'll miss the last plane out. Is it a symposium in Rome? An exhibition in Málaga? A conference in Budapest? Whatever it is, he's in a hurry. He's one of a dozen or so public figures in Spain who are called the Ubiquitous Ones. It's not his fault. There are simply too few people of his caliber around. The scarcer the resource, the more intensively it's exploited. He drops me at the center of Gijon and takes his leave with a cheerful sigh: "If only one weren't indispensable!"

Darkness has fallen. It's drizzling. The shops have let down their shutters. The cafés on the Calle Corrida are quiet. The citizens of Gijon are staying home. Are they short of money? The old main street is deserted. Only two figures withstand the constant rain, one armed with a sword and a cross, the other with a book. They are the patrons of Gijon: King Pelayo of Asturias, who drove out the Moors, and Jovellanos, the man of the Enlightenment. They don't glance at one another. Each looks helplessly across the dark, crisis-shaken town from his own end of the empty street.

THE MONUMENT
....

The Valley of the Fallen is the largest war memorial in the world. Is this self-portrait of the Franco regime worth visiting?

"Appearances never deceive. Architects lie, but architecture tells the truth. The more monumental an object is, the more clearly it betrays the nature of those who commissioned it. You must go there for that reason alone."

The literature on the place is full of figures: the cross that rises above the valley alone weighs 201,740 tons. The bronze door of the basilica is 34 feet high. The crypt is 852 feet long; the square in front of the entrance measures almost 100,000 square feet. Fifty thousand dead are accommodated in the necropolis. It took thousands of forced laborers 19 years to build the monument.

"What do you want to go there for?" asks a Catalan friend, anti-clerical to the core. "If you've seen the Moscow subway, you already know what it's like. Only it's ten times bigger, and it says 'Fallen for God and Fatherland' above the entrance. The truth would be, fallen for nothing at all. So much concrete to perpetuate a lie! I've never been there. I won't go with you. I wouldn't dream of it!"

"It's pointless to polemicize against a temple," says a Socialist politician. "If you ask me, the Mexican pyramids are no less obscene. But the right has always had a better nose for symbols. The right are the experts on delusions. That's why there's no point in arguing about monuments, flags, and street names. It can even be dangerous, because the stupidest arguments always win. You can save yourself the trip."

"You must put your prejudices aside," I was advised by the wife of a German industrialist, an exuberant blonde who in next to no time has transformed herself into a Spanish patriot. "I think the Valley of the Fallen is magnificent. I go there again and again, and it's more beautiful each time! The landscape is breathtaking, and as for the architecture—you'll see for yourself how unpretentious and authentic it is, and all in real stone! I know you don't have a good word for Franco; I don't either—how could you imagine such a thing!—but while politicians come and go, Spanish *grandeza* remains. Believe me, it's worth it. I take all my visitors there!"

"The Valley of the Fallen? For me it's a childhood memory," I was told by one of the best minds in Madrid. He is the son of a high-ranking Falangist. As a student he was a cofounder of a Marxist-Leninist party; today he is one of the most perceptive commentators on Spanish politics. "It must have been in the mid-fifties. We drove up in a long black limousine with a chauffeur. Cars were a rarity in those days. At most there were six cars per thousand inhabitants; now, I think, it's a hundred and sixty. Mother was wearing a pink dress and a large hat. I thought she was overdressed. The construction work was in full swing. I remember very clearly the prisoners resting on their shovels. They looked me straight in the face. It was a strange feeling—I suspected that I was a prisoner too. Anyway, if you really do go there, you should walk a couple of hundred yards into the forest. I've been told that the barracks for the forced laborers are still standing. I've never been there since."

It was all true. Even the remains of the barracks were still there. The stars in the travel guide are well deserved—it's worth seeing. It's as if the Pharaohs had hired Walt Disney; as if Stalin had become pious; as if the Mafia had decided to build a necropolis for the Honorable Society; as if Albert Speer had planned a Vatican without the Pope; as if Paul Getty had commissioned a gang of forgers to build a Renaissance fallout shelter.

Tourism, however, wears down even the hardest stone. It normalizes everything by taking a snapshot of it and covering it with paper cups. Tourism gives a purpose to this pointless construction, which loses its terror when reduced to the size of a souvenir, of an ashtray. And so I can guarantee that no ideological dynamite lies hidden beneath the foundations of this monument.

The cog-railway immediately makes a reassuring impresson. It runs from the parking lot to the base of the 460-foot-high concrete cross, where the four cardinal virtues gaze despairingly into the distance. It's closed "due to mechanical failure" and seems to have been shut down for the last six months. In the valley whole busloads of Americans are lining up at the toilets. At the bar you can buy German-made Pralinen-Freude chocolates, or a liqueur bottle in the shape of a flamenco dancer. The video games available are Fenix, Crash Road, Space King, Moon Cresta, and Piraña—not a bad selection for such a sacred place. The venerable lucky-crane game offers an old-fashioned kind of thrill. Anyone who is willing to invest fifty pesetas and is skillful enough can maneuver the arm of the crane over a heap of rubber balls, ball-point pens, and packs of cigarettes so that these desirable objects fall into his lap, as it were—for a fraction of their usual cost. However, a Texan who tried it was effortlessly beaten by the machine and left the bar cursing.

A souvenir stand has been set up in front of the entrance to the basilica. Holy Virgins in plastic bags are on sale here, and small plaques with the brass inscription ¡La muerte es un acto de servicio! Death is duty! Business is slow.

A retired NCO offers his services as guide. The man is bloated by decades of army stews, and the outline of his suspenders is visible underneath a green knit cardigan. He reveals his hallucinatory view of history beneath the mosaic decoration of the cupola. Heroes, he says, are heroes; he won't change his mind about that. Even Primo de Rivera lies buried here, and he was against Franco. Everyone makes mistakes sometimes, even Franco, but here there is room for everyone. I can barely make out what the pensioner is mumbling. Perhaps it's because of his strong dialect, or perhaps because the man is already drunk, though it's not yet midday.

The entrance hall too lacks a solemn atmosphere, despite the giant candelabra. The porters have established themselves here. They inhabit a plastic-and-board booth reminiscent of an East Berlin customs hut. The two porters are sitting there in their shirt-sleeves. They've laid their sweaty caps beside the half-empty beer bottles on the table in front of them. A fuse box, a green fifties-style wastebasket, a couple of brooms. It's hot. There's a smell of soiled underwear. The shack's architecture tells the truth. Appearances never lie.

ROMANTICISM

After the bullfight Don Antonio Ordoñez gives a small reception in his townhouse in Seville. Strictly speaking—and the distinctions are strictly observed here—this is not a reception or a party but a *tertulia*. This traditional form of old Spanish hospitality now survives only in the provinces. Etymologists maintain that the word derives from the name of a father of the Church. Quintus Septimius Tertullianus is long dead, but the elegance of his language, which is said to have been "dark and shining like ebony," his belligerence, and his taste for splitting hairs must have made a deep impression on the Spanish—otherwise it would be difficult to explain why they still empty their glasses in his name today.

The host of the evening is a heavy, red-faced man who moves with surprising grace and displays an unusual sensitivity to etiquette. Although he has hired two waiters, he personally tops off his guests' sherry. Here the gesture and the courtesy that fame demand count more than anything else. Don Antonio was once a celebrated *torero*.

With only a few red ornaments painted on the walls, the triangular, whitewashed room is austere to the point of starkness. Two giant bulls' heads, a devotional picture of the

"Canonical Coronation of the Hopeful Picture of Tirana" ornamented with twigs, and a couple of paper lanterns are the only other decorations. And yet the scene has all the elegance of a salon.

As far as I can see, the guests have only one thing in common: their knowledge of everything having to do with bullfighting. It's their universal text, and they all share in its exegesis: the historian in designer jeans who never removes his dark glasses; the lady from the broadcasting station; the builder who has transformed himself overnight into a Socialist politician; the sociologist who used to concern herself with feminism but is now more interested in problems of fashion; the dean of the summer university; and the pale, ill-informed, fatalistic student from a good family. "If it happens, it happens," she whispers in my ear. "I've got no plans. I'm nobody. The future doesn't exist." Generously silent, the host listens to the metaphysical interpretations of bullfighting that his friends elaborate between ham rolls.

But how has the French tourist stumbled into this circle? She is dressed up as an Andalusian. Completely wrapped in black lace and throwing shameless glances around the room, she talks about her favorite author, the Marquis de Sade, on whom she is writing a thesis. But the petty bourgeois in her easily defeats the demonic and the folkloric: with ecstatically shut eyes and a shaky voice, she puts everything she's got into Carmen's aria, displaying a double chin in the process. Everyone applauds enthusiastically. Ancient Spanish virtues that some had given up for lost reappear this evening: an admirable patience and boundless courtesy.

The pilgrimage to the bulls at El Judío, Don Antonio's ranch, takes place the following day. The layout of the corral is labyrinthine: a complicated system of trap doors, boxes, little weighhouses, and passageways leads out into a small arena. The buyers and their ladies can admire the bulls from a box. Attentive whispering. For every nuance of color in the coat, for each gradation of age, for every bodily flaw, and for every movement the animals make there is a special expression. Most are not to be found in the dictionary of the Royal Academy; they are part of a language known only to initiates. Don Antonio's ranch is one of the two hundred that keep bullfighting supplied, but only fifteen of these breeders are taken seriously. "The others have only gotten involved out of vanity. They lose much more money than they earn. They have become breeders the way other people become owner of a football team, with checkbook in hand." It's the omniscient university professor who passes this information on to me.

At lunch—lobster, game hen, and rice—Don Antonio begins to talk about politics. "I am," he declares, "independent, right-wing, and liberal." The king is a coward, and as for Felipe González, he has never even seen a bullfight—that alone lets you know what kind of man he is. The young intellectuals look anxiously at one another. What the maestro is saying is not at all *comme il faut*. The left-wing sociologist quickly tries to change the subject. But the old *torero* won't let himself be sidetracked. "Yes, yes, my friend, we are living in a left-wing dictatorship!"

Will Don Antonio enter the ring once more? Will he run for Parliament, and if so, for which party? I was unable to find out. But if he sets out to tilt against the windmills of Socialism, then there is only one place on earth where he would stand a good chance of being elected, and that is Ronda, his native town. The relics of his cult can already be seen in the bullfighting museum there: his baptismal picture; a photo in which, as a boy of five, he swings the *muleta*; a dreadful oil painting depicting the whole "Ortoñez dynasty"; photographs that show him with Orson Welles and the inevitable Hemingway; a document naming him a "favorite son of the town"; and, mounted on a brass plaque, the ears he cut from his last bull in 1980.

"Andalusia fascinates me because it's so romantic," he tells me as I take my leave.

Is there such a thing as an Andalusian culture? I always had the impression that it had disappeared under a thick, sticky layer of imitation long before the word "kitsch" was invented. But no! Its defender, an earnest secondary-school teacher, puts me right. "Our culture," he says, "conceals itself by displaying itself; it survives by allowing itself to be overwhelmed. This strategy has defeated every conqueror: the Phoenicians and the Romans, the Vandals and the Visigoths, the Arabs and the kings of Castile. We corrupted the Napoleonic invaders, and we'll deal with tourism as well. Adaptation is our strongest weapon—it makes us unconquerable."

I have difficulty following him, for, like every bar in the beautiful city of Seville, the small restaurant we are sitting in is overrun by tireless hordes of musicians disseminating their thudding version of the flamenco.

"Don't pay any attention to it! I've collected and recorded twenty thousand genuine *coplas*. No one else really knows what flamenco is! A single lifetime is not enough to understand the poetic power of this country." The staring eyes behind the glasses betray the fanatical patriot. His omniscience is evident even in a tirade. Prehistory and hydrography, mythology and botany, literary history and mineralogy, they all demonstrate the uniqueness of his homeland. "Without us the witches of Europe would have been lost, because the mandrake root grows only here, on the lower reaches of the Guadalquivir. Without Andalusia there would be no Spanish civilization and no European culture." The evidence for his thesis is drawn from the Ice Age and the Middle Ages, from Roman antiquity and the present day. Everything speaks and signifies, everything is synchronous, everything becomes a divining rod in the fanatical documentation of folklore.

"Just between you and me, the flagbearers of Andalusian identity get on my nerves," said an old trade unionist whom

I'd asked for some information. "More than a year ago there was an outburst of enthusiasm in the regional press. A paleontologist had come across some bones during an excavation, and his expertise proved that these must be the oldest human remains in the world. So there, at last, was the proof that Andalusia was the cradle of humanity. After a few weeks it turned out that they were donkey bones. I haven't been able to find a single retraction in the local press. These people study every little variation in dialect, but they won't mention the word 'agrobusiness.' Two percent of the agricultural businesses in Andalusia cultivate half the total acreage. Big capital from abroad is buying up estates from the old, corrupt landlords and mechanizing agriculture. Unemployment in the region is at twenty-three percent, and that number will double in the next few years. I say to hell with Andalusian culture!"

THE EXTREMISTS

No movement, no voices, no smoke, no noise of machinery. The living corpse is laid out on a bed as large as several football fields. Behind barricaded iron gates and high barbed-wire fences lies the site of Europe's largest and most modern shipyard. No visitors, no press, no photos allowed—orders from above. Madrid wants no publicity. The AESA yard belongs 100 percent to the Spanish state. This white elephant of Franco's industrial policy was completed in 1973; it has brought little benefit to the impoverished southern tip of Spain.

The forty thousand inhabitants of Puerto Real, near Cádiz, are hostages of the dying monster. The little town is 90 percent dependent on the shipyard, says José Antonio Barroso, the mayor, a thirty-three-year-old with the childlike, chubby face of a seminarian.

"I used to be a pipe fitter in the yard," he tells me, "but

politics is like a one-way street. Even if there were work again, I couldn't go back. No one would take me on. I don't even have a high-school certificate."

The people of Puerto Real don't care how long their mayor sat behind a school desk. As we walk through the town he embraces an old woman, shouts a greeting to the men working—unregistered—in a back court, chats with the unemployed sitting in a café watching the bicycle race on TV, and treats Teté the smuggler to a glass of wine. The smuggler is ninety-one years old. One of the twenty-four children he's left behind on four continents is a member of the Central Committee of the Cuban Communist Party in Havana. Before the shipyard came, smuggling was the most important industry in the district, and Teté, a master smuggler, remains a respected man. It's the politicians who are considered dishonorable in Puerto Real. The Madrid parties don't stand a chance against Antonio Barroso.

And yet the baby-faced mayor is a well-known extremist. He owes his ideological education to a long-defunct ultraleft splinter party. Coffee cup in hand, he explains the teachings of Marx and Engels to me at length; he looks forward especially to the withering-away of the state. Yet his voters couldn't care less who Marx and Engels were. They don't even know who Pablo Iglesias* was.

Their view of politics is not shaped by programs. They know Francoism and they know unemployment, both in great detail. They can show the visitor the wall against which the opponents of Franco were shot, the places where the bullet holes were plastered over, and the lumps of cement that somehow always seem to fall out of the holes. Or Los Rosales, a property behind the station. One man wanted to open a bar there, another one an auto repair garage; but everyone who has tried to set up shop there has failed. The place is

* Considered the founder of Spanish socialism. (Trans.)

unlucky: the Falangists tortured their victims there. *El verdugo*, the hangman, is not forgotten either. In those days he used to visit women when their husbands were at work, in order to blackmail them: money and half an hour in bed, or else their husbands would be arrested. When he'd gotten what he wanted he denounced the couple, getting rid of both victim and witness.

"Nevertheless, we don't want to put anyone against the wall," says José Antonio. "It's the right who don't want reconciliation."

But as far as unemployment is concerned, he believes the Socialists' successes were undeserved. "In my eyes they're cowards. They've only done a fifth of what was possible. The greatest political service to this country was performed by an old Franco boss, Suárez. He dismantled the whole apparatus of the dictatorship. The fruits just fell into Felipe González's lap. And what have the Socialists done with them? Just look at what's happened to our shipyard. It was originally supposed to employ eight thousand workers; by the time it was completed the figure was down to forty-five hundred. The management sits in Madrid, gentlemen with waiting rooms and official cars but without a single idea among them of how to adapt production to the world market. There are two ways of getting rid of a big plant that's losing money: either with a single blow—but they won't do that, because it would put their own jobs at risk—or by slowly starving it out. And that's what the Socialists are doing. But you can't preserve human labor in a jar for years on end. The men become demoralized, they lose their skills. We have four thousand employees 'on rotation'—that is, they're on the payroll but they aren't *doing* anything. The only ones who are actually allowed to enter the yard are employed as caretakers. They oil the machines, knock off the rust, or play night watchman. The yard doesn't make anything! It's embalmed! It's just madness."

Then, unfortunately, the mayor must take his leave to see

to his animals. He lives alone in an old house outside the town. He has converted it into a menagerie, with three dogs—one of them a giant mastiff as big as a calf, named Tovarich—lizards, peacocks, chameleons, and three parrots, whose vocabulary is unrepeatable.

"My cockatoo's little wife just laid six eggs," says the extremist, and a blissful smile spreads across his angelic face. "I can't wait to find out if they're going to hatch."

It's peaceful in Marinaleda too, although the village lies in a part of Andalusia where 60 percent are illiterate and unemployment is endemic. The inhabitants who work are almost entirely day laborers. Many have escaped their misery by moving to Barcelona or emigrating. The houses of the homecomers display the fruits of their hard work. Their bright-patterned tiles are the only private status symbol that is tolerated in Marinaleda. All the other improvements are the result of collective initiative. There are little green benches everywhere, and above, on top of a small victory arch, stand the words *Avenida de la Libertad* (Liberty Avenue), in hand-forged letters. Even the curbstones are painted red and white, although only a moped occasionally sputters by here. The atmosphere reminds me of a kindergarten or an old-folks' home. Marinaleda is a symbolic village; for years it was a place of pilgrimage for the Spanish left. Its name was in all the papers because of repeated land occupations.

However, these actions were very different from the rural laborers' revolts of the Andalusian tradition. No one was killed and no town hall was burnt down. The land takeovers were completely symbolic, and the land was given up without resistance as soon as the Guardia Civil appeared. A pacifist breeze blows through Marinaleda. That's due to the experiment's originator, a dreamer with a Christlike beard called Juan Manuel Sánchez Cordillo. This tireless man is inspired by the hope that a good example will suffice to persuade mankind to change its ways. It is easy to laugh at this apostle without a messiah. Yet he has been able to secure for his flock every grant and subsidy available from the Spanish state.

You can learn to read and write in the town hall of Marinaleda, and take courses in dental care and nutrition. Today a comrade from the city has arrived. He's explaining to his audience the wolflike nature of capitalism and the unscrupulousness of its lackeys, among them the Madrid government. A few elderly women dressed all in black sit with grandchildren on their laps on the folding chairs beside the iron stove, listening silently.

It's noisier in the Casa del Pueblo. The walls of the spacious shed are covered with posters whose style and content are a reminder of more militant days: "Agricultural workers, arise! Never bow your heads!" In another picture a young land-owner poses nonchalantly in silk cravat and black sombrero, cigarette in mouth; beside him stoops a worker bathed in sweat, while behind the worker a red sun is rising. The legend of a more recent banner conveys the provocative thought of the Marinaleda commune's founder: "Anyone who wants to be a revolutionary must begin by shooting his own egoism!"

Whether melancholy or militant, the customers in the bar pay no attention to the slogans. Their shoes and shirts show that they are close to the poverty line. They appreciate that everything in this bar is cheaper than anywhere else. The fan on the ceiling creaks, the dominoes clatter, the sports program drones out from the television. There's no woman anywhere in sight, no land, no money, and no liberation.

THE MODEL BUSINESS

"Measured by growth rate of net profit, the most successful companies in Spain have very little to do with manufacturing," the gentleman from the chamber of commerce tells me. "In third place is a company that makes slot machines, a fashion house is second, and first is a company that calls itself PRISA, which stands for Promotora de Informaciones S.A.—Information Promotion Ltd."

The most important PRISA plant is so out of the way that most taxi drivers are puzzled when you give them the address. It's a carefully guarded, windowless industrial building to the east of Madrid. The most important newspaper in Spain is produced in this building, which is studded with concrete ornaments of a quite Romanian ugliness.

In less than ten years *El País* has become a central institution of Spanish democracy. The newspaper's short history sounds almost like a fairy tale. In 1978 its founder, Jesús de Polanco, who hardly looks like a press baron—his plain suits and his little briefcase suggest rather a minor civil servant—invited a few friends and acquaintances to a meeting. (Generalissimo Franco still enjoyed unbroken health at the time.) Among those invited were Manuel Fraga, a conservative politician; Ramón Tamames, a Communist economist; and a few industrialists, Christian Democrats, and academics. It was agreed to set up a company with the aim of publishing an independent daily newspaper. The only useful thing the Spanish press produced at this time was wastepaper. Its servility and incompetence were proverbial, its production standards primitive. It was clear to the founders of PRISA that the regime would not be willing to grant them a license. But they began to lay the foundations of their enterprise. Following Franco's death, they struck at just the right moment. Political parties were still banned and from one day to the next *El País* became the sole forum for political discussion. Its success exceeded all expectations. Within a very short time the paper had won over the majority of literate Spaniards. Today *El País* is not only by far the best newspaper in Spanish but one of the best in the world. By comparison, other great newspapers appear a little old-maidish (*The New York Times*), unreliable (*La Repubblica*), leaden (*Le Monde*), or reactionary (*Frankfurter Allgemeine Zeitung*).

That's remarkable enough if one considers the conditions under which *El País* began. When one also takes into account the circulation of the paper, it looks extraordinary. For with a print run of 350,000 (570,000 on Sundays) *El País* reaches more readers in Spain than anything else in print; its most successful competitor has a circulation of 190,000, and the popular press is far behind, with smaller editions of around 100,000. This success is unique in the western world; in every other country a newspaper's sales figures are in inverse proportion to the information it contains.

One can point to a number of obvious factors to explain this anomaly: the inefficiency of the competition, the political instincts of the editors, the sheer ability of the journalists. But *El País* is, moreover, one of the most advanced industrial companies in Spain. The newspaper sees itself as a pilot project not only in terms of its content but also its production process. Editorial work is carried out entirely on word processors. Setting, make-up, and printing are computer-controlled. The office in Barcelona, where a local edition appears, is linked to the head office in Madrid by cable and satellite. This model capitalist business contradicts all the traditional Spanish ideas about work. The organization's perfectionism is almost pedantic. Every year the newspaper produces a handbook for internal use that lays down whether it's "Gaddafi" or "Kadhafi" and whether NATO should be printed with or without periods.

But all these explanations are inadequate. Ultimately, the role *El País* plays is comprehensible only by reference to the peculiarities of the Spanish situation, to the fragility of democratic structures, and to lags and deficits that cannot, even with the best will in the world, be made good in a single decade. The events of the night of February 23/24, 1981*

---

* The date of an attempted military coup. (Trans.)

were symbolic of the role the press must play under these circumstances. The state television was silent. The country was close to panic. In this emergency the editor-in-chief, Juan Luís Cebrián, brought no fewer than four special editions— opposing the tanks and in support of the Constitution—to the streets of Madrid. The failure of the coup was attributable not least to this hazardous action. This example shows that in Spain a newspaper with the political stature of *El País* not only has influence, as in every other democracy, but can exercise quite substantial power. It's no wonder, then, that *El País* has occasionally been described as the *gobierno alternativo*, the alternative government. This characterization is not meant to be entirely flattering. In fact, with the increasing normalization of political life the newspaper's symbolic role is becoming precarious.

A certain disenchantment has become noticeable among the journalists recently. "In the long term our quasi monopoly is unhealthy," says one. "A first-class journalist has nowhere else to go in this country, and the management knows that all too well. Cebrián rewrites the lead articles of the best people as much as he likes. He doesn't allow anyone else to rise to the top. He's an enlightened despot."

"Do you know who the three most important people in Spain are? First is Felipe González, second is the king, and third is Juan Luís Cebrián. In the editors' offices they say that without a smile. I'm pessimistic about an outfit that over-reaches and overestimates itself like that. Don't you think that the paper has become duller, less witty, more officious? That's its punishment. Breakfast reading for the self-righteous!"

"Don't take it so hard," says a third. "The heroic age is over in journalism too. *El País* is now quite an ordinary media business. It no longer has to help Spanish culture to its feet or save democracy. It has to sell copies. It has to get control of commercial television. Just the same as in Bonn, Paris, and Rome.

"But it's *not* the same."

"Come on! I really don't know what's supposed to be so Spanish about Spain."

THE POPE

....

Anyone who wants to see the pope drinking his aperitif only has to turn up in the Golden Tower Tavern at about half past one in the afternoon. At the long wooden bar of this spacious restaurant you'll find a bearded, muscular, forty-five-year-old man who looks a bit like a doorman or a butcher: His Holiness Pope Gregory XVII, easily recognizable by his broad-brimmed Jesuit hat and his scarlet sash. The visitor, however, should not expect a benevolent glance from the prelate, for since an accident ten years ago Gregory XVII can no longer see. He does not give interviews, either, and his retinue, which consists of Cardinal State Secretary Padre Manola and a half-dozen bishops who look like bodyguards in disguise, protects him from troublesome questioners.

The pope does not come from an affluent background. He worked as a bookkeeper in a small company for many years, until one day the Mother of God appeared to a couple of schoolchildren in a desolate, loamy field near El Palmar de Troya, thirty-five kilometers south of Seville. The Catholic Church was indifferent to this vision of Mary. But Clemente Domínguez, for that was the bookkeeper's name, had heard the voice of the Virgin. What could he do but obey? His first task was to raise the necessary start-up capital; its sources remain obscure. In any case, there was enough for a journey to Rome. There Clemente was able to get hold of an aged monsignore who was willing to ordain him: the isolated Vietnamese bishop Ngo Dinh Thue. Once a priest, always a priest! For according to canon law the ordination of a priest can never be revoked, not even by a formal excommunication. The bookkeeper from Seville promoted himself to bishop and then appointed a whole host of followers to other eminent positions.

In 1978, after the death of Pope Paul VI, Clemente convened a council in Bogotá, which opened with a hailstorm of encyclicals and bulls. To the astonishment of Christendom, it turned out that the Roman bishop Woytila was a fraud—was, in fact, the Antichrist himself. In this serious situation the Council of Bogotá had no alternative but to declare itself a conclave and elect a new pope. So the bookkeeper from Seville became head of the "Catholic, Apostolic, and Palmarian Church."

His new Vatican is situated on the very godforsaken field that had achieved a certain notoriety because of Mary's appearance there. A sixteen-foot-high concrete wall seals off the sanctuary from the outside world; the Berlin Wall looks like a garden fence by comparison. An iron door, without a nameplate or a bell, without a hint as to what's behind it, opens only once a day; a tiny peephole allows for the inspection of visitors. Behind the wall, armed guards with trained dogs are ready to protect the new St. Peter's. Four towers and a giant cupola of reinforced concrete soar into the sky alongside the steel frames of several incomplete towers and domes.

The mass held in this megalomaniac village church is an extravagant spectacle. It's celebrated at twenty-six altars simultaneously, and because this number is inadequate to accommodate the thirty-nine officiating bishops, the sacrament of the mass takes place alternately, in a kind of relay. While the priests swarm around the altars, the congregation in the elongated nave looks quite lost. It consists of a few heavily veiled nuns, who have arrived from Seville in a minibus, and a small crowd of old women from the neighboring village, who from time to time kiss the plastic covers of their scapularies.

With a pleasurable frisson of horror, the people of Seville recount old and new rumors about the apostolic concentration camp of El Palmar de Troya. There's talk of pregnant nuns, of priests castrating themselves, of homosexual cardinals, and of African monks who were committed to the mental hospital with delirium tremens. There are also rumors about shady bequests, about Texas millionairesses and English aristocrats said to be hidden away in the Andalusian Vatican.

It seems that the citizens of Seville lack the proper faith, a readiness to follow the pontiff. After the last anecdotes have been told, they just shrug their shoulders. The smell of the stake has blown away. Gregory XVII can offer his countrymen only a parody of ancient ecstasies, a pale shadow of the old Spanish madness.

A few faded newspaper clippings from 1978 recall the former bookkeeper's most extravagant idea. On the instructions of the Holy Virgin in El Palmar, the pope had several thousand Spaniards canonized. Among them were Saint Luís Carrero Blanco, Saint José Antonio, and Saint Francisco Franco. The bartender at the Golden Tower doesn't seem to remember this solemn act. He calmly pockets the tip, while His Holiness knocks back his fifth glass of wine.

THE IMPENETRABLE

The fun stops in Arrigorriaga. Here the Spanish consensus comes to an end. For just thirty-five pesetas the suburban train from Bilbao carries me into enemy territory. Arrigorriaga is ten kilometers upstream from the Basque metropolis on the Nervíon River. The whole valley was devastated decades ago by an industrialization that advanced more brutally than a tank division. The district looks like a trash dump. At six o'clock in the evening the working-class streets—in Arrigorriaga all the streets are working-class—are deserted.

Dogs bark. The last palm tree died long ago. The walls are covered with slogans.

Here, unlike in Madrid, painting graffiti is no sport for outsiders; it's not an outlet for sectarians, not an alibi for students from the lower middle class, but a collective obsession. The writing on the wall only expresses what everyone thinks, and, whatever the signature, the words—which I can understand, though I don't speak a word of Basque—always say the same thing: "Clear out forever! Out!" The addressee, the Spanish state and its representatives, is nowhere to be seen.

The customers in the smoky bar subject the stranger to a test in a fraction of a second: friend or foe? Anyone who's neither one nor the other doesn't register. The hatch opens for only the blink of an eye and then shuts again. From the outside this society appears compact; inside it is full of divisions that the outsider suspects but cannot understand.

A man who walks like a pensioner though he's not yet fifty—he works in a paper mill that may soon be closed down—shows me the sights of the place: the old abandoned school, the town hall, the House of the People. All were built in the days of the Republic. They are constructed in a unique regional style, half folkloric, half monumental, examples of an artistic tradition born of adversity.

The explanations my companion gives me are a little confused. Money rules the world, Reagan is a deadly enemy of the Basques, we can hold out for another hundred years, the Holy Virgin protects us, the Spanish must be expelled, if NATO left us in peace we'd all be rich. Then he points to two windows in the top story of a shabby tenement. "Do you know who lives there? Argela's mother!" He pronounces the name with reverence, as if speaking of the Pope or Einstein or Lenin. Who is Argela? A saint? A genius? I don't dare ask. It's inconceivable to my companion that there might be people to whom the name Argela means nothing.

Later I learn that he was talking about Beñaran Ordeñana, the founder of the military wing of ETA, the militant Basque liberation movement. Ordeñana organized the assassination of Franco's regent, Carrero Blanco. Later he himself fell victim to a car bomb probably planted by an agent of the Spanish police. Since then he has been honored as a martyr.

In the evening the train station at Arrigorriaga is deserted. One employee is asleep, another is reading the newspaper, a third is on the phone. No one wants to sell me a ticket.

When, in an exclusive restaurant in the center of Bilbao, I mention the name of the gentleman with whom I have an appointment, I am solicitously—no, almost obsequiously—received. Xabier Arzallus makes an impressive figure, gray-haired, highly educated, distinguished. He owes his authority less to his political prominence than to his intelligence and to the courage he has shown. The left calls him the Pope of Basque Nationalism. There is indeed something clerical about his language; one might almost say it is unctuous. His German is perfect, his syntax reveals a Jesuit training, his carriage a closeness to power. But there is something else as well, a hardness that doesn't fit the manner of a lawyer or a diplomat.

"If one is used to living in the jungle," he explains to me, "then one forgets about fear. Read what Humboldt wrote about the Basque character in 1800 and you'll understand what I mean. My great-grandfather went to prison for insurrection. That was in the 1860s. I found his musket when I was rebuilding my country house. The whole country is full of hiding places for weapons. Under Franco we smuggled many people across the border who are now our enemies—Communists, Christians, Socialists. I'm telling you this so you'll understand that history is more important to us than anything else. We have always been oppressed and we have always lost."

"And so you always feel you're in the right. Even if only a

quarter of the inhabitants of the Basque Country understand Basque, even if a third of the population consists of immigrants who are indifferent to the Basque question."

"I am a separatist, and I want our language, Euskara, to play the leading role in our country again. But there is no quick and painless route to these goals. My party is therefore ready to form alliances. The Nationalist Party follows every practicable path, including the parliamentary one. We have already achieved a great deal: regional autonomy, a native Basque police force, powers for the Basque regional government that would still have been unthinkable ten years ago."

"And what do you think of the activities of ETA, which are becoming more and more brutal and incomprehensible?"

"As you know, we have nothing to do with ETA. They accuse us of being collaborators and traitors. I'm not frightened of them. Our political differences are obvious. But don't expect me to morally condemn their supporters. Our common bonds are not as easily broken. The present generation of the military wing are our grandchildren. Their impatience with the government's broken promises, torture, and dirty tricks is understandable. Any attempt to break their will by force is hopeless. It's hard to defeat someone who is ready to die at any time."

Do I understand him correctly, this intellectual with the manners of an abbot? The silverware gleams, the wine in the glasses glistens. "So terrorism is not a problem of conscience for you as a Christian?"

"Violence is a strategic question, not a religious one," replies Xabier Arzallus tersely. I think of the Islamic ayatollahs, whom the Western press likes to portray as crude troublemakers and bloodthirsty hoodlums when, in fact, they are dignified, sober men with a great reputation for wisdom.

"But why does no one think of solving the Basque question through a plebiscite?"

"I would have nothing against it, but neither ETA nor

Madrid would accept a plebiscite. They block each other. ETA would have to expect a disastrous defeat, and the government in Madrid could count on facing a coup."

"Do you believe that an independent Basque state would be at all viable? I've noticed that the Nationalists' programs are fairly vague in this respect. I don't see how you intend to solve the region's economic problems."

"There are more important things than the economy. We're not Marxists. Basque militancy has increased with greater affluence, not declined. We are not as easily corrupted as the government in Madrid. We are ready to pay any price to get rid of the Spanish government—and we would also put up with a lower standard of living."

And then, with a mephistophelian smile, the *éminence grise* of the Basque National Party allows himself an ironic remark over coffee that takes the edge off the pathos of his argument. "If we ever became a sovereign state—and that would be possible only by some practical joke of history—I have no idea what the result would be."

Herri Batasuna (the Party of Popular Unity) is considered the political arm of ETA. Its spokesman, Iñeki Esnaola, a member of the party executive, and a lawyer like Arzallus, carefully avoids every outward sign of radicalism and is as glib and innocuous as if he were advocating the Basque version of a moderate Social Democratic Party. He deliberately plays down the party's left wing: "We are a coalition of various groups, so we also have to put up with the Marxist-Leninists. Anyway, they're only a minority. We don't want to make our country an Albania on the Bay of Biscay; we're more interested in the Swedish model."

"But it's said that ETA has the last word because it's got the guns."

"Well, you know, no one gets by without myths to fall back on when it comes to the Basque question. The Nationalist

Party needs us as bogeymen and men of terror. We need ETA because without it no one in Madrid would take us seriously. And it's the same the other way around. Where would the Guardia Civil be without ETA? Where would the army be without the Guardia Civil, which does all its dirty work? Where would the government be without the army? It allows the government to present itself as the lesser evil, as the guardian of threatened democracy. Do you know Journey to Jerusalem,* the children's game in which you have to change places as quickly as possible? One chair at a time is taken away. That's what Spanish pluralism is like. Of course, it's a pretty violent game. Yet all we want is the right to self-determination. Everyone's entitled to that. We're saying, Give it to us and you'll have peace and quiet. Refuse it and you'll have to take the consequences. And we're not going to give way on that point. It's sacred to us."

I ask him the same question I ask every Basque: What is it that's so intangibly distinctive about the Basques? What kind of secret "essence" do they want to assert? What does this metaphysical substance, which can't be defined but can only be felt, consist of? Mr. Esnaola could not explain it to me, and neither could the writer I visited in prison.

Martuene, a few miles outside San Sebastián, is a "soft jail." I had left my I.D. behind in the hotel by mistake and was admitted on trust, a liberality unimaginable in Germany. I was left alone for two hours with the writer Joseba Sarrion-andía, a small, friendly, bearded man who was born twenty-seven years ago in Durango, in the heart of the Basque country, not far from Guernica. In Durango his picture hangs on the wall of every house. He is the hero of the little market town; it is said that four-fifths of the inhabitants call for his release.

* A game similar to musical chairs. (Trans.)

He seems gentle, almost naïve, and although his stories are considered difficult and artificial, the Basque public buys them enthusiastically. It's a relatively inexpensive gesture. The literary prizes that delegations from several Basque communities have presented to him in his cell are not only recognition for his prose but also for the calm obstinacy with which he refuses to renounce ETA.

Ideological abstractions hardly interest Joseba. His writing is more important to him than anything else. He would rather talk about poems than politics. When I ask him about his illegal activities, he glances resentfully at me. He speaks quietly and his answer consists of only four words: "I did not kill." I believe him. Factually, without emphasis, speaking almost in a monotone, he recites the litany of his experiences. The arrest, the journey in the green patrol wagon of the "well-deserving" (as the Guardia Civil, without a trace of irony, calls itself), the mock execution during transport, the blows, the nine-day-long interrogations, the electrodes on the genitals, the nine months of solitary before the trial, standing at attention against the cell wall for three hours a day. "There's nothing special about it. I am only one of three hundred Basque prisoners. Nothing has changed in Spain. The military and the police are still in charge." The sentence of the court was thirty years' imprisonment for taking part in a kidnapping. "I could go home tomorrow if I signed a paper renouncing the armed struggle. But I'm not signing."

Then, shyly, and full of enthusiasm, he again talks about the poems that have helped him to survive five years of prison and torture unharmed, and about Kafka, German literature, and Alfred Kubin's novel *The Other Side*. He has no doubts about his cause. He is friendly, modest, and quite impervious to argument.

"They have turned out the lights, I must stop," he wrote to me from prison afterwards. "I find it difficult to continue with a candle in one hand and a pen in the other." I would have liked to reply to him, but Joseba Sarrionandía is now a man without an address. Disguised as a musician, he mixed in with the members of a band who had played for the prisoners of Martuene. There has been no trace of him since the concert.

The daily newspaper *Egin* is the organ of the Marxist-Leninist-influenced separatists in Euskadi. Criticism of ETA's activities is not to be expected from it. The paper advocates the hegemony of Euskara, but four-fifths of the articles in it are written in Spanish. A newspaper that promoted the Basque language in Basque would be unsellable. "The only real difference between us and the Spanish is our culture," says *Egin*'s manager. "It's more important than sovereignty."

I can't get that statement out of my head. An old narrow-gauge railway links Bilbao and San Sebastián, but no one wants to travel on it. Everyone goes by bus. It's brand-new, luxuriously equipped, air-conditioned; the seats are adjustable, the windows are tinted. The driver's pride and joy, though, is the video system. American, English, Spanish, and Basque pop groups bawl out their throbbing songs in the passenger's ear for seventy minutes. No one can even read a newspaper with this hellish racket. Conversation with a neighbor, in any language, is impossible. The passengers don't look at the green hills of their homeland but at an endless series of idiotic video promos. I keep an eye out for a CIA agent or an emissary of the central government in Madrid—in vain. To liquidate Basque culture the driver has only to press a button. He knows what his passengers want.

THE CENTRIFUGE

Somos una nación—We are a nation! This declaration can be read on the walls of many houses in southern Spain. It presents the visitor with a number of problems. For one thing, its logic is questionable; if it's true it's superfluous, and if it is without substance then it only reflects the impotence of its authors. Nor is it clear from the slogan which nation is meant. For in Spain there are an indefinite number of nationalities, and their number seems to increase year by year.

"For decades," writes the heterodox thinker and essayist Fernando Savater, "we suffered from the pathetic delusions and the late-imperial arrogance imposed upon us by the improbable character of Spain. But now we see ourselves confronted by the equally improbable character of the Basque country, Catalonia, Andalusia, and Galicia. Soon it will get to the point where we'll be arguing about the immortal spirit of Zaragoza or about the historical obligations that come with being born in Fuengirola . . . I don't know, but it all seems like a waste of time to me."

Everyone wants to be special, all the more so since there are fewer and fewer differences between us; every little village has its local patriotism and looks down on the next village. Such desires are comprehensible in a banal world, perhaps even legitimate—but can they be realized if every choral society behaves as if I were the Vietcong? The autonomists' shrill tones parody the rhetoric of the national liberation movements in the Third World. I cannot pass judgment on their motives, but any package tourist is in a position to conclude that Galicia is not a second Nicaragua, nor Catalonia a second Afghanistan. To me such comparisons seem somewhat exaggerated even in the case of the Basque country.

Of course, Spain has never been a homogeneous country; of course, Madrid's centralism is bureaucratic folly; of course, the Franco regime suppressed every independent impulse for decades. Reason enough to look around for a viable form of federalism but hardly to surrender to a cult of provincialism.

As far as I can see, every person in Spain today can speak

or write in whatever language he chooses. However, that doesn't stop the inhabitants of the country from engaging in linguistic civil war. With the end of the great building boom, enough construction capacity seems to have been freed for a new project: the erection of a Spanish Tower of Babel. "The Asturian language, 'Bable,' will soon be used by Iberian Airways flight crews to announce takeoffs from or landings at the airport of the Autonomous Principality of the Asturias" (*El País*, May 17, 1985).

It's a harmless diversion. It's also entirely reasonable for the inhabitants of Barcelona to demand that the city have street signs not only in Spanish but in the language of the country too. Yet hardly has this goal been attained than the local language guerrillas set to work obliterating every single Spanish word. These self-appointed language police are by no means marginal. Heribert Barrera, a leading politician of the Republican left in Barcelona, put it to me quite bluntly: "We reject bilingualism in Catalonia. One of the two languages will win, and the victor will be Catalan. It is unacceptable for the language of the colonizer to keep the upper hand here. And we want the hegemony of Catalan to be guaranteed by law. If it were up to me, English would be our second language in the future, not Spanish."

The spokesman of Herri Batasuna can hardly afford to be less militant. Without any regard for the wishes of parents and pupils, he demands that instruction in the schools of his region be conducted entirely in Basque.

Such demands show that the revolt against central authority remains transfixed by its authoritarian opponent. Liberation can be realized only by force. The autonomists have merely changed the target: now it is their own local governments that are supposed to provide the remedies, through laws, regulations, and decrees. They fail to observe that it's always society, never the state, that is decisive for the vitality of a culture and the strength of a language.

* * *

I told my conclusion to a psychoanalyst in Barcelona. "You're right," she said, "but your explanation doesn't go far enough. Haven't you noticed how extraordinarily artificial all these disputes are? The degree of hysteria shows that there must be something else involved, that it's a compensation, a displacement.

"The true nationalist knows, of course, that the victories of the Castilian central government were always Pyrrhic, that the Spanish state is really rather weak, that our politicial parties are houses of cards, and that our institutions are strangely isolated islands in the sea of reality. The true nationalist isn't plagued by doubts about his own identity. You see his self-confidence in the shoulder-shrugging tautology of our [i.e., Catalonia's] president, Jordi Pujol, who says *somos quienes somos*, we are who we are, and leaves it at that. Of course, the old demagogue is delighted to use the linguistic dispute for his own ends; but he also knows that our culture and language—and you know that I am Catalan with all my heart and soul—is far too rich and vigorous to need the poisonous artificial fertilizers the state provides."

"You're getting away from your argument. You mentioned compensation, displacement. Displacement of what?"

"It's so obvious! Just take a look at our country! The thoughtless vulgarity with which the countryside is being destroyed; the subhuman housing; the crisis of the old industrial areas . . . And yet despite these problems a local patriotism is developing that can think of nothing better to do than wave flags and overturn road signs! A local patriotism that doesn't care about clean water or housing, that doesn't know anything about industrial policies, on-the-job safety, infrastructure, or ecology . . . It's the same old Spanish madness, only now it no longer feels at home in the center, where it hatched, but has built its nest on the periphery, on the walls of the Spanish centrifuge. The managers are in charge in Madrid, but in the meantime the Basques and the Gallegos, the Asturians and the Canary Islanders, the Andalusians and the Catalans have themselves adopted the old heroic cantankerousness, the zealotry, the national self-importance and sensitivity and fanaticism. Eternal Spain is a senile mystification. The only people who still cling to it are the very ones who would rather die than be Spanish!"

THE SHARDS

The Intersection Known as The Crossroads of His Eminence (El Encruce de Su Eminencia). A fire in the middle of the road, children standing around burning car tires. The suburban ghetto consists of cheap new buildings with subsidized rents. Threatening faces. It's like driving through Harlem. A bride, dressed completely in white, in front of a shabby bar. A donkey beneath a kitchen balcony. An abandoned merry-go-round; no one here has the desire or the money to ride on it. This is where the Spain of the travel agencies ends. Drugs, gypsies, child prostitution.

The traffic lights at the intersection are red. The wheels crunch. The road surface is covered with tiny glass splinters. The experts are waiting nearby: emaciated sixteen-year-olds holding the wrenches they use to smash the back windows of cars stopped at the lights. The robbery only takes a few seconds. They've hesitated a second too long, the light changes to green, the driver accelerates, as we drive off with screeching tires, the terrain of the suburb is left behind in the dusk.

My picture of Spain, a heap of shards on a street intersection. I saved my travel bag, but the young highwaymen have, in a few seconds, stolen my slim emergency pack of preconceived notions, my stereotypes and prejudices.

Bouvard and Pécuchet. One week after he has taken up his post, the newly appointed director general of the Ministry of

Culture is trying to ascertain the number of his subordinates. Some turn up only twice a month; others don't even bother to pick up their salary. Whispering insiders offer their estimates: the ministry employs four thousand civil servants in the capital, seventeen to twenty-one thousand in the whole country.

Four months later, while walking down the ministry corridors, the director general stumbles upon a little room in which six censors are working. Censorship was abolished a long time ago, of course, but these gentlemen are by no means idle. They leaf zealously through the books that, in accord with venerable tradition, continue to be sent to them.

Philip Marlowe in La Mancha. The editor has sent him to a remote provincial capital. The journalist, a former sports writer, is not to be envied. Local politics are complicated. He finds not one but three, four, five closed societies, all as suspicious, vain, and opaque as in a Balzac novel. The newspaper pays badly. The reporter is paid not for what he writes but only for what Madrid chooses to print. The apartment looks as if its tenant had been away for a long time. The cheese in the refrigerator is moldy, the butter rancid, the ham green. But the correspondent displays the tenacity of a terrier. Soon he knows a great deal about tender offers and contracts and the strange coalitions and maneuverings within the local council. But after several months there are still questions he cannot answer. Who is the man in the very long Mercedes, always wearing dark glasses, whose chauffeur is allowed to park anywhere, even in the space reserved for the chief justice of the court? Why doesn't the mail arrive? Who is the destitute widow who holds a reception at her villa every Saturday? Everyone pays court to her as if it were she who decided who gets promoted. Why is the light on in the journalist's room when he comes home late? The lamp shade is gone, and a naked light bulb swings above the table. He took good care to lock up when he left the house. And the whiskey bottle is lying empty in the shower. Who finished it off? Is this meant to be a final warning?

Oral Tradition.   The White Book of the Ministry of Education and Science states that there are exactly 11,418,724 functional illiterates in Spain. "I ask myself who counted them," says my friend the critic, "and whether whoever it was thought of including themselves. Please don't think I have anything against illiterates. My professional experience tells me that our country's best poets must be among them."

Society of Abundance.   How many doormen are there on the Iberian peninsula? Half a million? Three-quarters of a million? A million? They sit and gossip under the stairs, or they have a little room to themselves, or they visit other doormen and play cards. What they are there for remains obscure. They don't bother about the heating, they have no idea what to do with a broom, even the police can do without their information. The private doormen are idle but harmless. The janitors become a nuisance as soon as they infest a public building.

I count four at the entrance to the town hall of the place where I have some business. One, who registers nothing, nevertheless sits in a glass box with the sign "Registro." Another stands at the door. Two others wait in their own room, fidgeting with their pistols. On each floor yet another sits apathetically at a little table, facing an empty coffee cup, a full ashtray, and a blank form that will never be filled out. In every anteroom yet another two guards stare off into space. Their job is to make life difficult for anyone who enters the building. Their directions, if they give directions at all, are invariably wrong. Their philosophy of life is Soviet-bureaucratic. They are the bodyguard of inefficiency, the praetorians of idleness, the guardian angels of red tape.

No one can fire a million doorkeepers. And what would be the point, anyway? They're cheaper than the superfluous general secretaries and presidents they guard, than the fourteen hundred superfluous generals and admirals, than the superfluous Guardia Civil. The superfluous is a mysterious category, without which no society can survive. The janitors are as troublesome as a goiter, but not fatal like a tumor.

Haunted Time. There is perhaps no other country in the world with so many ruined buildings. Theaters in which movies stopped running long ago, empty signal towers, collapsing breweries, apartment houses where only rats make their home, factories, dockside granaries, palaces, garages: their doors blocked up, façades blackened, windows nailed shut. Sometimes only the steel frame of a building is left. Occasionally a door bangs in the wind.

Then, when one least expects it, some of these ruins show signs of life. Poisonous smoke pours out of a dilapidated factory, a welder's blue flame glows inside a rusted shed, an ancient crane begins to move, someone steps onto the balcony of an abandoned villa. And right next door a new supermarket, an industrial building faced with golden mirror glass, a luxury apartment house.

The local inhabitants are taken aback when you ask them about the ghost architecture in their neighborhood. They mutter something about rent laws, about property speculation. But their explanations are half-hearted. The truth is, they don't notice the dead buildings.

The ruins are stubborn witnesses to a silent civil war no one pays any attention to. The smell of the old and abandoned also clings to many institutions: the trade union headquarters of the Franco period, the offices of "corporations,"* the clubs,

---

* *Trade associations established for the purpose of "harmonizing" the interests of employers and workers. (Trans.)*

and the barracks. One walks past their dark walls and senses that, yes, perhaps there is still life in them, but it is a life after death.

A Silent Change of Power.   In San Vicente, a sleepy lane just behind the cathedral at Oviedo, there is a remarkable café: the Home of the Blue Division.* The lamps at the entrance are decorated with the Falange's bundle-of-arrows insignia and with German helmets from the Second World War. The glass is broken. Two three-foot-high artillery shells greet the customer on either side as he enters.

Written on the walls of the building: *¡Viva la droga!* Down with NATO! Reagan is a murderer!

The café looks as bare and dark as a soup kitchen. A priest in an old-fashioned habit chats with the veteran behind the bar. There's a stuffed wild goose on top of the television. Some relics of the Blue Division are preserved above the bar: a battered mess kit, a helmet, rusty cartridge cases. On the wall, the Caudillo extends a welcome from the left and José Antonio Primo de Rivera from the right; the king is in the middle. No one even glances at them or thinks of releasing them from their *ménage à trois*.

The Home of the Blue Division has fallen to a band of conquerors. The invasion took place without bloodshed. The victors feel so secure that they don't bother about the decor; they ignore it. At the plastic tables high-school girls are writing out their homework in notebooks, tongues pressed against upper lips out of sheer eagerness and concentration. A bearded hippie spoons up his lentil soup and leafs through a volume of poems. Philosophy students play cards. A rosy-cheeked girl listens ecstatically to her Walkman. A meal—

* *A volunteer force sent by Franco to fight against the Soviet Union alongside German forces during the Second World War. (Trans.)*

soup, hamburger, fries, bread, and wine—costs just 250 pesetas. It's the cheapest meal in town. The past has become a backdrop, a stage set for a play that's no longer in the repertory. The grandchildren can't be bothered to sweep away the shards.

EPILOGUE:
THE SEACOAST OF BOHEMIA
BY TIMOTHY TAYLOR

....

(*THE NEW NEW YORKER*, FEBRUARY 21, 2006)

RAMSTEIN

I pushed open the door, and a shudder ran down my back. Nothing had changed. The one-armed bandit against the wall flashed and rang as it had done twelve years before; the mustard jar was in the same place on the checked tablecloth; in the dim, reddish light the same pale rolls were drying up in their wicker coffin. An aroma of beer and fries hung heavy in the air, the yellow bull's-eye panes rattled every time a freight train passed outside, and anyone unfamiliar with the whims of German *Gemütlichkeit* unfailingly bruised his knee on the crossbeams that lurked under the heavy rustic tabletops.

The menu, in a fake-leather folder as heavy as a prayer book, was also unchanged: pork chops with mashed potatoes, I read under the yellowed plastic sheet, schnitzel Hawaii, sausages with potato salad, sweet wine by the glass, dry wine by the glass.

My heart sank, but at the same time I was overcome by a perverse feeling of satisfaction: this German bar was my Archimedean point, the only corner of Europe I knew inside out. For two years I had spent every free evening in this place. I knew that time stood still here, that with the schnitzels of Frau Leininger (a.k.a. "the Walrus") world history had bitten off more than it could chew. My research had to begin in this godforsaken place.

"Is it really possible? Are you back in this country again, Mr. Teilohr?" The proprietress came rolling toward me like a steamer in a heavy sea, put her hands on her hips, and gave me a glance full of ghastly flirtatiousness. She subjected everything American to the rules of Rhineland phonetics, so I had become, and remained, Mr. Teilohr. It was close to a miracle that she recognized me at all, for I hadn't set foot in her bar, her village, her country, or her continent for twelve years.

I was as little prepared for her hearty welcome as for the silence in the bar. The Golden Gate of my memory was quite different: loud, packed, and violent. In its best days there was never a single seat empty after nine, the music was deafening, the black GIs were thumping the slot machines, and the little ratlike pushers went from table to table with their goods. The foreign-exchange rate was murderous for the soldiers, and they could afford only the cheapest bars and brothels. The whiskey the proprietress sold tasted dangerous. It probably came from a chemical factory, yet Frau Leininger always poured it from old Johnny Walker bottles from the PX—she took care to maintain appearances. My superiors didn't like my hanging around in the Golden Gate—as a lieutenant, I was more or less duty-bound to get bored in the Officers' Club. But I felt like a convict behind the barbed wire of the base, and so, my boots caked with clay after the long days of the autumn maneuvers, I usually wound up in Frau Leininger's cozy purgatory. No one paid any attention to me, I didn't pay any attention to anyone. I sat there showing all the symptoms of chronic depression, got drunk silently and methodically, and waited for the obligatory fight. Then the Walrus calmly elbowed her way through the crowd, separated the knife-wielders, and threw her guests out. She didn't need any military police. Cursing, the GIs reeled out to their battered cars, slammed the doors, revved up the engines, and disappeared into the darkness. None of them had the faintest idea why they had been sent to this inhospitable place. I was always the last to leave the Golden Gate. I watched the taillights disappear and waited for the liaison staff driver who usually picked me up. I too felt as if I had been exiled to Europe.

The imperturbable Frau Leininger obviously saw things differently. After bringing me my beer and sausages, she planted herself in front of me, beamed, and said, "You know, Mr. Teilohr, when you were here—those were the days! Do you still remember when you tried to put out the Christmas tree lights with gin?" What could I say? I couldn't recall such amusements, even with the best will in the world.

On the other hand, my misgivings about Germany never went as far as those of the attaché at the American embassy in Bad Godesberg, whom I had called on shortly after my arrival in Europe. He looked thin and haggard, and the little red veins in his unsteady eyes gave him a somewhat harassed appearance.

"Mr. Taylor, please be careful! That's a warning!" Those were his first words.

"Careful of what?" I asked. "Are you afraid of the few surviving terrorists who are still running around?"

"They can't stand us!" he exclaimed. "They hate us!"

"But who can't stand us?"

"All of them. The Germans. The French. The Spanish. They're all anti-American. We have virtually no friends left here anymore."

I tried to calm him. "But the alliance still exists, doesn't it?" I said.

"The alliance exists only on paper! It's not an alliance anymore, it's a bad joke."

"What do you expect? After we withdrew our troops . . . God knows the two hundred men in Berlin don't count . . ."

"Exactly!" he cried.

"But it was our decision. Congress . . ."

"I was against it from the start."

I felt sorry for him but I didn't know how to console him. And, after all, it was his job to help me, not the other way around. He pulled himself together and asked what he could do for me.

"I assume you need a couple of contacts. But the politicians here . . ."

I assured him that I was far from eager to elicit anti-American remarks from the Bonn statesmen. "Talking to politicians is never very productive," I said. "They're condemned to bore the world."

"Don't underestimate these people," he whispered. "They're capable of anything. You know, Taylor, the West Germans were always two-faced."

"Is that the official CIA assessment?" I asked.

"For Christ's sake, if you quote me I'll deny everything."

"I don't understand why you're complaining. The bosses in Bonn hung on every little word from Washington for decades . . ."

"That was a long time ago. In those days they just didn't dare to show what they were really thinking."

"You're getting pretty worked up about it, Murphy."

"Does that surprise you? The whole downtown is crawling with Russians. Ever since they've been allowed to travel, you trip over Russian tourists everywhere in Western Europe . . . It's a very serious security problem."

"Yes, I understand. You've got your hands full. But ultimately it all comes down to business."

"You can say that again! They use every trick in the book to force us out of the market. The European Community . . ."

"That's enough, Murphy! You're talking about it as if it were a world power. You know as well as I do that the European community is a henhouse, a snarled-up ball of states that get smaller and smaller—if you can still call them states at all."

"But they all manage to agree when it comes to putting us down. And then if you thump the table they hide inside their tangled mess. No clear statement, no long-term perspective. No offense to anyone at all. All their imagined complexities, privileges, and minorities have to be respected. Sometimes it's the environmentalists who have to be featherbedded, then it's the Moslems or the Basques or the retired Communists. A while ago they even wanted to print their banknotes in twelve languages. It would drive you crazy! I'm glad I'm being transferred to Seoul soon, at least the situation there is clear right from the start."

It was a good quarter of an hour before I managed to extricate myself from his tirades. He even wanted to see me to the door.

"Please don't bother," I said. "You've been very helpful."

No wonder we've got problems, I thought on the way to the station, with diplomats like that . . . Nevertheless, I felt sorry for Murphy, and ultimately, like all paranoiacs, he wasn't completely wrong. After all, I knew only too well what it was like for an American to be stationed in Europe for years on end.

Although the population had declined in recent years, I had the impression that everything was even more cramped than before on this side of the Atlantic. The crowds in the pedestrian precinct were unbearable. Free movement in this country was impossible. Compulsory travel by train contributed to the feeling. The train to Kaiserslautern was good, even luxurious, but I would rather have gone by car, and the bureaucratic limitations on road travel exasperated me. I prepared myself for a boring journey. My fellow travelers brought out their books. That too was a European fad. At Koblenz a Bulgarian or Yugoslav family got on and immediately unpacked their delicacies. I spent the rest of the journey in a cloud of garlic.

"Yes, the Golden Gate has certainly seen better days," continued the proprietress. She had sat down at my table, breathing heavily. "I might just as well close down for all the business I get since the base was deactivated, Mr. Teilohr." I was indeed the only guest. "But what else can I do at my age? The new shopping mall went under five or six years ago, and Elsie's place, you remember, the big disco with the laser show, it shut down a long time ago too. A disaster for us, Mr. Teilohr, a terrible shame! The whole district has gone down the drain! Did you enjoy your meal?"

At least one person mourns us, I thought. Then I took a room on the second floor. There was a musty smell, as if no one had lived in it for years. The next morning I took a walk through the town. The proprietress hadn't exaggerated. The deserted gas stations and the boarded-up store windows made it look like a ghost town.

I crossed the empty freeway and followed a track through the woods for a while. The concrete fence posts were still standing, but the rusty wire netting was lying on the ground. The huge area of the former base was obviously unused. I worked my way through the undergrowth and reached the compound I had lived in.

The house was still there but the weeds were a yard high in the porch. The banisters were broken. I tested the steps carefully. The floor in my living room was rotted. The ceiling evidently leaked. The skeleton of a refrigerator stood in the kitchen. Not even a tramp could have found shelter here. I startled a herd of deer between the munitions depot and the helicopter hangar. The airfield control tower had collapsed. On the way back I tripped over a pair of tank tracks in the grass. Were there any unexploded bombs here? Buried poison gas?

I shivered. I remembered the bunkers and tank barriers, remains of Second World War fortifications, that I had stumbled across during our field training exercises years ago. And I asked myself whether this landscape of ruins was the right starting point for my European expedition, or whether my first step had already led me into a labyrinth of déjà vu.

THE HAGUE
....

There are still a couple of taxis at the station, but they only go to the suburbs. As in most European cities, the center of town is blocked off. After a week I already have a corn on my foot. The Indian summer here is tropical, my shoes are in danger of sticking to the soft asphalt.

The mixture of dignity and vulgarity one finds in the Netherlands is unique. The transition from slum to palace is fluid. The male prostitutes wear green-plastic ID cards around their necks, guaranteed AIDS-free. Exotic ragouts simmer on the street outside cheap Asian restaurants. Drug dealers, as persistent as mosquitoes, swarm around the passersby. Right next to them, old ladies with stern expressions examine the fruit in old-fashioned grocery stores. Once their daily shopping rounds are done, they revive themselves with heavy cream cakes in a homely cafe. The Renaissance houses are perfectly restored. Corpulent civil servants chat on the steps. I force my way through a melee of mulattos, Surinamese, and Moluccans.

Finally, at exactly 11:00 A.M. I reach my goal, a cool, spacious, classical villa in a quiet street not far from the Parklaan. Its pearl-gray pillars and pilasters suggest an embassy. This is the home of the van Rossum Auction House.

The room on the first floor is crowded, there's no chance of finding a seat. Yet there's not a single camera, and no blazing spotlights. This auction is nothing like the media spectacles in London, New York, and Tokyo. Most of those present are very old gentlemen, with only a scattering of young bankers. Women are almost entirely absent. The models who surround the auctioneer at Sotheby's or Hitocha's are missing too. No bids are displayed. Here business is conducted discreetly and in complete silence. A glance is enough. It can seem like an outburst of unrestrained passion if a bidder goes so far as to raise his card. The prices leap upwards under the mumblings of the auctioneer. A Château

Cheval-Blanc 1991—not even a particularly outstanding year—is knocked down at sixty-four hundred dollars. A magnum of Pétrus, 1993, reaches nineteen thousand, and even lesser wines like a fifth of Cru Classé from the Médoc effortlessly reach eighteen hundred to two thousand dollars. The highest prices of all, of course, are paid for the vintages from the late seventies. After a long fight, a Château Palmer, one of the lengendary '78s, goes to an elderly, frail-looking man dressed in black, who looks like a figure from a Velázquez painting. After two hours it's all over. The auction has brought in three to four million dollars—and all for a few hundred dusty bottles.

Robert van Rossum receives me courteously, with outstretched arms, in his paneled office. I have to sit down in a large wing chair. The green-glass lampshades give the room a touch of old-fashioned comfort. But van Rossum does not look like a *bon vivant*. His heartiness seems false, and I sense a thin, puckered miser hiding inside the body of the fifty-year-old man, like the doll inside the doll.

"Of course not," he responds to my first question, "I don't drink Bordeaux. I couldn't afford it. Most of these wines are no longer drunk nowadays, they're collected. They're museum pieces, souvenirs of a vanished culture. No doubt there are still some spendthrifts who open them. Your own countrymen are particularly prone to such ostentatious gestures. It's regarded as the ultimate extravagance. But by and large we're dealing with one of the many cults our civilization produces and which are so difficult to explain. Anthropologists compare it to the medieval veneration of reliquaries. Perhaps they're right. I don't really understand what they're getting at. All I can say is, I saw it coming."

He leaned back and, to my dismay, lit a cigar. It's one of the repellent features of a European journey that in private homes, even if not in public, one is frequently subjected to this disgusting and dangerous vice. I clenched my teeth and said, "I suppose that your house looks back on a long tradition."

"The company was founded in 1878, in these very rooms. Its activities were interrupted only by the Second World War. But the van Rossums had nothing to do with the wine trade. My great-grandfather began as a collector of graphic art, and he became a dealer almost inadvertently. Then in subsequent generations our activities expanded, first to painting and then to Asiatica and Greek and Roman jewelry as well."

"No modern art?"

"Never! We avoided that temptation at least. My father always took an anticyclical view. As a result, of course, he missed out on the great boom thirty or forty years ago. But then he was also untouched by the collapse of the market at the beginning of the nineties, when the bubble burst and no one was prepared to pay a penny for all the daubings of the twentieth century put together. When the wind changed, our holdings were suddenly worth millions. Virtually anything that was older than 1850 was torn out of our hands. You'll no doubt remember that at the time every little piece of junk became valuable, provided it was baroque or Renaissance junk. The problem was supply. The market soon dried up completely, high-quality material was simply no longer to be found. Well, that's beside the point. At any rate, I'd had enough of art dealing. Perhaps that's why later, I mean in June 1996, I immediately realized that a unique opportunity was presenting itself."

It was quite obvious that I was talking to a hard-boiled cynic.

"Do you think I'm cynical?" he asked, blowing out a fresh cloud of smoke and giving me a suspicious sideways glance.

I answered him with another question.

"How did you react when it happened? Can you remember any details?"

"Of course, very well. The first announcement came on a

Saturday. An explosion in one of the four reactors at Le Blayais. No cause for alarm. The usual attempt to cover up. As you know, it had already happened that Friday evening, at ten-fourteen.

"The authorities didn't begin to evacuate the Médoc until midday on Sunday. Bordeaux was evacuated on Monday morning. I immediately sat down at the phone and called my partners in Paris, London, Germany. I also bought up whatever I could lay my hands on in the Netherlands. I'm not a gambler by nature, but on this occasion I staked everything on a single card. The risk was enormous."

"Why? What do you mean?"

"Well, it was possible that, for once, the French government was telling the truth. For days Paris claimed that the situation was under control. In that case, as an art dealer with relatively modest reserves, I would have been left high and dry sitting on the biggest cellar of Bordeaux in the world. The company would have been buried under an inconceivable avalanche of debts."

"You were lucky."

"By Wednesday it was clear that there had been a meltdown in at least one reactor."

"You no doubt greeted the news with tears of gratitude."

"Your sarcasm is misplaced. The whole thing was hardly a joke. It was soon clear that the second reactor could no longer be controlled either. I'm still surprised that I was the only person to think of it . . ."

"At that moment people probably had other worries."

"Of course. Anyone who was here at the time won't forget it easily. The panic-stricken flight, the jammed roads, the shut-down airports, the shooting. When the army was finally sent in, the soldiers deserted *en masse*. And then the lynching of scientists, engineers, and industrialists . . . You'll remember it only from television."

"And you sat in your office and called up wine merchants?"

"I kept my nerve. Don't forget that usually the wind comes from the Atlantic and blows from west to southwest. It was an improbable stroke of luck that in the days immediately following the accident at Le Blayais a cold front moved up over the Pyrenees and a wind from the southeast drove the cloud away from land. Otherwise, we wouldn't be sitting here now. If the wind had turned 90 degrees then, the whole of Western Europe, not just the Bordelais, would be uninhabitable today."

"A few hundred thousand dead, but you made the deal of a lifetime."

"After years of nail-biting, don't forget that! Months went by before it became clear to the customers that not a single grape would be harvested in the Bordeaux region for generations to come. Then came the energy laws, the forced expansion of solar and hydrogen technology, the crisis of 1997 . . . Nobody was thinking about buying wine."

"But then came what you call the reliquary cult. When did you hold your first auction?"

"Just before the turn of the millennium. First we had to overcome a degree of ill feeling, a degree of distrust. On top of that there was the American competition, which we underestimated for a long time. Between you and me, apart from a few top estates perhaps, the best California vintages can easily hold their own with what I have to offer . . . The Spanish have made progress too . . . But, as I said, ultimately this has nothing to do with drinking."

I coughed. Although he had crushed his cigar into the ashtray, the butt was still glowing, spreading a penetrating stink through the room.

"I'd like to ask one last question," I said quickly. "What guarantee can you offer your customers that the wines you acquire are irreproachable in origin and condition?"

"A good question! Given today's prices, suspect goods are, of course, constantly coming onto the market. When they're not forgeries, they're looted stocks or smaller lots that have been smuggled out of the contaminated provinces. But remember that my basic stock left the region of origin long before the catastrophe. Nevertheless, as a matter of policy we never auction a single bottle without having first of all tested it in our own laboratory." He stood up and took a sealed bottle from a shelf.

"Here, you can see from this computer printout that the contents are absolutely untainted. We've made great progress in dosimetry. We are able to detect each isotope individually. Our levels are lower by a factor of three than those laid down in the European guidelines. So you can take this '83 Saint-Julien home without any risk whatsoever. Perhaps a bit too much tannin, but it keeps well and is not without finesse. I hope you'll like it."

I rose. The lie came easily. "Thank you," I said. "But I don't drink."

BERLIN

Not much is left of the broken charm of this city. Little of the heroic decadence that was a backdrop for so many films is still to be seen. The moles of culture, who once unearthed old and new myths from the rubble of history, left years ago. The city's air of debauchery disappeared with the end of its extraterritoriality. Pleasure and terror have given way to normality, and normality, wherever time is on its side, conquers everything.

The four white-helmeted men in the jeep who now, as before, cross Marx-Engels Square and circle the Gedächtniskirche are merely a quotation, a piece of folklore, a reminder of the Occupation and the city's four-power status. No one turns to look at them. Only the Japanese tourists bother to take a picture.

And the house in which we met, on the shores of the

Wannsee, might just as well have been in Copenhagen or Hannover. The postmodern clinker building bore no resemblance to that notorious villa in which, in 1942, another Wannsee Conference* had taken place. In fact it could be seen, gray and half hidden behind weeping willows, through the huge round sash windows, but no one gave it a glance. This was a meeting of a very different kind. On the agenda here were not Jews and other "alien races" but otters and hawk moths, larches and frogs. On the flawlessly printed cardboard sign that the uniformed hostess had placed in front of me were the following words: "Permanent Species Protection Conference of German-Speaking Countries / Panel of Experts / Timothy Taylor / Accredited Correspondent."

I was interested in this meeting because this was the only issue that other Europeans ungrudgingly left to the Swiss, the Austrians, and the Germans. The protection of endangered species was a Central European obsession. I knew that. Nevertheless, I was taken aback by the passion that the participants displayed.

Even the mayor's well-intentioned speech of welcome was interrupted by shouts, whistles, and boos. At the opening session there was a fierce argument over the agenda. And from the very first moment, masked demonstrators from the eco-anarchist milieu clashed with officers of the environmental police. A representative of the chemical industry, who made profuse ritual protestations of humility and reassurance, was shouted down. The new nature religions had also, of course, sent delegates—bizarrely dressed priests and one or two bishops in sunrobes. An aged veteran of the seventies, the founding period of the movement, got so worked up about a proposal presented by the Association of Bioethicists and Environmental Engineers that he had to be carried out of

* *I.e., the conference that set the "Final Solution" in motion. (Trans.)*

the hall, looking as red as a lobster and close to a heart attack.

If, despite all the uproar, I managed to understand the proceedings correctly, then the following points were being discussed: a bill to protect weeds in public and private green spaces, parks, and gardens; a general ban on skiing in the Alpine foothills; the construction of tunnels under railroad lines to allow the passage of small animals; the rebreeding of extinct species of butterfly and the setting up of artificial scent paths for the red-bellied toad (*Bombina bombina*); in addition, there was the question of agreeing on a location for the Community's Artificial Rain Forest Project.

All very interesting, but the noise in the hall was so unbearable that I decided to claim a minimum of species protection for myself. I left the meeting and went into the garden. A paradisiac stillness lay over the lake. Motorboats had been banned here for decades. At the bottom of the garden the slope to the shore was lined with tall bushes. I wanted to push my way through to the water. As I was doing so, I surprised a plump lady arguing passionately with her companion, who was wearing a baggy gabardine suit and looked like a retired bookkeeper. I would have taken it for a marital disagreement had I not been struck by the conspiratorial expression of the lady in the blue tailored two-piece. I mumbled an apology and went on.

"Aren't you the American reporter?" she called after me in her cheery girl's voice. I turned around and introduced myself. "But I didn't mean to disturb you," I said.

"Don't worry about that! How did you find the session?"

My reply was evasive, and a certain lack of enthusiasm was probably evident in my voice, for the two exchanged worried glances. There was an embarrassing pause.

"Have you been to the Wall yet?" asked the gentleman in gray eventually. For a moment I didn't know how to answer this surprising question.

"No," I admitted reluctantly. "I don't think there's been anything to see there for a long time."

"Ah," cried the lady—she had some of the mannerisms of a kindergarten teacher—and turned her lively, slightly protruding eyes on me, "but there you are very much mistaken! We have a very interesting situation at the Wall right now! By the way, my name is Ohlmeyer, Dr. Sabine Ohlmeyer of the West Berlin Senate, Nature Conservancy, and this is Professor Sturz of the GDR Ministry of the Environment."

While I was getting through the unavoidable handshakes, I remembered the pictures that had once gone around the world: the blasting of the concrete obstacles, the razing of the barriers, the bulldozers, the demolished customs huts.

"Why?" I asked. "What do you mean by 'a very interesting situation'?"

"You'll soon see!" exclaimed Dr. Ohlmeyer happily. "If you like, why don't you join me for a walk along the border this evening? Perhaps Professor Sturz can also spare you an hour. Won't you, Professor?"

We met near the former Checkpoint Charlie. The area behind the towers of the new banking quarter has kept something of the old Kreuzberg shabbiness. The smell of the postwar period still hangs over the old fire walls. An illegal bazaar has established itself on one of the last bomb sites. Here Turkish vendors sell slippers and stolen computers; there are stray dogs, crumbling sex shops, decrepit sausage stalls, and tramps sleeping in doorways surrounded by empty Chianti bottles.

The traffic on Friedrichstrasse was sluggish. The border policeman was a lonely, bored monarch in his glass box. He waved the few vehicles past. I watched him as, Walkman on his head, he nodded in time to the music, and I asked myself why I had let myself in for this appointment. But then I saw the fence. A brand-new, gleaming, silver chain link fence, at least nine feet high, set about twenty paces back from the street.

Dr. Ohlmeyer laughed. "You didn't expect that, did you?

Actually, the fence has been up less than three weeks. I'm afraid it was a wearisome business getting the consent of all the relevant authorities on both sides before we were allowed to erect the enclosure. Wasn't it, Professor?"

"I don't understand . . ."

"You'll see in a moment."

Flanked by the two experts, I crossed the border, a white line in the road. The former death strip has been fenced in on both sides. As we stalked on, zigzagging along it towards the Potsdamer Platz and the Brandenburg Gate, I saw the remains of old border installations through the fence: searchlights, ditches, and occasionally one of those crumbling watchtowers that send a shiver up anyone's back because they are so reminiscent of the concentration camps of the forties. And behind it was the Wall. It was still here, even if in places there were gaps where the piping along the top had fallen off. Professor Sturz handed me his binoculars, and I discovered that a lengthy section of the Wall disappeared under a wooden protective gallery—a brand-new casing roofed with the kind of board often put up on building sites.

"Isn't it fantastic?" chirped Dr. Ohlmeyer. "A unique biotope! Where else in the world is there such vegetation right in the middle of a metropolis?"

All I could see on the fenced-in area, which broadened out at this point were broom, lupines, and nettles as tall as a man.

"There are wild rabbits here," continued my companion, "hedgehogs, opposums, even blindworms! And as for insects, we've already counted six different varieties of parasitical hymenopter. We hope that bats and night birds will colonize the towers in time."

"But the Wall," I said. "Why hasn't it been torn down? What is that wooden construction for? It looks just as if . . ."

"That's just it, Mr. Taylor! This interference makes a mockery of all our efforts! And yet the whole site has been designated a nature reserve! This obstruction is the work of the architectural preservationists. They say the Wall must be preserved, that it's historically important and mustn't be abandoned and forgotten."

"Such opinions are voiced even in the GDR," claimed Professor Sturz, "although there has been considerable debate in the various government committees. But the provisional encasing undoubtedly means the architectural preservationists have achieved a partial victory."

"The art historians are the worst. They regard the Wall as a work of art because of the graffiti, which are, however, only to be found on the western side. The Senator responsible for the arts would like to make a twenty-mile-long open-air museum out of the biotope. But you know what that means nowadays, Mr. Taylor! Our museums are nothing but fairgrounds! If the architectural preservationists get their way, then this untouched landscape will be finished and everything that has developed here over the decades will be brutally trampled underfoot. That's why we need the support of the media, abroad as well, and we would be very grateful if you could draw the attention of the American public to our cause."

They looked at me in perfect harmony. All that was missing was for them to hold hands. I didn't know what to say. Perhaps, I thought, my first impression was not so wrong. Perhaps I had an inter-German pair of lovers before me. I didn't have the heart to disappoint them.

"Certainly," I said. "Berlin's giant knotgrass has my full support."

The Foreign Press Club was deserted. Berlin didn't make the headlines anymore, and the big electronic papers had pulled out their correspondents long ago. I had arranged to meet a British journalist I knew from New York, who was holding the line here because he was married to a German. He absentmindedly stirred his cappuccino as I told him about my experiences at the Wall. "That's just the thing," he said finally. "You absolutely have to use it. Sentimental and soft-headed, it's exactly what people want to hear. And, like all good news items, your German-German story is completely wrong."

"That wasn't my impression. On the contrary, the two of them are dead serious. That's what's so funny about it."

"Agreed," he replied. "Neverthelesss, you're on the wrong track altogether with your story."

"Why?"

"Because this inter-German harmony is a fiction. Putting aside your professor and his girlfriend, who probably have nothing in common apart from their obsession, the fact is, the Germans can't stand each other. East and West—they're like cat and dog!"

"I thought they'd settled their differences."

"Officially, yes. But the moment you stop taking their declarations at face value, you stumble into an undergrowth of complexes, rivalries, and resentments. It's significant that the number of inter-German marriages, of mixed marriages, if one can call them that, has remained minimal. Or take soccer. Without a massive police presence, there would be deaths at every GDR—Federal Republic match. To say nothing of the political apparatuses. And I mean parties of the same leanings on either side. They hate each other like poison. And when I hear my young friends talking about the other side—I'm telling you, they loathe each other! The Westerner swears by his Lufthansa cosmopolitanism, while the Easterner feels morally virtuous, as if he were automatically immune to every kind of decadence, corruption, and cynicism. In short, each feels superior to the other."

"And the famous reunification?"

"All just coffee and cakes. You see, we were all barking up the wrong tree for decades. Do you still remember how frightened of the Germans everyone was in the nineties?

Especially the French, of course, but the English were worried too—not to mention the Poles, who saw the Third World War looming on over the horizon. And what's happened? Nothing at all. Since then the German bogeyman has very quietly been laid to rest. We fell for it because we didn't know the first thing about German history."

"But wait a minute! It was German history that made us nervous. And with very good reason."

"Sure. But we didn't understand that German unity was only an episode. It lasted less than a hundred years, and what did it do for the Germans between Bismarck and Hitler? One crash landing after another. Instead, they've remembered their past: a millennium of patchwork. More than anything else, they'd like their provincial kings and princes back. Particularism is the true home of all Germans! And that's not just true of Germany. It's really a European phenomenon, apart from the French, who continue to stand by their centralism. The Europeans are proceeding according to an old motto: Divide but don't rule. By God, I know what I'm talking about! To hell with Great Britain! I'm not English, Tim. I'm Scottish!"

HELSINKI

Erkki Rintala had disappeared, disappeared without a trace. "No idea what's become of him."

I hadn't expected that. The president had resigned only two months before. The whole of Europe knew his giant, broad-shouldered figure, his enamel-blue eyes, his white-blond hair, his broad red face, and the impassive expression, as stoical and superior as a silent-film comic's, with which he had guided the fortunes of the European Community for years.

Helsinki in early autumn, when the September light falls obliquely and dazzlingly on the blue bay, on the pink sandstone façades and on the white pillars of the cathedral, is a pleasant, accessible city. No one stands much on ceremony here, and the only security problem is liquor. Also, I'm not a professional journalist, only an amateur—I regard journalism as a kin of masquerade—so I had failed to write to Erkki Rintala in advance. I opened the telephone book. As I had suspected, the most famous living Finn was listed with his full private address. I let the phone ring for a while, in vain— he didn't even have an answering machine. Since I had nothing else to do, I walked along the Esplanade and the boulevard to the given address. The president lived in one of those elegant houses faced with yellow plaster and built before the Frist World War that are found in every European capital. There was even a nameplate. The view from the third floor across the harbor of Sandvika must be magnificent. But, of course, no one was at home. The old concierge who finally opened the door for me spoke only Finnish. With a sweeping gesture he let me understand that Rintala had gone away on holiday, to the North. The old man's paddling movements indicated an Arctic distance.

No one knew anything at the Foreign Ministry. The embassy was shut because the staff was on strike. At the editorial offices of the *Helsingin Sanomat*, the country's leading newspaper, I was received with reserved politeness and referred to a hunchbacked gentleman who was sitting thoughtfully in front of his computer screen.

"Let's go," he said, after I had made my request. He led me through the courtyard to a side street, entered a shabby tenement, and made his way purposefully to the cellar steps. "Top secret!" he whispered. In the cellar there was a primitive bar. We sat down at a makeshift table, and without being asked the proprietor placed a bottle of vodka and two glasses in front of us. Out of the speakers came a Finnish version of "Cannonball Blues." I felt as if I were in a thirties film. I had heard that the sale of alcohol was subject to strict and complicated regulations in Scandinavia. But it was news to me that in Helsinki there were illegal drinking dens, real speakeasies, as in Prohibition-era Chicago.

The editor pouted out an excessively generous measure of vodka for me. Then he began to interrogate me. He wanted to know what I thought of the Detroit uprisings, of the obligatory prayers on American television, of the holographic reproduction of the Louvre on Coney Island. He also asked me who had commissioned me. I had the feeling he thought I was a spy, but perhaps it was only the way he held his head to one side that made me think so. When I assured him I was traveling on my own acount, he nodded, drew out a sheet of paper, and scribbled a rough map on it. The directions were fairly confusing. Because there wasn't enough space, they had to be continued on the other side.

"At this turnoff you'll see the little church of Rääkkylämäki. Keep the church on your left. After a mile or so, a track leads off to the right, there's no signpost, only a letter box. The track will take you right to Erkki's cabin. Throw the map away. Erkki will be angry, so you must on no account say that I sent you."

I sighed, and although I didn't in the least feel like it, I invited my friend to share another round of vodka.

Finland is one of the few European countries where you can rent a car without any great difficulties. For geographical reasons, the railroad mania never took hold here. One can't reach the more remote areas even by electrobus—and almost everywhere is remote here.

I drove in a northerly direction for almost three hours, and after I had lost my way twice I eventually reached the place with the unpronounceable name. The landscape was attractive, if a little monotonous. The villages looked shabby. There were many shut-down shops and abandoned school buildings. The map proved very accurate. Following the birch-lined track, I came to a small lake. I left the car by the shore.

The man I was looking for was bent over a table working with something behind a large shed. When he heard me coming, he raised his head, gave me an ill-humored glance, and returned to his task without saying a word. I came closer and saw that he had set up a small workbench in the open air. A pedantically ordered row of machine parts, which he clearly wanted to assemble, lay in front of him. At least ten minutes passed. Finally, without looking at me, he muttered. "What do you want?"

His voice was surprisingly soft. He spoke faultless but somewhat halting Oxbridge English. I hesitated.

"American," he grunted. "That's obvious. Sociologist or newspaperman. You've come all this way for nothing. I don't give interviews. I have nothing to say. Apart from that, as you can see, I'm busy."

I simply stood and watched as he cleaned a screw thread with a gas-soaked rag.

"All right," he said at last. "Come back in two hours. Then I'll give you something to eat. Otherwise, you'll starve in this district. There aren't any hamburger restaurants near here."

I thanked him. There was nothing for me to do but explore the neighborhood. A nice spot, plenty of undergrowth, ideal for Professor Sturz from East Berlin, but impassable and also marshy in places. Finally I sat in my car and had a short midday nap.

When I went back to the house, the light was already beginning to fade. The workbench had disappeared into the shed. The cabin, an old shack, looked tiny to me. Still, there must be electricity, because two windows were lit up.

"Come in," called out my involuntary host. He was sitting in an old rocking chair. The room was stuffed with bookcases. As far as I could see, he had specialized in two kinds of reading: poetry, in every possible language, and technical

handbooks and manuals. Besides that, there were two antiquated pieces of equipment on the shelves: a record player
of a very ancient model and a television set with the green
frog's-eye that served for a screen in the fifties. He poured
me out a glass of bitter, black coffee. I was careful not to ask
him any questions and observed the North's unwritten law
of silence.

"The things work perfectly," said Rintala. "I've got hold of
a reserve of old tubes from Soviet stocks, and I've constructed
a digital adapter that transforms the satellite signal into the
old six-hundred twenty-five-line standard. It's all just a hobby,
of course."

"How many channels do you receive?" I asked.

"I never watch television," he replied.

"There was a longer pause. Then my host suggested the
unavoidable visit to the sauna, "before it gets too dark."
Fortunately, hot blasts of steam at 90 degrees Centigrade
don't worry me, and I had nothing against jumping out of
the glowing wooden booth and into the cool lake. I offered
to chop wood while he cooked the supper of reindeer steaks
and fried potatoes. To go with it, Rintala brought out a bottle
of '94 Listrac.

"Van Rossum?" I asked.

"Oh, do you know about van Rossum? An unpleasant
fellow, but what can one do? I can no longer afford such
extravagances now. I'm living on my assets, at least as far as
Bordeaux is concerned—well, what do you want to know?"

"Mr. President . . ."

"Just forget about the President! I'm glad to have those
four years behind me."

"You are only fifty-six and, if one can believe the press, in
perfect health. Why did you throw in the sponge?"

"What you should be asking is why I got mixed up in the
whole masquerade at all. Brussels is nothing but a monkey-
house. I'm sure I'm not giving away any secrets when I say

the president of the European Community has no weight. In Europe the president is not the imperial figure he is in the USA but only a cardboard ruler. We have a kind of fixed-term elected monarchy. And besides, there was a very simple reason for my candidacy. It was necessary to elect a Finn in order to reassure the Russians. Though I don't know what's so reassuring about me."

"Well, perhaps it's an example of the famous Fin-landization?"

"Don't give me that nonsense! Even in the seventies that wasn't true, and today the term has become completely meaningless. The Soviets have got other worries since the Central Asian civil wars. Then on top of that there's the conflict in the Far East. Quite apart from their internal problems."

"The Europeans have simply been lucky. More luck than judgment."

The plates had been rinsed, the birchwood blazed in the fireplace—the moment I had been waiting for had arrived: sitting in his creaking rocking chair, Erkki Rintala prepared to make his case.

"Who does have judgment in world politics? As an American, you should know how rare that quality is. You are the citizen of an empire, a superpower. This status has its advantages but it also has certain drawbacks. The more powerful a society feels itself to be, the less it understands what is going on in the outside world. There's no escaping such a loss of reality. Please don't misunderstand me! I believe the Americans to be a very intelligent people. But the stupidity I'm talking about is something objective. Every nation that achieved the status of world power proved itself to be cretinous as a collective—the Romans and the Chinese, the British and the Russians, the Germans and the Japanese."

"As a Finn," I threw in, "it's easy enough for you to talk."

"Quite. Our follies could never be so great. That was our

good fortune. Today it is also the privilege of the small peninsula we call Europe."

"A fairly modest privilege."

"Do you think so? I am of a quite different opinion. We can look back on sixty years of peace. That has never happened before in the three-thousand-year history of this continent. And even more astonishing is the fact that no one finds it astonishing. Since the armaments were melted down and the superpowers withdrew, war in Europe has become unthinkable. There are no longer any disputed borders or threatening minority problems."

"And what about the Basques, or Ireland, or Transylvania?"

"Sentimental memories."

"You see the great powers as troublemakers. May I remind you that it was the Americans and the Russians who kept the peace in Europe for thirty years after the Second World War? Wasn't it Big Brother who stopped the Germans from taking back their eastern territories? And what Silesia meant to the Germans, Transylvania meant to the Hungarians, Kosovo to the Albanians, Macedonia to the Bulgarians, and Karelia to the Finns."

"Very well. If you insist, I'm perfectly willing to thank Messrs. Stalin, Roosevelt, and Churchill posthumously for Yalta, even if there's an ironic undertone to my gratitude. However, now we can get by without guardians."

"But not without never-ending squabbles, petty horse trading, and senseless extravagance."

"You don't need to tell me, Mr. Taylor!"

He threw a couple of blocks of wood onto the fire and leaned back comfortably.

"You see," he continued, "for decades we pursued a chimera called European unity. The idea orginated at a time when the whole world still believed in technological progress, in growth and rationalization. The whole so-called European idea amounted to the attempt to oppose the two big blocs with yet another big bloc. In other words, nothing but big science, high tech, space travel, plutonium—all those bad jokes. For decades the politicians backed this Europe of managers, armaments experts, and technocrats and held up Japan as a shining example to us. Only they didn't take the inhabitants of our beautiful peninsula into account. From County Cork to the Bukovina, I have never met anyone who had the slightest intention of becoming a white Japanese.

"The unavoidable consequence was that Brussels became a giant supranational hydrocephalus. In their glass boxes the commissions, committees, and subcommittees played an absurd billion-dollar bridge game. All entirely without democratic legitimation: those who had power had not been elected, and those who had been elected—I mean the Strasbourg Parliament—had no power.

"I don't wish to deny that there were some achievements. We agreed on common food dyes and the customs forms were standardized. But inevitably the whole Brussels folly had to end in massive bankruptcy. We're still paying for it today. But one pays for everything in politics."

"So, if I understand you properly, you want European unity without unity?"

"One couldn't put it any better. Do you know Burckhardt?"

"The Swiss historian?"

"Yes. He said something very sensible: 'The only thing that was always fatal for Europe was a stifling monopoly of state power, wielded either domestically or externally. Every leveling tendency, whether political, religious, or social, threatens our continent. Forced unity and homogenization are bad for us; it's our diversity that saves us.' I'm quoting from memory."

"But Burckhardt—that was in the nineteenth century!"

"If ideas have to be new, what about Mandelbrot?"

"Mandelbrot?"

"Yes. He's a mathematician who, by the way, worked in the U.S.A. for a long time, for IBM, I believe. He became famous because of his research into fractals."

"I don't know anything about mathematics."

"Neither do I. But the thing is quite simple. Classical geometry was concerned with regular areas and bodies, with triangles, sections of spheres, Riemannian spaces, and so on. However, Mandelbrot attempted the mathematical analysis of the irregular. He is the Columbus of irreducible diversity."

"I don't see what you're getting at."

"Then please consider this map of Finland, which is on a scale of one to five hundred thousand. Look at the coastline. It's rather complicated. If you look at it more closely, through a magnifying glass, the shapes on the map become simplified and it looks more regular. In reality, of course, it's exactly the reverse: the more closely you look at the coast, the more irregularities you find. And you can pursue this game right down to the microstructures. In other words, strictly speaking, it's impossible to make a precise measurement of the length of the Finnish coast at all."

"So?"

"Surely the implications are obvious? On any map of Europe, whether it shows income distribution, electoral behavior, religions, educational standards, migratory movements, eating habits, you come up against the same pattern: figures whose dimensions are no longer integral. Hausdorff demonstrated, as long ago as 1919, that in such cases it's appropriate to express the dimension by means of a break . . . In short, Europe is a fractal object."

"If I understand you correctly, you want to provide a mathematical justification for federalism."

"Nonsense! I was only leading you up the garden path. But as far as European society is concerned, it really is irregular, right down to its microstructures. Any attempt to create order here in the traditional sense is bound to fail. That's also true of the constitutional framework of the Community. It's possible, however, to lay down certain limits. This hodgepodge is our final shape. That's true even of our economy. The result is P.O.D., that is, the abandonment of mass production. Production on demand—we do it better than everyone else, and that's the reason we're still important in the world market. The Italians were the first to understand this—despite, or because of, their shaky infrastructure, their incompetent administration, and their jumble of institutions. But, as you can see, Italian improvisation also works here in the North."

"It all seems rather chaotic to me."

"What you call chaos is our most important resource. We need our differences. Of course, for politicians who are supposed to reconcile all the conflicting opinions at least to a certain extent, these conditions are hell. And that's why, Mr. Taylor, you find me here at the end of the world, and not in Brussels . . . You've had an exhausting day. I've made up a field bed under the roof for you."

The next morning I found the room empty. The coffee was being kept warm. Outside, light squalls were driving across the lake. The ex-president of Europe, in a blue parka and high wading boots, came back from his morning walk—he had already caught two trout for his lunch.

"Perhaps you would like to see the workshop before you leave," he said. "This place used to be a smithy. You can still see the old chimney here on the wall of the shed." He opened the barn door. A silver Jaguar XK-150 from the fifties gleamed in the semidarkness.

"I had to dismantle the whole compressor. The cooling system was leaking. But it's working again now."

He sat down at the steering wheel and let the engine roar. I bent down and looked at the undercarriage.

"Immaculate condition. Looks like new."

"The car is hardly ever used," said Erkki Rintala. "It's beautiful but useless. A souvenir of modernism."

BUCHAREST
·····························

Supper in the Super Nova, the brand-new luxury restaurant sixty-six floors above the roofs of the Romanian captial. The whole starry sky can be seen through the giant transparent dome. The Mozart coming out of the speakers never repeats itself. The microcomputer unceasingly composes new piano concertos. Mickey Woolstone, the manager, is proud of his new house.

"It's all American-style," he said. "It's a good thing we're showing the flag in this corner of the world at last." In his semitransparent body suit, his Romanian assistant, Tudor, a golf professional who has decided to make a career in the hotel trade, looks as if he came from California too. The menu features patriotic dishes: Long Island lobster, baked Virginia ham, turkey à l'américaine, lemon meringue pie. Even the wines are from San Francisco.

"Bucharest is an ideal location on the whole," observed Woolstone, and pointed at the panorama outside. The architecture is extreme: skyscrapers made of light-metal alloys and carbon fiber that display the hallmarks of their Spanish architects. The bizarre Gothic fashion triumphs here. "This is the Wild East!" exclaimed Mickey. "A town for gold diggers! Of course, the European competition tried every dirty trick in the book to keep us out, but for once America got its foot in the door in time. No building regulations here. The Romanians are happy to let us tear down their old slums. There wasn't much to save here anyway."

"Still," Tudor broke in, "we do have our churches. You absolutely must see Stavropoleos, the patriarch's church, and the Curtea Veche, Mr. Taylor."

"But that old gangster Ceauşescu—I guess you know all about him—tore down everything he could, before his own people shot him down. And the great earthquake took care of the rest. For fifty years—right, Tudor?—Romania was the asshole of Europe. The only thing that worked was the *Securitate*, the secret police. Everything else went down the drain. No meat, no lightbulbs, no electricity. In winter people froze to death in their own homes. Fifteen years ago the Romanians were still starving. Unbelievable. And today . . . Well, you can see what's happening now. An economic miracle like in the old days. It'll take them twenty years to catch up! The East European market is a horn of plenty.

"Of course, it was the Germans, the Germans and the French, who cashed in. When the dictatorship got booted out they had their foot in the door the very next day with the 'second Marshall Plan'—only this time they took care of business without us.

"Look over there, the guys in beige are East German construction engineers. They always wear beige suits . . . And the Romanian women they've dug up aren't exactly the pick of the crop either. At the next table, Italians here for the fashion week. At the back there, a consortium from Luxembourg. I don't know what they're trying to get rid of. And then the Russians, over by the window. Till ten the Russians watch every penny, but then, once they've warmed up, they practically throw their money out the window."

"All right for you," I said.

"But it still annoys me," grumbled the hotelier. "What was I saying? Yeah . . . We let the Europeans walk all over us. It's a disgrace."

I laughed. "The empire just isn't what it was, Mickey. You've got to be a good loser if you want to play poker. And as far as I can see, the Super Nova is a gold mine."

When the coffee arrived—even *it* was American, thin and decaffeinated—Woolstone excused himself, and I watched as he did the honors, first with the Italians, then with the bawling Russians. The French bankers, as arrogant as ever, pretended they didn't understand English. I suddenly felt sorry for Mickey. He seemed like a man fighting a losing battle. I remembered the attaché in Bad Godesberg, and I understood his persecution mania. Nowhere could an American feel more like a stranger than here.

Mickey's assistant looked at me out of the corner of his eye, as if he had guessed what I was thinking.

"What do you expect?" he said quietly. "This is the Balkans. We remain what we've always been. Forget the backdrop outside. Where I come from, an hour's train ride from Bucharest, everything is still the same."

"I know your country only from vampire movies," I said.

"If only there were vampires at least! No, there's not much in the place that could be put in a film script. A couple of policemen, a village boss who keeps everyone under his thumb, sleeping dogs, childhood diseases, shacks. It's the Third World. The Romanian miracle is only another form of bankruptcy. But don't say anything to Mickey. It would only depress him."

The next day I was lucky. The "Café Old Vienna" on the Boulevard of the Republic was packed. The 1890s marble bar, the billiard lights, the waitresses' little aprons and caps— it was all brand-new, of course. The designer had even thought of wooden newspaper holders, and I wouldn't have been surprised to find facsimiles from the Habsburg period in them. But the only thing jammed into the unwieldly antiquities were computer printouts of the lastest stock prices. As the orchestra leader struck up a waltz, a young woman sat down at my table. After a minute of small talk it turned out that she was taking a course in American studies. An unlikely coincidence, since it was considered an exotic subject here. She assured me that there were only nine "Americanists" in the whole of Bucharest, and "seven of them were only interested in getting a scholarship."

Carola was a pale, pretty, determined person. When she was thinking, she raised her thick eyebrows and furrowed her forehead. She was extremely intelligent, as I was soon to find out. I treated her to a cup of real Viennese coffee. She declined cake because it was too sweet.

"I would like to hire you as an interpreter," I said. "Since I don't speak a word of Romanian, I would like you to show me the city."

"That's completely unnecessary," she replied. "There are no sights in Bucharest except the whores, and you don't need an interpreter with them."

"That's not a very patriotic response," I said.

She shrugged her shoulders.

"If you don't like Bucharest, why do you stay here?" I asked.

"Why not? I've been to Paris and New York as well, if that's what you mean. But if there's corruption everywhere, then I prefer our own. I admit it's the worst, but we can cope with it. Apart from that, as far as the foreigners are concerned, we're at their feet, and we hate that too. We hate the Russians and the Germans, we hate all our neighbors, especially the Hungarians. Do you know why we're so chauvinistic? Because Romania isn't really a nation at all. Supposedly we can look back on two thousand years of history. At least that's what the schoolbooks say. But it's all made up! A ridiculous junk novel fabricated by hacks. And because we don't know who we are, we get taken for a ride every time. We don't need any foreigners for that. Our own kings, our parliaments, our officers, our Fascists, our Communists have been virtuosos in this respect, and we've never been short of hangmen."

"Even the worst regime is overthrown one day."

"True. But what happens then? Ten thousand people are dead and a few old scores are settled, and three days later the whole country gets back to normal. The personal files are stuffed into the stove, the medals are thrown into the garbage can, you open a little shop, you hoard and barter. What happened to the Ceauşescu people? The court cases all petered out. A couple of laughable fines followed by an amnesty. And now these criminals are being handled with kid gloves! We guarantee them their villas and their pensions. Anything at all to avoid trouble! The apparatchiks make up at least 8 or 10 percent of the population, the fellow travelers 60 percent. They mustn't be provoked—on the contrary, they've got to be mollycoddled so they keep quiet.

"So you see, one can survive even with a broken back. And like all cripples, the Romanians are crafty, stubborn, and don't listen to anyone else. The Communists spent fifty years trying to reeducate us. Just look at the result!"

She pointed at the boulevard outside.

"Not even a hint of Sverdlovsk or Petrozavodsk. It was all a waste of time! We are what we are. That's the terrible thing."

I looked at her carefully from the side. I was slowly beginning to suspect she was making fun of me.

Carola laughed. "Don't take it so seriously. Do you know what? I'll prove to you that I'm right. If you want, we can go to the operetta this evening."

"Do you mean it still exists? I thought operetta had died out twenty years ago."

"Not here. It's something you've got to see."

And a couple of hours later Carola did indeed take me to a wedding-cake-style theater hemmed in by a prisonlike office building and a garage on a dark side street. A huge line was besieging the box office, but Carola triumphantly pulled two tickets out of her pocket. "Don't be shocked," she said, "the house is fairly down at the heels. Our government would not put a cent into this theater, and the company has to get by without any subsidy. Despite that, *The Queen in the Pigsty* has been playing to sold-out houses for four years."

The stage set displayed a delirious vision of the nineteenth century, half *Freischütz*, half Moulin Rouge. Apart from the heroine of the title, the cast consisted of a village smith, an evil countess, a drunken village mayor, and an avaricious cattle dealer who was clearly a Jew. Then there was the prince disguised as a swineherd, who appeared in sackcloth at the beginning and in top hat and tails at the end. A chorus of girls in pink tutus constantly interrupted the story, which I was unable to follow. Verbose speeches and ribald stories followed one another relentlessly and were greeted with cheers. The smell of mothballs, the sugary violins, and the enormous mustachios swept the audience away. Even Carola seemed to have forgotten her sarcasm, she laughed and applauded enthusiastically.

Not until the curtain had fallen did she lean over and whisper in my ear, "You see? Now what did I tell you?"

PRAGUE

The city is unchanged. The twentieth century has left it untouched. What on earth forces me to make such a statement? I am in Prague for the first time. But the iron shutters with which the elegant shops in the alleyways of the Old Town are shut up at evening seem familiar to me, like a childhood memory. I recognize the window gratings, the heavy bolts, the case locks, and the crossed strips of cast iron on the medieval doors. Only I remembered everything darker and dirtier.

Beer fumes and the smell of frying wafted out of the pubs. There was something heavy mixed in with the elegance of this metropolis, as if the boundary between temptation and nightmare were fluid. The cobblestones glistened in the rain under the dull glow of the streetlights as I looked for the entrance to the catacombs of Prague.

I wasn't looking for one of those old-fashioned nightclubs where a morose pianist accompanies ladies in pink garter belts as they throw their legs up in the air on a pink stage. Prague was the capital of the Ecstatics, and it was because of them that I was here. The Ecstatics couldn't be overlooked. Wearing their long white robes, they mixed with the crowds in broad daylight. A strange sight!

They were occasionally to be seen in Berlin and Amsterdam too, as were Arabs in burnooses and Indian women in bright-colored saris. But here in Prague they were everywhere. Small groups populated the ticket offices and the supermarkets. They were even present in the suburbs and the poorer districts. Although they were often ridiculed—the commentators on the big networks called them "angels in nightshirts"—I found them sinister, and I was quite taken aback when, a day after my arrival in Prague, three of them sat down next to me on the streetcar, humming quietly. Outstanding scientists were supposed to have joined them. In Prague it was even rumored that two members of the Czech cabinet were Ecstatics.

"Well, that may be so," my landlady, Mrs. Grögeróva, had hold me—I was staying in a small, somewhat crooked house in the Lesser Quarter—"but, you know, the government isn't very important to us. It's like the garbage disposal. Nowadays most people have no idea who the president of the republic is."

I felt I was in good hands with Mrs. Grögeróva. Her pension had only three rooms. She liked to emphasize that she didn't need the money but that keeping a guesthouse helped pass the time. Whenever I returned, exhausted by my walks through the city, and entered her little drawing room, in which a marmaladelike coziness reigned, she was always ready for a chat. Then she poured herself a glass of mulled wine and sank back happily against one of the countless small cushions on her couch. Above the decorative cups on the sideboard hung the framed portraits of the Stalinists who for decades had tried in vain to ruin Czecho-slovakia forever. Mrs. Grögeróva was the widow of a high-ranking official who had put a bullet through his head when the party dictatorship had ended—evidently the only one to take this course. She gave the impression of being a good-natured but shrewd woman, incapable of any kind of fanaticism, and I wondered how she had managed to live with a man who presumably had been a killer in the service of state security.

Anyway, as far as the Ecstatics were concerned, my landlady had been unable to give me much help. It was easy enough to get hold of the right addresses. The Ecstatics didn't keep their meeting places secret. Yet for two evenings I had failed to gain admittance.

My first attempt had led me to a gloomy palace behind the Hradčany Castle. I could see white-robed figures standing in the inner courtyard. A woman Ecstatic stepped up to me in front of the illuminated cellar stairs and, without saying a word, grasped my head with both hands—I felt her cool fingers on my ears—and scrutinized my face, as she might have examined a head of lettuce. Her gaze was strangely neutral. I can still see the small pupils of her dark-blue eyes in front of me. She let me go and shook her head almost imperceptibly. That was all. Immediately I felt the athletic grip of two white-clothed men, who led me out into the street. The Ecstatics clearly had their own bouncers to protect themselves from intruders.

A second attempt, which I made late in the evening near the Old Town Square, had ended even more ingloriously. An old man, who despite his white robe reminded me of a rabbi, suddenly came up to me. He raised both hands in the air—like a figure on an altar painting—as if I were the devil in person. I was forced to leave without a word being spoken.

"I don't understand it."

"What don't you understand, Mr. Taylor?"

"The Ecstatics. If I wanted to set up a conspiratorial club or a secret lodge or a Mafia, then I wouldn't let everyone on the street see who belonged to it and who didn't."

"That's nonsense," said Mrs. Grögeróva, "the Ecstatics are completely harmless. The conspiracy theories have just been invented by the media. The Ecstatics aren't interested in power."

"But then why is it so difficult to get into their meetings? What's all the mystery for?"

"They're just not interested in missionary work. Quite the opposite."

"But there are more and more of them. There are supposed to be almost fifty thousand in Prague now."

"That's right."

"And how do they know who's right for them?"

"I have no idea. But in your case they weren't mistaken. You only went there out of curiosity, didn't you?"

"Who really is their head guru? Does anyone know?"

"In that respect the Ecstatics are really original. You have to grant them that. They have no founders, no hierarchy, and no priests. When a congregation grows too large, it splits voluntarily. Then one half leaves and starts a new parish."

"And why do they always meet below ground?"

"That has worried a lot of people, but it doesn't really mean anything," said Mrs. Grögeróva. "With the rents that are being asked in the center of town today, a cellar room is simply cheaper. Apart from that, it's quiet down there."

"And what do they do in their caves? Do they pray? Do they have a ritual?"

"Don't you know? The Ecstatics say that the true religion has yet to be found. That's why they have no doctrine and no liturgy. They just sing."

"I've already noticed the constant humming, you can even hear it on the street. A kind of quiet whining."

"Yes. They keep it up for hours, without a definite tune, and without a text, of course, and always falsetto. It sounds somehow genderless. A kind of angelic chorus, rising and falling. After a while they apparently go into a kind of trance. They call the state 'the inspiration.'"

"Hm. And why do you think the Ecstatics have emerged here in Prague, of all places?"

"Well, that's an old story. Once, in the Kingdom of Bohemia, people flocked to the Hussites, to the Taborites, and to the Bohemian Brothers. Then we looked to politics for our salvation—Pan-Slavism, Young Czechs, Nationalism, Stalinism, Socialism-with-a-Human-Face. And what was the result? Nothing but thirty-year wars, coups, defenestrations, and occupations. People are sick of politics. Now they're looking for something else. Does that surprise you?"

"But we can't just hum to ourselves, Mrs. Grögeróva, can we?"

"I'm not the right person to ask, Mr. Taylor. Ecstasy isn't the thing for you and me, is it? Just between us, I have no taste for the spiritual." With a little jerk of her curled hair she indicated the pictures on the wall. "Even when my late husband still believed in world revolution, I just shook my head and had my own thoughts. "You'll have another little glass of mulled wine, won't you? Would you like a piece of apple strudel with it?"

As I drained Madame Grögeróva's hot, sticky love potion, I felt as if I were going to suffocate among her cushions. But perhaps she was right.

I woke up with a bad hangover the next morning. My feet were sore. There were blisters on my heels. I was a failure as a reporter. I'd had enough of Europe.

All the planes to New York were booked up, and I had to beg for a long time before a supervisor, a charitable compatriot, put me at the top of his waiting list.

With a sigh of relief I sank into the taxi that was to take me to the airport. It was a ramshackle old Škoda. The driver was a pasty-looking type, perhaps forty-five, with a thoughtful baby face. There was a pile of books, notes, and pamphlets on the empty front seat.

"Please close the window," he said, "or all my literature will blow away."

"Are you a writer?"

"Student," he answered, unruffled, as if that were quite normal for a man of his age. "General and comparative literature."

"Do they still teach that?"

"Apparently so," he replied impassively. "I study in the taxi while I'm waiting. I'm an Austrian but I've been living in Prague for ten years. I'm prone to asthma and the sea air suits me."

"The sea air?"

"Yes, don't you remember? The seacoast of Bohemia."

We were just crossing the Vltava Bridge. He pointed out the window. "Look over there, the seagulls!"

"I don't understand a word."

"You're an American, aren't you? Then you're excused. But maybe you read German?"

"A little," I replied.

"Here," he said, "have this. You can read it later." And he pushed a crumpled piece of paper into my hand. We were passing Vokovice Solar City, a low, zigzag development of glass and aluminum. There were children in white caftans everywhere. There was even a group of Ecstatics in front of the airport terminal.

"Have a good journey," said the taxi driver. "Come back soon."

Perhaps it would be a kind of solution, I thought, just to hum to oneself. But the woman who had turned me back at the entrance to the catacombs was right. I'm afraid I don't have a singing voice.

Ten minutes after takeoff, as the news from New York appeared on the little monitor in front of me, a weight fell from my heart. Home again at last! Riots in Chicago. Primaries in Massachusetts. Designer drugs in the Pentagon. A wrecked baseball stadium. I felt I had returned to reality. Even the church service in the White House reassured me. After dinner I remembered the scrap of paper the taxi driver had pressed into my hand. I unfolded the grubby photocopy and read:

"If Bohemia still lies by the sea, I'll believe in the sea.
And if I believe in the sea, I can hope for land.

If I'm the one, then anyone is, he's worth as much as I.
I want nothing more for myself. Let me go under now.

Go under—that means to the ocean, there I'll find Bo-
    hemia again.
From my ruins, I wake up in peace.
From deep down I know, and am not lost.

Come here, all you Bohemians, seamen, harbor whores
    and ships
unanchored. Don't you want to be Bohemians, all you
    Illyrians,
Venetians and Veronese. Play the comedies that make
    us laugh

to our tears. And go astray a hundred times,
as I went astray and never stood the trials.
Yet I did stand them, each and every time.

As Bohemia stood them and one fine day
was pardoned to the sea and now lies by water.

I still border on a word and a different land,
I border, like little else, on everything more and more,

a man from Bohemia, a vagrant, a player,
who has nothing and whom nothing holds,

> *granted only, by a questionable sea, to gaze at the land
> of my choice.**

Under the poem was scribbled "Ingeborg Bachmann."

Bachmann? Never heard of her. "But that's nonsense—
Bohemia by the sea!" I had protested to the eternal student,
that lump of lard at the wheel. "You call it nonsense?" he'd
exclaimed. "Look around! It's madness!"—here he made a
vague gesture, which included the steep alleyway leading up
to Hradčany Castle, the city of Prague with its Ecstatics,
Bohemia, the whole continent—"It's complete madness! You
should learn it by heart, even if you don't understand a
word!"

* *Translation: Mark Anderson,* In the Storm of Roses: Selected
Poems by Ingeborg Bachmann *(Princeton, N.J.: 1986).*

AFTERWORD

....

I express my gratitude to everyone—friends and opponents, acquaintances and strangers, throughout Europe—who has helped me.

Without the hospitality of the following newspapers, publishers, and radio stations, which printed and broadcast my reports either whole or in part, this book would not have been written: *Die Zeit* (Hamburg), *Dagens Nyheter* (Stockholm), *L'Espresso* (Rome), *Universitetsforlaget* (Oslo), *El País* (Madrid), Süddeutscher Rundfunk (Stuttgart), Norddeutscher Rundfunk (Hannover), and Sender Freies Berlin.

The two chapters "Polish Incidents" and "The Seacoast of Bohemia" were first published in the German edition of *Europe, Europe.*

Munich   H.M.E.
Spring 1987

Stephen Brook
The Double Eagle

'Brook has an alert eye for foreign scenes, an acute ear for dialogue, a sympathetic temperament to absorb the cultural cornucopia of abroad. *The Double Eagle*, a report from Mittel Europa, is his best effort and my candidate for Book of the Year ... much more than a top notch guide book – it's a secret autobiography' EVENING STANDARD

'All the energy and detail of his American travel books, *Honky Tonk Gelato* and *New York Days, New York Nights* are here ... a richly-seasoned, densely-packed book ends on a note of seething fury as he finds an explanation for Austria's present terminal mediocrity in its neglect and loathing of the Jews who gave it distinction' THE OBSERVER

'Well written, thoroughly readable and thoughtful ... Brook's vein of humour, where satire and anger lurk beneath the good-natured surface, has strange echoes of Musil, Kafka or *Schweik*' THE INDEPENDENT

'Stephen Brook was wine correspondent for the *New Statesman*: his three cities of the Habsburg Empire are sipped and rolled about the palate; their bouquets sniffed with the assurance of the traveller who knows his vintages' THE GUARDIAN

'As Stephen Brook makes clear, the Habsburg Empire was not so much "a coherent national unit" as something to be "handed down from ruler to ruler almost as though it were a personal inheritance, an heirloom" ... he approaches three of the greatest Habsburg cities not just as a tourist but as the descendant of generations of the Empire's persecuted Jewish subjects. Politically he is an old fashioned libertarian of the socialist persuasion who dislikes the right wing authoritarianism of Roger Scruton (whom he meets in Budapest), as much as he does the organised state oppression he encounters in Hungary and Czechoslovakia. Part history, part politics, part travelogue, his book is intelligent, well balanced, highly informative and very readable' THE LISTENER

Robert Byron
The Road to Oxiana £3.95

In 1933 Robert Byron went to Persia and Afghanistan, and the result was
this vivid record of his journeys with its exact observation of people and
places and very funny dialogue. With an introduction by Bruce Chatwin.

'An improviser of genius, a natural player-by-ear. Into *Oxiana* went
scholarly essays, aphorisms, farcial playlets, wonderfully exact notations of
moments of time . . . along with documents like visa forms and newspaper
cuttings . . . a portrait of an accidental man adrift between frontiers'
NEW YORK TIMES BOOK REVIEW

'What *Ulysses* is to the novel between the wars and what *The Waste Land*
is to poetry, *The Road to Oxiana* is to the travel book' PAUL FUSSELL

F. Gonzalez-Crussi
Three Forms of Sudden Death £3.50
and other reflections on the grandeur and misery of the body

In this companion volume to his highly acclaimed *Notes of an Anatomist*, Dr Gonzalez-Crussi offers a new collection of essays on the human condition in terms of that greatest of common denominators, the human body. The topics that provoke the good doctor's comment and speculation are varied and often bizarre. The anecdotes he chooses to enrich them are drawn from sources as diverse as the Chinese classics and the *Journal of Pediatrics*.

Considering the hermaphrodite condition in *Sexual Undifferentiation*, he produces the sad tale of Maximiliana von Leihorst who died in 1748 aged forty-four after a long and successful military career. The cause of death – cancer of the breast – revealed hitherto unexpected attributes. In *Our Predaceous Nature*, we learn of a 5th-century Chinese general who, chopsticks firmly in hand, consumes the well-cooked flesh of his disloyal son under the gaze of that unfortunate's severed head.

Readers of *Notes of an Anatomist* and devotees of such writers as Oliver Sacks will reap rich rewards from these eminently informed and immensely literate pages.

'Informative, enlivened by apt anecdotes and written with a literary grace, these philosophical essays range from the demographic and social dislocations that control of birth and sex may cause to the inevitability of the body's senescence and the poor comfort that philosophy affords the aging' PUBLISHERS WEEKLY

Jonathan Raban
Coasting £4.99

'*Coasting* is half travel book, half autobiography, half novel (never mind the arithmetic) marvellously written and superbly constructed. The author's intention was surely to sail through time and place, to chart the coast-line of his own past, to take soundings of his future while bobbing around the edges of Britain ... The result is a triumph, and should be read for its evocation of childhood and awkward adolescence, its portrayal of his father, its descriptions of places and sunsets, of incidents and accidents. In short a writer's view of England and the English, including himself. It's the sort of book you put among those favourite books you keep on your desk or your table, the ones you pick up over and over again to re-read with undiminished pleasure, the sort you wish you'd written yourself'
BERYL BAINBRIDGE, SPECTATOR

'Sharp ... funny ... a marvellous attempt to discover the meaning of home'
IAN JACK, OBSERVER

'Passages of beautiful boat-writing float between complex confessions and trenchancies' RONALD BLYTHE, GUARDIAN

'Mr Raban tells it well. Nobody of his generation writes more subtly and imaginatively on travel. His day-to-day coasting produces an inexhaustibly vivid record of sea-changes ... He evokes the small societies of town or village with an acid incisiveness. His eye for the betraying detail, for the outer sign of the inner malaise, is lynx-sharp. The poetry is in the pitilessness' COLIN THUBRON, THE TIMES

'Miraculously inventive with sea and shore descriptions'
RACHEL BILLINGTON, FINANCIAL TIMES

'The fineness of Raban's style, and the acuteness of his sensibility, are backed by an impressive memory for the ingredients of lost times. The splendours and miseries of the novice single-hander make a compelling adventure for the reader to follow'
CHARLES TOWNSHEND, TIMES LITERARY SUPPLEMENT

'Jonathan Raban is a marvellous stylist and *Coasting* is his best book'
A. ALVAREZ, OBSERVER BOOKS OF THE YEAR 1986

Bruce Chatwin
In Patagonia £3.99

Patagonia – 'the uttermost part of the earth' – at the tip of South America.
The name calls to mind giants and outlaws, Magellan's dog-headed
monsters, natives whose heads steam. This book is a quest, a wonder
voyage – about wandering and exile. The narrator's quest for a strange
beast is marked by encounters with other people whose stories delay him
on his road.

'A brilliant travel book' OBSERVER

'Pure pleasure – full of incident and anecdote and the oddest facts
imaginable . . . vastly enjoyable' PAUL THEROUX, THE TIMES

Bruce Chatwin
The Viceroy of Ouidah £3.99

In the early 1800s a poor Brazilian, Francisco Manuel da Silva, sailed to Dahomey, to make his fortune in the slave trade. Armed only with a iron will, he became a man of substance in Ouidah, and friend to the mad African king. From this relationship fraught with danger da Silva never made the triumphal return to Brazil he dreamed of. But he did found a remarkable dynasty, an enormous brood of mulatto da Silva children, a highly miscellaneous clan over a century later.

'A sad, barbaric, decadent story told beautifully and brilliantly'
NEW STATESMAN

'Slips from the hilarious to the macabre, celebrates the comedy and plumbs the tragedy of Francisco's life – and of Africa – in prose that grabs you with its precision' OBSERVER

All Pan books are available at your local bookshop or newsagent, or can be ordered direct from the publisher. Indicate the number of copies required and fill in the form below.

Send to: **CS Department, Pan Books Ltd., P.O. Box 40, Basingstoke, Hants.   RG21 2YT.**

or phone: 0256 469551 (Ansaphone), quoting title, author and Credit Card number.

Please enclose a remittance* to the value of the cover price plus: 60p for the first book plus 30p per copy for each additional book ordered to a maximum charge of £2.40 to cover postage and packing.

*Payment may be made in sterling by UK personal cheque, postal order, sterling draft or international money order, made payable to Pan Books Ltd.

Alternatively by Barclaycard/Access:

Card No. ☐☐☐☐☐☐☐☐☐☐☐☐☐☐☐☐☐☐☐

Signature:

Applicable only in the UK and Republic of Ireland.

While every effort is made to keep prices low, it is sometimes necessary to increase prices at short notice. Pan Books reserve the right to show on covers and charge new retail prices which may differ from those advertised in the text or elsewhere.

NAME AND ADDRESS IN BLOCK LETTERS PLEASE:

....

Name————————————————————————————

Address—————————————————————————————

————————————————————————————————

————————————————————————————————

————————————————————————————————

3/87